T0300743

Praise for *The Hollow Crown*

"In *The Hollow Crown*, Dr. Eliot A. Cohen blends his deep knowledge of Shakespeare with his decades of senior experience in public service and academia to produce a unique and compelling look at how Shakespeare's themes about power and leadership continue to recur throughout history. Whether looking at unchecked ambition and the corrupting nature of power seen in *Macbeth* and *Richard III*, the manipulation and deception of Iago, or the integrity and moral clarity of Brutus, Dr. Cohen finds striking parallels throughout different chapters of American and world history. Cohen is one of the rare people who (like Hamlet) can rightly claim to be a man of thought and a man of action. Few can match his remarkable career chapters of public official, historian, writer, and educator. He is now bringing all those experiences together to reflect as Shakespeare did on the nature of power—how it can be used for good, how it can corrupt, and how it can be fragile and transient. Seeing the Civil War, World War II, and the war in Ukraine through the Shakespearean lens provided by Cohen is both illuminating and educational, as is considering how Vladimir Putin's utter lack of a moral center is not unlike Richard III. Readers who love literature and history will love this book."

—General James Mattis, former United States secretary of defense

"A terrific book by a thoughtful, articulate, and exceptional teacher-practitioner. In government and out, Cohen has consistently been one of the shrewdest observers of the exercise of power, and now we know one reason why: his mastery of Shakespeare. *The Hollow Crown* is a great read that is as instructive as it is enjoyable."

—David H. Petraeus, former director of the Central Intelligence Agency

"The acquisition, holding, and loss of power in every realm of life are subjects of enduring fascination, most especially to William Shakespeare. Cohen, no stranger to power himself, in *The Hollow Crown* has written a remarkable book delving into Shakespeare's unique insights into the psyche and arts—dark and otherwise—of those who wield power. Cohen brings his own perspective to the lessons Shakespeare offers about leadership for our own age, above all, 'the preeminent importance of character in all of its complexity.' *The Hollow Crown* is a must-read for self-understanding by all who seek or hold power and for those who seek insight about them from the greatest observer of human nature in the English language."

—Robert M. Gates, former United States secretary of defense

"Cohen has come up with a genius idea for an entirely original book on leadership. Drawing on his encyclopaedic knowledge of Shakespeare—mainly the history plays, but also some of the tragedies—he weaves in his profound knowledge of modern politics to produce a subtle, scholarly, and highly convincing account of what it means to be a leader. This book represents an intriguing, insightful, witty, and often unsettling tour de force."

—Andrew Roberts, author of *Churchill*

"After a career spent walking the corridors of power, Cohen now turns to Shakespeare to explain what he saw and experienced. Witty and erudite, this book relates Shakespeare's heroes, rogues, and tyrants to the modern world, producing lessons all of us can use."

—Anne Applebaum, author of *Red Famine*

"To Cohen's many laurels earned as a public servant and scholar, add another: his deep reading of the West's deepest student of humanity has yielded perennially pertinent lessons about the challenges of governance."

—George F. Will

"*The Hollow Crown* is a book that's not just about Shakespeare—it's a guide to understanding power, and it should be required reading for anyone seeking to understand the mysteries of Washington in these troubled times. The book draws skillfully on Cohen's years of experience observing the foibles of leaders up close to add modern perspective to the iconic kings and tyrants, generals and demagogues, who populate Shakespeare's plays. It is insightful, fast-moving, and strikingly relevant to the present day."

—Susan Glasser, coauthor of *The Divider*

"Thank goodness there are still people in America who think and write with the subtlety of Cohen. His brilliant meditation on power and statecraft, *The Hollow Crown*, is a double helix; he takes us deep into Shakespeare's plays and emerges with vivid portraits of our modern political figures. In Cohen's reading, Shakespeare becomes a kind of Elizabethan Machiavelli—a man who observes power and politics with such a nuanced and unsentimental eye that his work is timeless. Cohen finds some astonishing Shakespearean moments on the American political stage—from Washington and Lincoln to Nixon and Obama—presidents whose ambitions and flaws match the characters Shakespeare's histories and tragedies. People worry that reading and critical analysis are dying arts in America. Here's powerful evidence it isn't so."

—David Ignatius, columnist, *Washington Post*

THE HOLLOW
CROWN

Also by Eliot A. Cohen

*Military Misfortunes: The Anatomy of Failure
in War* (with John Gooch)

*Supreme Command: Soldiers, Statesmen,
and Leadership in Wartime*

*Conquered into Liberty: Two Centuries of Battles Along the
Great Warpath That Made the American Way of War*

*The Big Stick: The Limits of Soft Power and
the Necessity of Military Force*

THE HOLLOW CROWN

SHAKESPEARE ON HOW LEADERS RISE, RULE, AND FALL

ELIOT A. COHEN

BASIC BOOKS

New York

Basic Books
Hachette Book Group
1290 Avenue of the Americas, New York, NY 10104
www.basicbooks.com

Printed in the United States of America

First Edition: October 2023

Published by Basic Books, a subsidiary of Hachette Book Group, Inc. The Basic Books name and logo is a trademark of the Hachette Book Group.

The Hachette Speakers Bureau provides a wide range of authors for speaking events. To find out more, go to www.hachettespeakersbureau.com or email HachetteSpeakers @hbgusa.com.

Basic books may be purchased in bulk for business, educational, or promotional use. For more information, please contact your local bookseller or the Hachette Book Group Special Markets Department at special.markets@hbgusa.com. The publisher is not responsible for websites (or their content) that are not owned by the publisher.

Print book interior design by Amy Quinn.

Library of Congress Cataloging-in-Publication Data

Names: Cohen, Eliot A., author.
Title: The hollow crown: Shakespeare on how leaders rise, rule, and fall / Eliot A. Cohen.
Description: New York: Basic Books, [2023] | Includes bibliographical references and index.
Identifiers: LCCN 2023015033 | ISBN 9781541644861 (hardcover) | ISBN 9781541644854 (ebook)
Subjects: LCSH: Shakespeare, William, 1564-1616—Political and social views. | Shakespeare, William, 1564-1616—Criticism and interpretation. | Political leadership in literature. | Political leadership—History. | Power (Social sciences) | Speeches, addresses, etc.—History and criticism.
Classification: LCC PR3017 .C595 2023 | DDC 822.3/3—dc23/eng/20230612
LC record available at https://lccn.loc.gov/2023015033

ISBNs: 9781541644861 (hardcover), 9781541644854 (ebook)

LSC-C

Printing 1, 2023

To my teachers

For within the hollow crown
That rounds the mortal temples of a king
Keeps Death his court, and there the antic sits,
Scoffing his state and grinning at his pomp,
Allowing him a breath, a little scene,
To monarchize, be feared, and kill with looks,
Infusing him with self and vain conceit,
As if this flesh which walls about our life
Were brass impregnable; and humour'd thus,
Comes at the last and with a little pin
Bores through his castle wall, and farewell king!

—*Richard II*, Act 3, Scene 2

Contents

INTRODUCTION

The Arc of Power

IT IS ALL VERY WELL TO SEE RICHARD II, GONERIL, AND IAGO ON the stage. I, however, have had to work with some of those people.

I am a military historian, a former diplomat, a dean, and an engaged participant in Washington policy circles for over three decades. I have closely observed and occasionally worked with presidents, senators, foreign ministers, counselors, spies, and generals at home and abroad, not to mention corporate executives, provosts, and university presidents. I have even exercised power myself, from time to time. Through it all, I have come to recognize that there are few guides more perceptive than Shakespeare who can illuminate our understanding of how people get, use, and lose power. Shakespeare taught me to read speeches with a discerning eye, to scrutinize how politicians dress and stage public events, and, alas, to understand ever more deeply the darker sides of the desire to rule. He even nudged me into anticipating a major war.

The idea of turning these thoughts into a book occurred to me after seeing a production of *Henry VIII* at the Folger Theatre in Washington, DC. *Henry VIII* is not a particularly popular play, and indeed for many years some thought that it might not be a legitimate part of the Shakespeare canon. The present scholarly consensus seems to be that it represents a collaboration with a fellow playwright, John Fletcher. Be that as it may, there is a passage in it that is all Shakespeare.[1]

Cardinal Wolsey, Henry VIII's proud, sagacious, and imperious chancellor, has been abruptly dismissed by his mercurial and in many ways opaque master. The shaken chief minister says to his understudy, Thomas Cromwell,

> Farewell? a long farewell, to all my greatness.
> This is the state of man: to-day he puts forth
> The tender leaves of hopes; to-morrow blossoms,
> And bears his blushing honours thick upon him;
> The third day comes a frost, a killing frost,
> And, when he thinks, good easy man, full surely
> His greatness is a-ripening, nips his root,
> And then he falls, as I do. I have ventured,
> Like little wanton boys that swim on bladders,
> This many summers in a sea of glory,
> But far beyond my depth: my high-blown pride
> At length broke under me and now has left me,
> Weary and old with service, to the mercy
> Of a rude stream, that must for ever hide me.

Hearing this passage occasioned a shock of recognition. Plenty of eminent persons in Washington have taken a boyish pleasure in swimming upon their sea of glory but are indeed far beyond their depth. I have seen some thrash, like Wolsey, when their floats have burst. I have even watched a few drown in the torrent.

The day after the performance, I had scheduled a get-together with some of my students. As graduate students at one of the country's leading schools of international affairs, they hoped to discuss Washington politics, of course, and registered some surprise when I suggested that we talk about Wolsey's speech instead. After a lively hour we agreed that we should explore further what Shakespeare had to teach us about power. So began a series of meetings to discuss other Shakespearean speeches, many of which feature in later chapters. A prod from President Ron Daniels of Johns Hopkins led to a short course for alumni, then to a longer one, on Shakespeare for policymakers, offered to graduate students and even freshmen at Hopkins. This book is the eventual result.

What gripped my students, and what grips me, is Shakespeare's preoccupation with and understanding of character, which is itself at the heart of the politics that I have seen and lived. Shakespeare knew that individuals mattered profoundly and that the key to understanding political behavior is understanding individual psychology. This is why, upon viewing the plays and reading and rereading them, we often feel that we know his heroes and villains as well as, or better than, many of our contemporaries. We find ourselves uniquely familiar with the protagonists and yet still baffled by them. The same is often true of powerful people in real life, because part of the dark magic of power is the way in which it causes those who wield it to show different sides of their characters, sometimes in bewildering succession. Abraham Lincoln's famously tender letter of consolation to a bereaved teenage girl, Fanny McCullough, in December 1862 was written just as he expressed regret that he had yet to find a general who would accept tens of thousands of casualties on a regular basis to win the Civil War. Kindness and ruthlessness, candor and deviousness, compassion and cruelty are more often intermingled than one might think.

Shakespeare shows furthermore that it is not merely we, the observers, who fail to fully understand the powerful. Often they do not know themselves, or only begin to do so too late. Cardinal Wolsey's anguished speech begins with a moment of bewilderment but ends with recognition that it was a failing of character that brought him to this pass:

O Cromwell, Cromwell
Had I but served my God with half the zeal
I served my king, he would not in mine age
Have left me naked to mine enemies.[2]

Shakespeare often employs what the Greeks called *anagnorisis*, the sudden, piercing recognition of the truth of a situation. It is often (though not always) a moral truth, in any case conveyed through a moment of wrenching self-understanding. The operators of our world sometimes experience *anagnorisis* too, which is why politically motivated fixers and lawbreakers sometimes become prison chaplains, as did Chuck Colson, one of Richard Nixon's key advisers, or charitable workers, like John Profumo, the British secretary of state for war who was felled by a dalliance with a nineteen-year-old model. It is why we should perhaps take their confessions more seriously than we sometimes do.

Self-recognition by those who have fallen from power is but one aspect of Shakespeare's political teaching. There are many Shakespeares, or rather, many Shakespeareans, each of whom looks for and finds different sides of his genius. When I expressed some doubt about writing one more book about Shakespeare to my friend Dale Salwak, a professor of literature, he countered that he thought everyone should have to write a book about Shakespeare. In this he follows the views of the poet, literary critic, and sometime professor W. H. Auden: "It has been observed that critics who write about Shakespeare reveal more about themselves than about Shakespeare, but perhaps that is the great value of drama of the Shakespearean kind, namely, that whatever he may see taking place on stage, its final effect upon each spectator is a self-revelation."[3]

Everyone looks for and finds something different in Shakespeare's work. Some study him in terms of the politics of his age, seeking to place him in the context of the emergence of English theater or the tangled struggles of dynastic succession and religious conflict in the late sixteenth and early seventeenth centuries. Others approach him through the prism of literary theory, in terms of gender or language. Actors and directors read him pragmatically, as befits their occupations. Still others have studied the plays as works of philosophy detached from the historical circumstances of his time. All of these approaches have their merits but do not satisfactorily come to grips with an issue that lies at the center of so many of Shakespeare's plays: power, and particularly political power. Moreover, one reads Shakespeare differently when one has seen politicians get, wield, and lose power close up. One reads with new appreciation as well once one has had something of that experience oneself.

The organizing concept of this book, which informs its structure, is the arc of power—namely, the ways in which it is acquired (by inheritance, struggle, or coup), how it is exercised (inspiration, manipulation, and crime), and how it is lost (arrogance, self-deception, and voluntary relinquishment). This approach differs from that of most of the classic commentaries on Shakespeare, which proceed by examining the plays one at a time. My unconventional organization offers some advantages. It is often in comparison of characters and predicaments across plays that Shakespeare's insights emerge most clearly. Both King Lear in the play of that name and Prospero in *The Tempest* voluntarily relinquish authority. For one, it ends terribly; for the other, we believe (we cannot be certain) it brings peace and even completion. Similarly, both Prince Hal in *Henry IV, Part 2* and Richard II in the play of that name inherit power, but again with very different outcomes.

Looking at Shakespeare through the prism of the arc of power also allows a view into how power works in the real world. Young men and women on the make eventually rise to the top. They are often different kinds of people when they begin their quest than when they have achieved their goals, and they may look very different—to us and to themselves—when they have held power for some time. Shakespeare saw this firsthand, as Queen Elizabeth I aged and declined, as her successor, James I, came to the throne, and as counselors and courtiers, some youthful and others venerable, rose and fell.

I have seen firsthand the danger of believing that any powerful person is static. In February 2022 the Munich Security Conference—an annual gathering of experts and officials from around the world, but particularly Europe and the United States—occurred in the context of an ominous concentration of Russian forces on the borders of Ukraine. US intelligence warned of an impending invasion. Yet, curiously, the predominant view among current and former senior officials and experts was that either the Russian president, Vladimir Putin, was bluffing or he would launch only a limited operation to seize a small part of Ukraine. The consequences of an all-out invasion would be out of all scale with the potential gains in the eyes of these prudent and experienced men and women. Besides, Putin might be cold and callous but was no adventurer; he had committed his murders on a retail, not a wholesale, basis. At worst he might level a city in obscure Chechnya, but he would not be mad enough to blow to pieces jewels like Odessa or Kyiv in the heart of central Europe. The costs would be utterly disproportionate to whatever gains might accrue to him and his country.

I was not so sure. My reasons had nothing to do with a reading of secret intelligence (my security clearance had expired some years before) or a deep knowledge of Russia (which I lack) and everything to do with Shakespeare. In particular, having just reread *Richard III* for the seventh or eighth time, I thought something much worse for Ukraine and for the West was in the offing.

For the first three acts of that play, Richard III, Shakespeare's consummate villain, commits a variety of deceits and crimes, including the murder of his own brother by having him drowned in a cask of sweet wine. But then in Act 4, immediately after his coronation, he commits his greatest crime, ordering the murder of his two nephews in the Tower of London. Yet something has changed. When he orders his loyal lieutenant Buckingham to kill the two princes, Buckingham has qualms. These take the form only of hesitation, not refusal, let alone rebuke. Still, Richard explodes:

Cousin, thou wast not wont to be so dull.
Shall I be plain? I wish the bastards dead,
And I would have it suddenly performed.
What sayst thou now? Speak suddenly. Be brief.[4]

This, Richard's first murder as king, is different from the earlier ones. He has, until this point, concealed his intentions and his motivations. He has been deceptive, clever, and witty. Now, however, he is direct, violent, and dictatorial. Kingship and the experience of successful murder have transformed him into one who thinks he no longer need conceal his crimes or his purposes—indeed, he now revels in doing in the light what he has hitherto done in the dark. When Buckingham fails instantly and thoroughly to fall in line with Richard's desires, he is, in effect, banished from the court, and his own murder becomes inevitable.

When talking to colleagues at Munich about Putin, I recognized a similar trajectory. Previously, the Russian dictator had acted ruthlessly but shrewdly. In 2008 he ripped away a chunk of Georgia and effectively crippled it as a potential member of the North Atlantic Treaty Organization. In 2014 he seized Crimea, but did so with "little green men," soldiers in uniforms without identifying insignia. This blurred for a time the world's recognition that this was a Russian coup de main, though Putin subsequently acknowledged that these were in fact Russian special operations forces. In 2014 he also launched operations to seize parts of Ukraine's Donbas provinces, but again he used a subterfuge: the supposed aspirations of local Russian speakers for autonomy. As Russian forces built up around Ukraine's frontiers during the fall and early winter of 2021 and 2022, many observers expected a similarly masked landgrab.

On February 24, 2022, just a couple of days after the end of the conference, the attendees were stunned by the scale and wantonness of an invasion of Ukraine on three fronts. Putin's speeches and writing began by expressing his intent to restore Ukraine to its status as a Russian province, or at the very least a protectorate, eventually giving way to a declared intention to eliminate it as a distinct nation-state altogether. The psychological pattern was the same as for Richard III. Having achieved tremendous successes with crime, a dictator lacking any moral center no longer felt inhibited about saying clearly what brutality would come next or dreaming of future, equally monstrous crimes. Indeed, like Richard, he positively relished it. "Like it or don't like it, it's your duty, my beauty," Putin remarked in early February 2022.[5] This threat, with its evocation of rape, is not unlike Richard's attempt to conquer women, although without Richard's more adroit efforts at seduction as well. For tyrants, rape and murder often seem to go together.

Shakespeare's political insights at their most powerful reveal how leaders evolve, for better or worse, and why easy assumptions about leaders becoming more seasoned and cautious as they age may be wrong. They may grow wiser or more foolish, cautious or more reckless, but they will change. For that reason too it seems to me wisest to explore Shakespeare's psychology of power as an arc. This provides another benefit, because some characters, particularly in the history plays, appear in more than one play. We see them change, and we also see different sides to their characters as the plays unfold.

The Hollow Crown spends most of its time on the better-known tragedies (e.g., *Macbeth* or *King Lear*) and the histories, particularly the eight-play cycle that begins with *Richard II* and ends with *Richard III*. Questions of power—how it is acquired and exercised—are present in many other plays, but these deal with those issues more directly and more accessibly than, say, *Timon of Athens*. Inevitably, and with regret, I have made less use of some of the best-loved plays (*Hamlet*, most notably), confining myself to those plays in which power is a central preoccupation.

This book assumes no deep familiarity with Shakespeare's plays, though such knowledge will, of course, add to the reader's enjoyment. Indeed, I hope that it may stimulate reading, or in some cases rereading, including of old favorites like *Julius Caesar* and perhaps more obscure plays such as *Cymbeline* as well. These plays look different depending upon the age and life experience one brings to his or her reading. That too is part of the joy of revisiting them—teaching them as well. It has been instructive to me that my younger students say that they would gladly follow Henry V after reading aloud his magnificent St. Crispin's Day speech, even after I have done my best to show them that Shakespeare reveals him as a selfish and cold-blooded deceiver. For that matter, they probably think of my sympathy with Belarius, the despairing tutor of exiled princes in *Cymbeline*, as just the kind of crankiness you would expect of a battle-scarred old-timer. That was the view the princes took of Belarius too, come to think of it.

Shakespeare's characters are often unnerving because he enables us to crawl inside the psyche of even the most repellent of them. William Hazlitt, one of the greatest of all Shakespearean critics, observes in his 1817 book *Characters of Shakespeare's Plays* that "Shakespeare was in one sense the least moral of all writers; for morality (common so called) is made up of antipathies; and his talent consisted in sympathy with human nature, in all its shapes, degrees, depressions, and elevations."[6] It is this quality of empathy—so extraordinarily executed that audiences can feel moments of sympathy with villains and revulsion for heroes—that makes Shakespeare so penetrating and at times alarming to a student of the politics of power. We like our heroes and villains straight up, as it were, and Shakespeare pointedly denies us that.

If there is one quality essential for understanding politics it is empathy, the ability to imagine the other and see the world as they see it, no matter who they are and what they have done. The historian John Lukacs once observed that Winston Churchill was a better war leader than Adolf Hitler because he could, to some extent, imagine what it was like to be Hitler, while Hitler could never imagine what it was like to be Churchill.[7] If we wish to understand the way powerful people behave, even if we loathe their behavior and mean to thwart their desires, we have to feel their passions and quirks, their ambitions and resentments, while temporarily suspending moral judgment. The study of Shakespeare's characters develops our ability to empathize with those who seek, use, and leave power. This is not always a pleasant experience and often an unsettling one. Who, after all, wants to suspend judgment and say, in a tone of cool neutrality, "Yes, I can imagine what it is like to be that pitiless monster"?

Using Shakespeare to understand power requires navigating a number of pitfalls. Because Shakespeare's characters are so remarkably distinct and well-defined, it is tempting to define our contemporaries too closely in terms of a particular Shakespearean character. Very few office conspirators are as wily and implacably malicious as Iago; not every indecisive president is as clueless as Richard II. Shakespeare's characters are sometimes so well known that they can be too easily invoked as simplistic shorthand for real people. The 2016 production of Shakespeare in the Park, for example, was off base in portraying Julius Caesar as Donald Trump. The Roman was indisputably a great soldier, the American politician anything but. Caesar was a fatalist and Trump a believer in his unique abilities to achieve whatever he wanted.[8] There were some points of resemblance, to be sure: the inflated ego (compare Trump's "I alone can fix it" and Caesar's "I am as constant as the northern star"), the superstitiousness, the quiet but fearful contempt elicited from their displaced rivals and subordinates. But too close an analogy is always bound to break down sooner or later, as have even wilder attempts to compare Trump with Richard III or Macbeth.

Shakespeare does not provide us a set of stereotypes but rather enriches our understanding of psychology and behavior more generally. We can see points of resemblance to contemporary figures (and this book will explore some of those), but we benefit chiefly from the broader and deeper understanding of human nature he grants us. And he does that by dealing not in archetypes but in variety and idiosyncrasy. Hazlitt again: "Every single character in Shakespeare, is as much an individual, as those in life itself."[9]

In an era when statues and their heroes are toppled from their plinths, bardolatry may still be reckoned at least a venial sin. I take refuge in the words of one of the shrewdest of commentators: "An over-strained enthusiasm is more pardonable with respect to Shakespeare than the want of it; for our admiration cannot easily surpass his genius."[10]

More than four centuries after his death, Shakespeare still has a great deal to teach. My own understanding of politics has been deepened by Shakespeare not only through his study of character but in how he can teach us to observe closely, to listen for not only what the powerful say but what they omit. Shakespeare understood moreover that power is almost always exercised through a kind of theater, and in pondering staging and the juxtaposition of scenes, one can learn about stagecraft as it shapes the exercise of power in corner offices as well as in the public square.

The reader will note a somewhat dark tone in what follows. That is not coincidental. Shakespeare beguiles us with the fascination that power exerts; through him, even if we do not aspire to exercise it, we can better understand those who do. But the more I have experienced and observed of power and its workings, something else has emerged from my study of Shakespeare. In a variety of subtle ways, his plays reveal just how much damage power does to all human relationships and to the souls of those who wield it, particularly those who wield it without constraint. It is for that reason that I end the book by looking at whether Shakespeare believes it is possible to exercise power without crippling one's soul and to relinquish it without, as does Lear, going mad.

There is, finally, a bit of a subtext in the book, which has to do with my own experiences with and observations of people wielding power in government, universities, foundations or institutions, and businesses. While I confess to a wry thought now and then, it would be foolish for anyone to suggest that in describing any particular Shakespearean character, be he or she hero, villain, or victim, I have some unnamed person in mind as a particularly compelling example, particularly of duplicity, arrogance, or some other vice. I almost never have. Besides, Shakespeare was a master at covering his tracks, and I have tried to emulate his example.

11

CHAPTER 1

Why Shakespeare?

O N AUGUST 17, 1863, NOT LONG AFTER THE BATTLE OF GETTYS-burg, Abraham Lincoln wrote a letter to James H. Hackett, an American actor of some note in both the United States and Great Britain. Lincoln admired Hackett's portrayal of Falstaff, but his letter grew particularly effusive when he described his love of Shakespeare's broader body of work: "Some of Shakspeare's [*sic*] plays I have never read; while others I have gone over perhaps as frequently as any unprofessional reader. Among the latter are Lear, Richard Third, Henry Eighth, Hamlet, and especially Macbeth. I think nothing equals Macbeth. It is wonderful."[1]

He concluded by inviting Hackett to visit him in the White House. When Hackett did so, however, he was treated to a presidential chewing out for having omitted the play scene between Prince Hal and Falstaff in his recent performance of *Henry IV, Part 1*.[2] The hapless actor learned, as have many since, that practicing politicians, including those of the first rank, have found in Shakespeare not merely diversion but truths about their chosen profession. He also learned that some of them do not take kindly to the cutting of their favorite scenes.

Lincoln had, like many on the frontier, been exposed to few books—but those he was able to acquire and read, he mastered. And one of those select volumes, for him as for so many others, was an edition of the collected works of Shakespeare. He carried cheap reprints of the plays with him in his early circuit-riding days and read and reread the plays to his final days, declaiming favorite speeches. During the war he often read aloud from Shakespeare to his somewhat bewildered young secretary John Hay, who noted his particular fascination with Richard II's nervous collapse in Act 3 of that play: "For God's sake let us sit upon the ground / And tell sad stories of the death of kings."[3]

Later in the war, Lincoln visited the former Confederate capital, Richmond, newly occupied by Union forces. There he witnessed the devastation of the fires that swept the city as rebel forces retreated and was acclaimed by the formerly enslaved citizens of the town, now freed by Ulysses S. Grant's army. On the steamer bringing him back to Washington, DC, he read this passage from *Macbeth* to his fellow passengers:

> Better be with the dead
> Whom we, to gain our peace, have sent to peace,
> Than on the torture of the mind to lie
> In restless ecstasy. Duncan is in his grave:
> After life's fitful fever, he sleeps well.
> Treason has done his worst: nor steel nor poison,
> Malice domestic, foreign levy, nothing,
> Can touch him further.

Five days later, treason indeed did its worst in Ford's Theatre.[4]

Why did Lincoln turn to Shakespeare? Fred Kaplan, in his study of Lincoln as a writer, says that Shakespeare was his "secular Bible," for in Shakespeare—whom Lincoln preferred to read rather than see on stage—could be found all the foibles and greatness of human beings.[5] Shakespearean rhetoric was the stuff of elocution primers of the time, which Lincoln surely knew well. Shakespearean tropes were common in political discourse. With an exceptionally retentive memory, he could reel off lines of Shakespearean speeches, and phrases found their ways into his own oratory.

But it is significant that the plays he named in the Hackett letter were *Lear*, *Henry VIII*, *Hamlet*, and above all *Macbeth*. These are all dark plays about men tormented by their relationship to power. In several cases, power leads them up to and even over the precipice of madness. Perhaps his choice of favorite plays mirrored his own preoccupations, obsessions, and temptations, for Lincoln was not merely a powerful man but one who had craved and pursued power, and wielded it to great effect, but with very little personal happiness as a result.

Lincoln, of course, was hardly alone among great democratic statesmen in his devotion to the Bard. Winston Churchill adored Shakespeare, and the British actor Richard Burton once described just how disconcerting it was to perform with him in the audience. He was playing Hamlet at the Old Vic and, shortly before going on, was told "the Old Man" was going to be in the audience. In 1953 there was only one "Old Man," and soon Burton found himself onstage, with Churchill only a few yards away in the front row. To his consternation he heard a rumble accompanying each of his lines: it was Churchill reciting Hamlet's speeches along with him. No matter whether he spoke slower or more quickly, "I could not shake him off," he recalled, and whenever the director had cut bits from the play, there was an eruption. Shaken, Burton returned at the intermission to his dressing room, to be startled by a knock: "My Lord Hamlet," Churchill said with a bow, "may I use your lavatory?"[6]

Churchill's writings teemed with Shakespearean references. From the epigraph to one of his first books, *The Story of the Malakand Field Force*, to his private letters, he quoted from memory not just the famous lines but others more obscure—as when he wrote home to his wife, Clementine, in early 1918, quoting (with slight inaccuracy) a line from *Henry VI, Part 3*:

> This battle fares like to the morning's war,
> When dying clouds contend with growing light.[7]

Churchill's rhetoric and often his prose were Shakespearean in inspiration and style. When the Oxford philosopher Isaiah Berlin reviewed the first volume of Churchill's World War II memoirs, he observed,

> The units out of which his world is constructed are simpler and larger than life, the patterns vivid and repetitive like those of an epic poet, or at times like those of a dramatist who sees persons and situations as timeless symbols and embodiments of eternal, shining principles. . . . The archaisms of style to which Mr. Churchill's wartime speeches accustomed us are indispensable ingredients of the heightened tone, the formal chronicler's attire, for which the solemnity of the occasion called. Mr. Churchill is fully conscious of this.[8]

The echoes of Shakespeare here are unmistakable, to include the use of heightened tone, which is the characteristic effect of iambic pentameter in Shakespearean speeches. For Churchill, as for Lincoln, Shakespeare taught not only truths about human nature but the art of rhetoric, the craft of persuasive speech essential to all politics, but particularly democratic politics.

And yet, if Lincoln admired Shakespeare without reserve, one must also note that his assassin, John Wilkes Booth, was a Shakespearean actor from a family of Shakespearean actors (his brother Edwin was a particular favorite of Lincoln's and of other contemporaries). More troubling, Booth framed the act of murder as a justified blow against an American Julius Caesar, and the Caesar of his imagination was Shakespeare's. Booth's own overblown rhetoric was unsurprisingly suffused with such imagery, revealing how Shakespeare's work could be fitted to darker purposes.[9]

Just as Churchill immersed himself in Shakespeare, admired his heroes, and celebrated his language, so too did the Nazis. There was a long history of German devotion to Shakespeare, particularly after the publication of an excellent translation by Wilhelm Schlegel and August Tieck in the nineteenth century. But Nazi opinion went beyond admiration of "our Shakespeare," as he was sometimes called. Nor was this merely a matter of a quest for usable literary icons when so many German writers—Johann Goethe, Heinrich Heine, and many others—were off limits on ideological grounds. The antisemitism of *The Merchant of Venice* appealed to them, although not, of course, the shrewder and subtler readings of that play as a critique of Christian Venice. The Nazis admired other plays too, particularly *Coriolanus*, which could be interpreted as the struggle of the lonely hero warrior against the corrupt and weak democratic mob. One can read in that play and others a contempt for an easily swayed mass that accorded with the Nazi leadership's view of the world.

Antony and Cleopatra was similarly appealing to Nazi readers, who saw it as exposing the weakness of a leader who indulged in sensual pleasures rather than waging war. Far more appealing was the coolly calculating Octavius, who, like many a Nazi hero, has ice-cold blood in his veins. *Hamlet* was, in their reading of the story, about a heroic young man deciding on a violent course to avenge injustice, rather as the Nazis were avenging the Versailles settlement and the betrayals by the Weimar Republic and so many others. Building on nineteenth-century German admiration for Shakespeare, the Nazi regime reaffirmed the notion that the Elizabethan playwright was, in his essence, German.[10]

That Shakespeare could be adored by both the heroes and the monsters of modern politics is disturbing. It is tempting to take comfort in the notion that the former understood him and the latter got him all wrong. That may be so, but it is also instructive to consider that sometimes monsters also see things that are true and deeply unsettling and touch emotions that are as powerful as they are universal. Indeed, that helps explain why Churchill quickly developed a salutary fear of what Nazism could mean. He knew that even a brute like Adolf Hitler had access to human truths that were deep and powerful and, in some sense, true not only in Germany but in human nature itself.

It is better to consider the possibility that Shakespeare is indeed, as Samuel Johnson wrote in a preface to his works, "a faithful mirrour of manners and of life." We like to think that whatever we see in the mirror is beautiful; Shakespeare forces us to realize that there may be ugly or even hideous things there as well. And through characters like Richard III, he shows that sometimes the bad guys understand their world and the characters of those around them better than the good guys do.

Very well: why should one think that Shakespeare knew anything about politics? One could flip this around, as some have done: he knew so much about courts that for centuries all kinds of theories have been advanced to suggest that the author of the histories, in particular, had to have been a statesman like Francis Bacon. Indeed, some eminent Shakespearean actors like Mark Rylance and Derek Jacobi have subscribed to this view. It is a bit of an odd notion, on reflection: as actors, presumably they can play Shakespearean kings without having ruled anything beyond a dressing room.[11]

Scholars have patiently and repeatedly debunked the notion that anybody other than Shakespeare authored his dramatic works. There is plenty of documentary and other evidence of his life and career; his contemporaries, including his friend and rival Ben Jonson, who were in a position to know, certainly believed that he had written his plays. The theatrical world of the time was a small one, and Shakespeare was in the thick of it. He did not leave a trace of his political or even his religious beliefs, to be sure, but these were dangerous times, and he was probably too canny to let those slip.

One thing we do know about William Shakespeare is that he was familiar with courts. Troupes of players, including the Lord Chamberlain's Men, of which he was a principal figure, often performed in aristocratic houses and before the queen or the king. Their patron was, as the name suggests, high up in the court, and indeed they eventually became the King's Men when James I insisted on taking that role. Their costumes were usually aristocratic cast-offs, and the Master of the Revels, acting as censor of the new and dangerous medium that was the Elizabethan stage, vetted their scripts. And on at least one occasion that we know of, Shakespeare had a close call.

In early February 1601 the Lord Chamberlain's Men received a request to perform *Richard II*, including the scene in which Richard is deposed, before the Earl of Essex. Essex, a former favorite of Queen Elizabeth I who had botched a campaign in Ireland and was sliding into financial ruin, was plotting a coup, which fell apart on February 8. He was subsequently executed, but not before the troupe was interrogated and exonerated of any part in the conspiracy. To this day it is unclear whether the players were witting to what was going on and even whether the play was tweaked afterward to make it less threatening to Elizabeth. But we can be fairly certain that it reflected Essex's understanding of himself and of Elizabeth and that the performance was intended to boost the morale of the conspirators before the planned putsch.[12]

Shakespeare came away without punishment, which has even led some to suggest that he was an informant of one of Elizabeth's powerful ministers, possibly Robert Cecil. But in any case, he saw the exercise of power up close in an era when failing to understand its workings could have lethal repercussions. He understood the nature of royal courts.

He was, in addition, a well-read man, having received an education comparable, some have said, to that of a top-notch undergraduate majoring in classics.[13] His schooling and probably his later reading included wide reading of the ancient authors, who were nothing if not immersed in Greek and Roman politics. Literary scholars have detected throughout his plays material incorporated from other authors, always selected, rearranged, and even distorted for his own ends, but again, steeped in the political history of the times. There is finally James Shapiro's frustrated exclamation at the end of his thorough demolition of the notion that anyone other than Shakespeare wrote his plays: "What I find most disheartening about the claim that Shakespeare of Stratford lacked the life experience to have written the plays is that it diminishes the very thing that makes him so exceptional: his imagination."[14]

Shakespeare, then, had not only seen power up close but also studied it through the classical authors and rather shakier British histories that were available to him. He knew, from both readings and at first hand, how power may be acquired, exercised, and lost. Across a range of different political settings, his plays reflect on these themes—in history plays, plays set during antiquity, and plays set in the realm of the imagination.

The history plays deal chiefly with the dynastic struggles of the last Plantagenet kings in the two cycles of the so-called Henriad. In chronological order (though not that in which they were written), they are *Richard II*, the two *Henry IV* plays, *Henry V*, the three *Henry VI* plays, and *Richard III*. This is the world that gave birth to that which he knew most directly: that of the last Tudor monarch, Elizabeth I, and the new Stuart king, James I, and their royal courts, with their courtiers and aristocrats and of course their queen and king. In these plays (and one may include others like *Henry VIII* and even *King John*), he deals with real events and people. However he takes considerable liberties in describing and interpreting their lives and circumstances, rearranging chronology and the facts of time and place as he does so. Thus, in *Henry IV, Part 1* Shakespeare sets up a rivalry between Prince Hal, the raffish and disappointing crown prince, and Harry Percy (Hotspur), the valiant son of the Duke of Northumberland, whom Henry IV wishes were his heir:

O, that it could be proved
That some night-tripping fairy had exchanged
In cradle clothes our children where they lay,
And called mine "Percy," his "Plantagenet";
Then would I have his Harry and he mine.[15]

Dramatically, it works for the two Harrys—Prince Hal and Hotspur—to be young men, of nearly identical ages. In reality, as Shakespeare almost certainly knew, Hotspur was born in 1364 and Prince Hal in 1386. The "night-tripping fairy" would have had to replace the infant Hal with a strapping twenty-two-year-old for the words to accord with the deed.

The second setting for Shakespeare's charting of the arc of power is the ancient world, particularly in the three great Roman plays, *Julius Caesar*, *Antony and Cleopatra*, and *Coriolanus*. These are portrayals of a republic in decline, or in transition to imperial dictatorship. They are in one sense historical—Shakespeare draws heavily on the Greek biographer Plutarch—and so he finds himself partially bound to facts. But he has more room to explore a different kind of politics, less bound by heredity and aristocratic notions of honor. He also has less fear of trampling on the sensitivities of the Master of the Revels, who oversaw new plays for their potentially subversive content, and none touching the sensitive topic of religion. These plays, with their odor of corrupt republics and scheming demagogues, have attracted particular attention from conservative political philosophers.[16]

The freest realm for Shakespeare to explore politics consists in the imaginary kingdoms of plays like *The Tempest* or *A Midsummer Night's Dream*. These are not about real places or times (notoriously in *Winter's Tale*, landlocked Bohemia, the present-day Czech Republic, has a coast). There may be bizarre coincidences, improbable plots, and fanciful irruptions by fairies and ghosts. These are monarchies, but the king may have gone off in disguise or been cast ashore on a desert island by a storm. Magic plays a part in shaping the central action of many of these plays, and while Shakespeare may not have believed in the absolute reality of occult beings such as ghosts and sorcerers, he took them seriously as a part of politics, as should we.

These classifications are rough, and many plays do not fit neatly into one category or the other. *Cymbeline*, for example, is a study of a court set in an ancient Britain that is at war with Rome. It is a kind of dislocated history play. *Troilus and Cressida* is a very dark retelling of the

Iliad. Macbeth is based loosely on a historical setting but normally classified as a tragedy. Such breadth of venues and circumstances allowed Shakespeare remarkable versatility in his exploration of politics.

A great deal of politics, including much that is relevant to the politics of our time, Shakespeare ignores. Economics he pretty much disregards. Popular revolts appear in his plays, but mass movements do not. While mobs may appear in the history plays (for example, the Jack Cade uprising depicted in *Henry VI, Part 2*), and peaceably inclined townsmen may deplore aristocratic violence, theirs is a world of thrones, castles, and battlefields. The people are more present in the Roman plays, but largely as an object of manipulation by the patricians than as independent actors, although in both cases the populace often displays a commonsensical aversion to the shenanigans of aristocrats scrambling for honor and power, which they achieve at the expense of the broken limbs and shattered lives of common folk.

Religion Shakespeare carefully steers away from, and indeed, ideology in general is of no particular interest. At most he pokes a bit of fun at the Puritans of his day in the person of Angelo in *Measure for Measure* and Malvolio in *Twelfth Night*, but for the most part he avoids the fraught religious controversies of his day. Needless to say, in Shakespeare there are no journalists and pundits, although there are plenty of acute observers such as Enobarbus in *Antony and Cleopatra*. Legislatures may exist in the shape of the Roman Senate, but they are more a venue for the exercise of patrician rivalries than a place for true legislation, let alone representative government. Judges, sometimes formidable ones, appear, but there is little sense of a legal system braking power. He gives us a world in which there are fewer rules than in our own. Legitimacy matters, but constitutional order as we understand it does not. Bureaucracy in all its forms is pretty much absent.

The select aspects of politics Shakespeare focuses on are nevertheless of acute relevance to us. The first of these is court politics. It is in courts that leaders emerge, exercise power, and lose it. Even in nominal republics there are courts: Julius Caesar is a king in all but name (he desires the title nonetheless), and he has his courtiers and adherents as well as his rivals for the top position. Courts are the central point in the vortex of power.

Strip away the trappings of robes, crowns, and scepters, and one realizes that today as well courts run almost all human organizations. If there were not something profoundly familiar even to the citizens of republics about court politics, we would read neither Leo Tolstoy's *War and Peace* nor Shakespeare. There is someone at the top who rules or reigns. There is often a designated (or aspiring) successor as crown prince, around whom factions form, as well as various nobles jockeying for position. The king or queen may be old and failing or young and inexperienced, besotted with power or too easily influenced to exercise it well. And surrounding all there are the artful behaviors of those who wish access, privilege, or power. "In the presence of kings," Tolstoy observes in *War and Peace*, "all men are courtiers."[17]

When I became counselor of the Department of State—the senior adviser to the secretary of state and indeed all of the senior officers of the department—a grizzled former ambassador greeted me saying, "Welcome to the Knights of the Round Table." It was a shrewd analogy, because Secretary of State Condoleezza Rice would pick from among the principal officers to go on diplomatic quests or beat back incursions from the bureaucratic borderlands. The seventh floor of the Foggy Bottom office building where I worked was indeed a court. As a dean, I soon realized that university headquarters was a court. Indeed, I ran a lesser court myself on the second floor of our Washington, DC, offices. Courts can be found in executive suites of any business, university, or charity. They are as universal a form of politics as patron-client relations or conspiracy.

In contemporary usage the word *court* is often intended in a pejorative way, connoting a world of flattery and insincerity. One encounters plenty of that in organizational life, but considered more objectively, this reflects the simple fact that most organizations have a person at their apex. That individual will have a certain aura, reinforced by setting (the throne room may be a corner office), dress, and rituals of collective engagement. Even ostentatious efforts to show the common touch (think of an open office plan) only reinforce the image of a benign king, or perhaps one who wanders the streets incognito, like Haroun al-Rashid in *The Arabian Nights*, but nonetheless remains a king.

All courts have a limited number of actors. There are formal and informal hierarchies (also described quite brilliantly by Tolstoy) in which an adviser of modest nominal rank and background will out-rank someone who appears to the outside world as superior in station and importance. The inhabitants of courts have complex motivations and, because one almost never rises without ambition, their own aspirations for success. Intrigue and backstairs politicking are entirely normal, and one encounters characters who are noble or sociopathic and many more who are interestingly in between. Moreover, courts are shifting places, which is why Shakespeare studies many different forms of corruption, from the harshness of a Henry IV, too long accustomed to arbitrary power, to the luxury and decadence of Cleopatra's court, which causes more than one great Roman general to lose his bearings. Sex scandals that bring down chief executives have been around for a very long time.

Looming over all is the perennial problem of succession. In Shakespeare's world, as in ours, a ruling monarch may think he has found an ideal successor or find himself trapped by having picked someone in whom he has lost faith. In that world, as in ours, an ambitious if talented subordinate can cut out those who stand in his way and rise to the top on a path strewn with real or metaphorical bodies. It is not just on the stage or in alleyways that knives get planted in noble backs. Julius Caesar's shock at his own abrupt exit from power is experienced in C-suites, corner offices in government buildings, and academic quadrangles as well. Nor is it uncommon to find leaders who have clung to power too long, only to find a hungry successor quietly hoping for their exit—or even accelerating nature's course.

Shakespeare brings to his study of this kind of power a profound metaphor: politics as theater. Politics can be understood as a kind of theatrical production, in which all the components of stagecraft can be found. Successful politicians have always chosen their stages. Think, for example, of the Versailles conference in 1919, placed in the Hall of Mirrors, a scene of French glory and humiliation (there Bismarck inaugurated the German Empire after the Franco-Prussian War). But stages need not be magnificent. They may be subtly luxurious or even bare. What matters is how the troupe makes them work. The bareness of the Elizabethan stage—a few props, little more—allowed Shakespeare's actors to fill it with audience members' imaginations, inducing them to conjure up castles and battlefields, storm-wracked ships and desert islands.

The playwrights of power are behind the scenes. Their scripts may succeed brilliantly, usually garnering them little fame, or fall apart in the hands of untalented actors. They are often the advisers and consultants, the counselors and strategists. The directors may be a bit more visible: think of Senate Majority Leader Lyndon Baines Johnson in the 1950s, directing, guiding, and shaping politics in ways that were quite clear to other senators although not to a larger public. There are actors, of course, because those in power are often self-consciously playing roles. They usually do best when their stage personas and real characters mesh, and they have a necessarily limited performance range. Margaret Thatcher was right for the battered Britain of the 1970s and 1980s and Golda Meir for the Israel of her time. Neither would have had much chance in the other's politics, and neither would do well in her starring role in the politics of a different time, as little as twenty or thirty years later. Both women too played their parts carefully, attending to matters of dress or minor gesture, be it Thatcher's handbags or Meir's personally tended coffeepot for her kitchen cabinet.

The audiences of power are also critical: after all, they make or break the play. And as in Shakespeare's time, when the groundlings who stood through the play craved bawdy humor and exciting sword play, while the richer folk seated in the balconies hoped for something a bit more cerebral, different kinds of people are watching the same performance. And the shrewd playwright, director, and actors will attempt to cater to all kinds. There are, finally, critics, which in the political world translates to journalists, historians, and observers of all kinds, whose judgments may not be fair but most definitely matter.

In Shakespeare's world the most talented leader combines many of these roles. Such is the case for Henry V, who carefully manages his moments of power, plays many characters (the dupe, the stern ruler, the everyman king, the simple soldier, and the ardent lover), and is very calculating about the drama he will stage. Richard III, the arch villain king, is engaging in part because he offers an acute running commentary for the audience on his own performance as deceiver. This is not merely entertaining: rather, it shows us how the business of deception, seduction, and political murder are done, and done well.

Power is exercised through theater. A spectacular example of that occurred on July 1, 2021, when tens of thousands of people gathered in Tienanmen Square in Beijing. There on the platform stood the Communist Party's general chairman and the president of the People's Republic of China (PRC), Xi Jinping. Around him were scores of faceless bureaucrats and functionaries in black suits and red ties. He, however, was dressed in a gray suit, of the cut made famous by Mao Zedong, the founder of the PRC. "To the 70,000 people in Tiananmen Square watching the Xi-Mao juxtaposition, Xi was sending a message: I am the only person who can accomplish this historic mission [the incorporation of Taiwan into the PRC] and thereby go down in history. For that reason, I will aim for Mao's status."[18] Xi had chosen a magnificent stage and made a statement with his costume.

The same technique has been used on a smaller scale and for far more benign purposes. When John F. Kennedy gave an inaugural speech that inspired a generation, he dressed the part, discarding the hat that presidents normally wore on cold January days in Washington, DC. The costume (or in this case, the artful and conspicuous removal of costume) added punch as he declared, "Let the word go forth from this time and place, to friend and foe alike, that the torch has been passed to a new generation of Americans." Without showing any lack of respect to the old war hero he was succeeding, his hatlessness suited his words: he wanted to convey youth and vigor, and he did so with admirable stagecraft. Kennedy, like Lincoln and Churchill, also used the English language in a Shakespearean manner. He consciously adopted elevated speech, which in Shakespeare's plays usually comes in the form of iambic pentameter, knowing that it was suited to the occasion and place.

Shakespeare's own use of the tools of theater makes our understanding of character and of power as stagecraft far deeper than one would derive from a learned article or the shrewdest reporting. If he did not invent the soliloquy, he most definitely mastered it as a way of letting us into the mind of a central figure. The soliloquy, a speech delivered by a character speaking to himself, or perhaps to an audience—breaking the so-called fourth wall of the stage, that which fronts on the spectators—is an unparalleled way of exploring a character. The soliloquy itself may misjudge reality, or the characters giving one may fool themselves, but in it they reveal not only what they really think but who they really are.

Consider, for example, Richard, Duke of Gloucester's soliloquy in *Henry VI, Part 3*. He will eventually become the monster king Richard III, but at the moment he is far from the crown and lays bare his soul. His brother Edward has become king after the tumultuous struggle between Lancastrians and Yorkists for the throne. The lecherous Edward has declared that he will be charitable to the widow of one of his enemies—although he clearly has seduction in mind as well.

Richard loathes his brother, who has just instructed his courtiers to "use her honourably." In disgust and fury, he reveals the ambition and despair at his core:

> Ay, Edward will use women honourably.
> Would he were wasted, marrow, bones and all,
> That from his loins no hopeful branch may spring
> To cross me from the golden time I look for.

Richard introduces himself to us as a man seething with resentments, capable not just of rivalry with his brother but of real hatred.

He hints at the sexual jealousy and frustration that form a critical part of his character and at the aspiration for success of a kind that few men can achieve.

Richard's golden time is one in which he can be king, but as he points out, between him and the crown stand not only Edward but his brother Clarence and his nephews. Richard then opens his mind to the audience:

> Why, then, I do but dream on sovereignty
> Like one that stands upon a promontory
> And spies a far-off shore where he would tread
> Wishing his foot were equal with his eye,
> And chides the sea that sunders him from thence,
> Saying, he'll lade it dry to have his way:
> So do I wish the crown, being so far off;

Richard, we discover, is not without self-knowledge. It is absurd to think that one can drain the sea that stands between him and the crown; it is absurd too to rant at inanimate objects.

> And so I chide the means that keeps me from it;
> And so I say, I'll cut the causes off,
> Flattering me with impossibilities.
> My eye's too quick, my heart o'erweens too much,
> Unless my hand and strength could equal them.

For Richard, like most intelligent megalomaniacs, there is a tension between desires that they know are indeed "impossibilities" and their desire for them. What distinguishes him from many like him is a certain degree of self-knowledge.

Richard's opening statement here is not outrageous. He is an ambitious man and, like many ambitious individuals, chafes at the distance between his desires and his apparent ability to achieve them. In and of itself, there is nothing awful about that; it is neither unusual nor reprehensible.

> Well, say there is no kingdom then for Richard;
> What other pleasure can the world afford?
> I'll make my heaven in a lady's lap,
> And deck my body in gay ornaments,
> And witch sweet ladies with my words and looks.

Richard is not unusual either in having a yearning for sex that is linked with his drive for power. But whereas that hunger will trap and sometimes even ruin other power-hungry men, in his case realism creeps in.

> O miserable thought! and more unlikely
> Than to accomplish twenty golden crowns!
> Why, love forswore me in my mother's womb:
> And, for I should not deal in her soft laws,
> She did corrupt frail nature with some bribe,
> To shrink mine arm up like a wither'd shrub;
> To make an envious mountain on my back,
> Where sits deformity to mock my body;
> To shape my legs of an unequal size;
> To disproportion me in every part,
> Like to a chaos, or an unlick'd bear-whelp
> That carries no impression like the dam.

That realism comes with a curse. Richard looks in the mirror and sees what is actually there, and he knows that it is ugly—externally and internally as well.

> And am I then a man to be beloved?
> O monstrous fault, to harbour such a thought!

At this moment one can—and most audiences probably do—sympathize with Richard, who assumes his physical deformities will repel women and believes (correctly) that he is profoundly unlovable. But there is a deeper point here. A tyrant, classically defined, is someone with an overwhelming lust for domination—*eros* out of control. That is true of Richard, but it is also the case that he is totally alone in the world. He can seduce people, but he can never have a loving relationship with anyone other than himself (and shortly before his death, he doubts even that).

> Then, since this earth affords no joy to me,
> But to command, to cheque, to o'erbear such
> As are of better person than myself,
> I'll make my heaven to dream upon the crown,
> And, whiles I live, to account this world but hell,
> Until my mis-shaped trunk that bears this head
> Be round impaled with a glorious crown.

Power may or may not be, as Henry Kissinger reputedly said, the ultimate aphrodisiac, but in Richard's case it is a potential solace and substitute for love. Yet this is a narrow and cruel conception of power. The kind of power Richard desires is a means of avenging himself on those who are more fortunate and better-looking. His heaven, moreover, lies not in accomplishment so much as in dreaming. He has no idea what he will do with power once he has it, other than to revel in and exert it. In that way he differs from a Lenin, Stalin, Hitler, or Mao, who had very definite ideas of how they would use it. Richard defines success with an unusual word: his "mis-shaped trunk that bears this head" will be "impaled"—a word that more usually connotes a particularly brutal kind of execution. Perhaps deep down Richard knows that even being crowned will not, in fact, bring happiness, even in that golden time that he looks for. At this point Richard exposes a streak of madness.

> And yet I know not how to get the crown,
> For many lives stand between me and home:
> And I,—like one lost in a thorny wood,
> That rends the thorns and is rent with the thorns,
> Seeking a way and straying from the way;
> Not knowing how to find the open air,
> But toiling desperately to find it out,—
> Torment myself to catch the English crown:
> And from that torment I will free myself,
> Or hew my way out with a bloody axe.

Richard is, like many desperately striving leaders, a peculiar combination of fantasist and realist. Here the latter has taken charge of his thoughts, as the claustrophobia of his aspirations becomes clear to him even as he dreams of escaping those constraints. The thorny wood of high politics is indeed a place of torment. But Richard does not end there.

> Why, I can smile, and murder whiles I smile,
> And cry "Content" to that which grieves my heart,
> And wet my cheeks with artificial tears,
> And frame my face to all occasions.
> I'll drown more sailors than the mermaid shall;
> I'll slay more gazers than the basilisk;
> I'll play the orator as well as Nestor,
> Deceive more slily than Ulysses could,
> And, like a Sinon, take another Troy.
> I can add colours to the chameleon,
> Change shapes with Proteus for advantages,
> And set the murderous Machiavel to school.

Richard understands but inflates his own political gifts, which, like those of many tyrannically inclined leaders, are narrow but deep. He has no conscience, and he is a talented actor (again, the theatrical metaphor). He is also utterly ruthless, without even the limited compunctions that make Macbeth a more sympathetic figure. Having taken stock of his talents, he concludes that what started as impossibility is now well within reach:

> Can I do this, and cannot get a crown?
> Tut, were it farther off, I'll pluck it down.[19]

Richard's certainty here has, again, a touch of madness. Having begun by noting in sober reality how difficult it would be to dispose of all those who stand between him and the crown, he now airily dismisses those obstacles. He is both right and wrong—his ability to deceive and his willingness to betray and to kill will enable him to seize the throne, but those qualities have a half-life. Once those around him understand who he is, the tide of power will turn against him.

Richard in this soliloquy has shown not only his motivations and his aspirations but also the shape of his future career. He will indeed manipulate, dissemble, and murder his way to the top. But he has also foreshadowed his ultimate misery and failure as a wielder of power. Unloving and unlovable, he will forever be clawing at those around him, trusting no one, ruling only by fear or, at best, deception.

Those delivering a soliloquy do not lie to the audience, although they may very well deceive themselves. They do, however, reveal themselves. We eavesdrop on their innermost thoughts and convictions. In the case of Richard, we learn enough of his psychology to pity him, to be horrified by him, and to both respect his skills and perceive his madness. We see him, in short, as a complicated human being.

In political life this is no small thing. Powerful people receive the admiration or the loathing of those around them; they may be dismissed as bumblers who somehow ended up in a position of power or respected extravagantly as master puppeteers. The truth is almost always more complex.[20] Their aptitudes and skills may be partial but profound; they may atrophy or grow; and they may be morally complex

as well. Empathy is the essential quality for those who desire to understand power, and if Shakespeare teaches nothing else, it is the ability
to inhabit the personality of someone utterly alien or even repugnant
to us. In a very different context, this quality of empathy is the artistry
of his portrayal in *The Merchant of Venice* of the usurious Jew Shylock,
who is unquestionably a villain but gets all the best speeches and is, as
W. H. Auden once argued, the only serious person in the play.

In real life soliloquies rarely occur—like all theatrical speeches, they
are contrived, and besides, it is difficult not to be aware of an audience that is watching. This is one reason why a play can provide more
insight into political characters than a formal biography. But there are
moments in real life that approach a soliloquy. One such is Richard M.
Nixon's farewell speech to the White House staff on August 9, 1974.

Nixon, one of the more complicated individuals to make it to
the American presidency, had been brought down by what others described as "a third-rate burglary"—the famous break-in at the
offices of the Democratic opposition, housed in the Watergate complex. The brooding president, hated by large segments of the political
and intellectual elite, had been extraordinarily successful in the conduct of foreign policy, extricating the United States from Vietnam,
opening relations with China, and stabilizing the US relationship with
the Soviet Union. On the domestic front he had actually supported
legislation that, in retrospect, repaired and strengthened the welfare
state. He had been reelected by a healthy margin. But facing impeach-
ment and trial in the Senate, he resigned.

Exhausted and broken, he spoke to his staff, his speech both trite
and poignant as he thanked the ushers and his personal White House
staff: "And I recall after so many times I've made speeches—some of
them pretty tough—you'll always come back or after a hard day—and
my days usually have run rather long—I'd always get a lift from them
because I might be a little down, but they always smiled."[21]

A Shakespearean Richard (II, not III) echoes the same sentiment
toward his own end, reflecting on the loneliness of a persecuted public man:

For 'tis a sign of love; and love to Richard
Is a strange brooch in this all-hating world.[22]

With Nixon's gratitude comes a sense of the opportunities he has missed: "And so it is with you. I look around here and I see so many of this staff that, you know, I should have been by your offices and shaking hands and I'd love to have talked to you and found out how to run the world. Everybody wants to tell the President what to do. And boy he needs to be told many times. But I just haven't had the time." He sounds like another king leaving power in circumstances of despair, King Lear on the heath: "I have taken too little care of this," or, again like Richard II, "I wasted time and now doth Time waste me."

But the most Shakespearean moment of all is at the end, when, after moments of self-pity, he pays tribute to his parents and reflects on Theodore Roosevelt: "We want you to be proud of what you've done. We want you to continue to serve in government if that is your wish. Always give your best. Never get discouraged. Never be petty. Always remember others may hate you but those who hate you don't win unless you hate them. And then you destroy yourself." The transition from the royal we of the opening sentence to the singular voice ("And then you destroy yourself") is striking. Here is a real-life moment of *anagnorisis*, for if anything destroyed Nixon, it was his own petty hatreds, his desire for revenge against those he believed looked down on him or had kicked him around. At that moment, one has to think, Nixon's audience was like that in a theater seeing a man come to terms with his own demons. Like Cardinal Wolsey in *Henry VIII*, the fallen president had acquired bitter wisdom too late to benefit from it.

Richard Nixon was notoriously loathed by his numerous enemies, but it is difficult not to be touched by that moment of revelation. Much like a soliloquy of a character as loathsome as Richard III, his farewell speech sparked empathy (and maybe even some sympathy) among those who mistrusted him. His remarks revealed how the powerful can be tormented by their unachievable longings and regrets. In the same way, one cannot read Shakespeare's plays closely and still think even of one's bitterest enemies as cartoon figures, monsters though they may be.

This is what Shakespeare has to teach us about power. He wields tools that permit us to understand power as an arc with a dynamism far beyond what any but the very best biographers, journalists, and historians can achieve. He can reorder time and space; he can invent people and occasions and throw them together as he sees fit; he can open windows into a politician's mind. The greatest conjuror of the English language that has ever lived, he has a magic wand of infinite versatility to create alternative realities in which we believe, even after the immediate enchantment of a reading or a performance. Insofar as politics is concerned, his focus is narrow: the dynamics of courts and the drama of power as theater. But that is room enough for us to learn whence power comes, how it is used, and how it is lost.

PART I

ACQUIRING POWER

In Shakespeare's world, power may be gained in three ways: by inheritance, by acquisition through cunning or skill, and by seizure through conspiracy or coup. In all cases, however, gaining power is but the first, and not necessarily the most difficult, challenge one faces.

CHAPTER 2

Inheriting It

THOUGH SOMETIMES EARNED, POWER IS MOST OFTEN INHERITED. We tend to think of that happening chiefly in monarchies, when son (occasionally daughter) succeeds father (occasionally mother) or even a cousin of some kind ascends to the throne. But the pattern is far more pervasive than that. Across all human organizations, there is a powerful tendency for the people in charge to want to perpetuate themselves, their vision, and their successes. This can mean passing the reins to their children or, if that is not possible, picking the person who will follow them—inheritance need not follow the bloodline.[1]

Human beings are programmed to value kinship. Spouses succeed politicians who have died in office, ambitious clan heads like Joseph Kennedy aspire to create political dynasties, and owners of corporate empires—Rupert Murdoch, for example—turn to their children to carry on the business. Yet even when the day-to-day realities include squabbling, rivalry, and perhaps fratricide, no tie is closer than that of parent and child—which is why dynasties persist.

The bias toward inheritance is also why leaders may seem not to have a great deal of choice about who will succeed them. American presidents who die in office are necessarily succeeded by their vice presidents, but even absent that final a departure, many a vice president has seemed an heir presumptive. For many of them it does not quite work out: Richard Nixon did not succeed Dwight D. Eisenhower (not immediately, at any rate), Hubert Humphrey failed to succeed Lyndon B. Johnson, and Walter Mondale did not follow Jimmy Carter. George H. W. Bush managed to succeed Ronald Reagan but only for one term, Al Gore did not succeed Bill Clinton, and Joe Biden only succeeded Barack Obama after numerous setbacks. Not only Shakespeare's kings but America's presidents demonstrate that succession in politics is fraught with difficulty.

Inheritance can take other forms too. Corporate titans may not have offspring who are interested in taking over, but they do often have favorites whom they would like to see take their place and whom they groom for succession. These may even be surrogate children, in a way, afforded all of the opportunities for filial devotion or parricide, as the case may be. Even when the process of searching for a new leader cuts out the incumbent for whatever reason, or when a new leader emerges from nowhere, there is still an element of inheritance. Corporate vice presidents wrangling to succeed a departing CEO, senior politicians competing to be their party's candidate in the next election, or deans angling to become provosts are all, in some measure, inheritors. What we sometimes think of as merit, or at least a rise to preeminence based on one's résumé, is in fact a form of privileged path to power.

Sometimes an inheritance can go very well indeed. The best example from the corporate world, Steve Jobs's grooming of Tim Cook to succeed him as leader of the computer giant Apple, is itself a Shakespearean tale. Jobs, an eccentric, irascible genius, founded Apple in 1976 and revolutionized personal computing by creating a company that made technologies easy for average people to use. His brilliance, however, was undermined by his own temper and micromanagement, his obsession with every detail of design, and a crippling lack of self-discipline as a manager. He found himself forced out of the company in 1985 by the man he had picked as CEO, John Sculley. Jobs created another company, NeXT, which failed, being bought out by Apple a decade later. But when Apple's revenue shrank from $11 billion in 1995 to almost half that in 1998, Jobs was brought back to lead the company through a crisis that some observers believed would be terminal.

Within a few years of taking the helm in 1997, Jobs had turned the company around, launching a series of revolutionary products, including the iPhone. He remained as quirky as ever, but after twice failing as a company leader, he had learned not only about the need for organizational process as well as inspired improvisation but also about his own weaknesses. And so he hired Tim Cook, an IBM executive, to run global operations for the company. Coming from a company that was the buttoned-down antithesis to Apple, Cook's success seemed unlikely at first. Yet, though Cook was in many ways Jobs's opposite—understated, methodical, analytic, and coolly cerebral rather than passionate, inspired, and intuitive—Jobs recognized that those qualities were exactly what Apple needed at that stage in its history. Over the next years, and particularly after his 2003 cancer diagnosis, Jobs mentored Cook for the top position. A decade after Cook took over as CEO, Apple was worth seven times more than when Jobs resigned.[2]

Jobs endured repeated, severe, and public failures and an illness that humbled him before it killed him. He contemplated his death sentence from cancer in his commencement address at Stanford in 2005. It was not a soliloquy but could easily be rendered as one.[3] "Remembering that you are going to die is the best way I know to avoid the trap of thinking you have something to lose. You are already naked. There is no reason not to follow your heart." Jobs was in effect describing a moment of Shakespearean self-recognition, including an understanding of his own failures and the reality of his impending death. He came through his ordeal with humility, learned at a high cost, and a resolve to be diligent in the education of his successor.

Such learning and growth resulting from self-knowledge is extremely rare among those who wield power, if for no other reason than that, unlike Jobs, they rarely get a second chance. Shakespearean kings often barely get a single crack at picking a crown prince: Jobs got two. Uniquely, too, Jobs had his moment of crisis-induced *anagnorisis* in time to do something about it.

Cook inherited from Jobs. But such transitions are usually far more problematic. When legendary GE chief executive Jack Welch, once named "Manager of the Century" by *Fortune* magazine, resolved to select a successor, a rigorous culling of candidates led to the appointment of Welch's handpicked choice. Starting in 1981, for twenty years Welch had devoted himself with unusual intensity to GE's processes for selecting and promoting leaders, taking a personal role as a mentor that was unusual in a corporation that size. GE had made a cult of its superior managers, all bred from within, like a large aristocratic clan. Welch had ample time to select the best inheritor, and he settled on Jeffrey Immelt.

It was a disaster. During Immelt's sixteen-year tenure, GE stock plunged some 30 percent, losing some $150 billion in market value. Even his departure did not staunch the bleeding. The year afterward, GE stock was dropped from the Dow Jones Industrial Average. Immelt's successor, John Flannery, lasted barely a year, only to be succeeded in turn by Larry Culp, an outsider to the company who split the conglomerate into three parts—the equivalent of dividing a unified kingdom into a set of dukedoms.

It was a spectacular fall, partly the result of circumstances beyond GE's control but also the product of an insular culture and a succession process that had simply picked the wrong leader for a changing world. Jack Welch's final decision as GE's leader proved to be the unraveling of his life's work.[4] Immelt and Welch concluded their careers with bitter mutual recriminations.

In the political world, such failures are even more numerous. Russia's Yuri Andropov succeeded Leonid Brezhnev as general secretary of the Communist Party in 1982 and had barely a year and a half to select a successor before his failing health caught up with him. He settled on Mikhail Gorbachev, whom he correctly assessed as a good Leninist who recognized that the Soviet Union was in need of change, even if neither man fully understood how sclerotic and unreformable the system had become. On paper, Gorbachev stood out for his confident intelligence, abundant energy and charm, and proven wiliness in managing party elites. And yet, after inheriting leadership of the Soviet Union, this stand-out leader ended up destroying it, presiding over the dissolution of its alliances and the breakup not only of the USSR itself but of what had been large elements of the Russian Empire before it.[5]

The reasons for such failures are numerous, and Shakespeare explores many of them.

An heir may simply be radically unqualified for the task. One of Shakespeare's later romances, *Cymbeline*, probably written around 1610, features one such inheritor, Cloten, stepson of the king for whom the play is named. King Cymbeline's daughter by his first marriage, Innogen, has been falsely accused by her husband, Posthumus, of adultery. Cloten, the son of Cymbeline's second wife by her previous husband, seeks to shore up his claim to the throne. The king may not have been his father, but his mother is a queen, and she wants her son to inherit the throne. As the heir presumptive (at least in his own mind), Cloten feels free to act on his impulses, beginning with his desire to rape Innogen and murder her husband:

She said upon a time—the bitterness of it I now belch from my heart— that she held the very garment of Posthumus in more respect than my noble and natural person, together with the adornment of my qualities. With that suit upon my back will I ravish her—first kill him, and in her eyes. There shall she see my valour, which will then be a torment to her contempt. He on the ground, my speech of insultment ended on his dead body, and when my lust hath dined—which, as I say, to vex her, I will execute in the clothes that she so praised—to the court I'll knock her back, foot her home again.[6]

The boorish, violent, and feckless Cloten's own counselors see him as a ridiculous figure, mocking him in asides to the audience as he boasts, threatens, and struts. They secretly despise him even as they feed his vanity and self-regard:

> That such a crafty devil as is his mother
> Should yield the world this ass![7]

And yet, as courtiers, they do nothing to stop him. Though they may mock the prince behind his back, they continue to flatter him and abet his desires—that is what courtiers do. Yet ridiculous and foolish as he undoubtedly is, Shakespeare makes clear that he is also deeply dangerous. If he had his way, he really would kill Posthumus, put on his clothes, and rape Innogen before dragging her off and beating her on his return to court. He has grown up with power and learned nothing about its prudent or moral exercise.

Cymbeline's own two sons have been abducted by a former soldier and courtier, who is bringing them up in the wild, unintentionally leaving the field clear for the queen's stupid and dangerous son. When one of the hidden princes encounters Cloten in the wild, a fight ensues, and he is neutralized at last. After cutting off Cloten's head, the prince remarks,

> This Cloten was a fool, an empty purse,
> There was no money in't. Not Hercules
> Could have knocked out his brains, for he had none.
> Yet I not doing this, the fool had borne
> My head as I do his.[8]

Like many real-life thuggish princes, Cloten is partly comic. Yet, from another angle, he presents a terrifying picture of the temptations to which an unprincipled and, let it be said, unintelligent inheritor is subject. Living his life in proximity to untrammeled power, such an inheritor feels none of the inhibitions and learns none of the prudence needed to rule.

In general, Shakespeare shows that inheritors are best brought up far away from the corruptions of city and court. So it is that Belarius, the abductor-protector of the real princes, brings them far from court to the mountains of Wales. Though fond of the quiet life, Belarius is a scarred veteran of wars both military and political, and the princes pester him for stories about the court.[9]

> Out of your proof you speak: we poor unfledged
> Have never winged from view o'th' nest nor know not
> What air's from home. Haply this life is best,
> If quiet life be best, sweeter to you
> That have a sharper known, well corresponding
> With your stiff age. But unto us it is
> A cell of ignorance, travelling abed,
> A prison for a debtor that not dares
> To stride a limit.

His response is the timeless rejoinder of embittered experience to youthful ambition.

> How you speak!
> Did you but know the city's usuries
> And felt them knowingly: the art o' th' court,
> As hard to leave as keep, whose top to climb
> Is certain falling, or so slipp'ry that
> The fear's as bad as falling; the toil o' th' war,
> A pain that only seems to seek out danger
> I' th' name of fame and honour, which dies i' th' search
> And hath as oft a sland'rous epitaph
> As record of fair act; nay, many times

Doth ill deserve by doing well; what's worse,
Must curtsy at the censure. O boys, this story
The world may read in me.

These are the realities of court politics. The higher one ascends in power and influence, the easier it is to fall. The pervasive fear of failure or being supplanted can be as painful as the fall itself. Good work is all too often met with abuse—and the need to pretend that the abuse is not resented or even undeserved.

Belarius is unusually candid in explaining to the princes why the experience of power, particularly in a court, is often painful. Many another careful teacher who has had his or her own bruising experiences and has taught ambitious young people knows moments such as this. The difficulty is that, in the words of Aaron Burr in the musical *Hamilton*, aspiring princes "wanna be in / The room where it happens." They may hear about, but do not understand, the terrors of life at the top, the battering and scarring that the Belariuses of this world have experienced. For a teacher there is a familiar feeling of frustration in one's inability to make them understand. They will have to learn it for themselves, and one only hopes that some of what they have heard but not fully grasped remains with them.

The great advantage that the princes have in this case is that they have been brought up not knowing who they are; for the very knowledge of princes (or princesses) that they are in fact inheritors most often causes the problem. In Cloten's case, that belief has a disastrous effect on a character that is already deeply flawed.

Of the Shakespearean princes who know that they are destined to rule, most handle that knowledge poorly: Richard II, arrogant and incompetent, has inherited power and loses his throne and his life to Henry Bolingbroke. Henry VI, another legitimate king, wishes he had had some other life than that of rule and ends up suffering a similar fate.

But Shakespeare is not solely fixated on cautionary tales. He presents us with one prince who becomes king by orderly succession to his father and is most definitely a success: Prince Hal of *Henry IV,*

Part 1 and *Part 2*, who becomes the glorious King Henry V in the play of that name.

And yet Prince Hal's path to competent kingship is even so an extremely difficult one. To learn to be a king he must, in effect, exile himself from the court, which earns a mistrust from his father that will endure to their last minutes together. We first meet him in *Henry IV, Part 1* through the unhappy words of his father. Henry IV not only despairs of his oldest son but in some sense despises him, particularly in contrast with Hotspur, Harry Percy, son of the rebellious Duke of Northumberland.

> Yea, there thou mak'st me sad and mak'st me sin
> In envy that my lord Northumberland
> Should be the father to so blest a son,
> A son who is the theme of honour's tongue,
> Amongst a grove the very straightest plant,
> Who is sweet Fortune's minion and her pride;
> Whilst I, by looking on the praise of him,
> See riot and dishonour stain the brow
> Of my young Harry.[10]

In this short speech we see what matters to Henry IV: honor (meant in the sense less of probity than recognized courage and high-mindedness); simplicity ("the very straightest plant"); and the favors of Fortune. But, importantly, he not only wants Hal to be an honorable prince but desires that he be seen as such. Shakespeare makes clear, therefore, that Henry IV has been taken in by externalities and reputation—not honor but "honor's tongue," for example. Henry IV looks "on the praise of him [Hotspur]" and compares it with Hal's well-earned reputation for riotous living. Though Henry IV is in some respects a shrewd observer, here he has erred by judging his own son and his rival Hotspur by reputation and superficial achievements.

The king does not want a prince just like himself. As Henry Bolingbroke, he rose to power by skill and subterfuge, not to mention murder.

As Henry IV he would prefer a successor who is dashing, ardent, and lucky. He gets instead someone who is just as cunning and conniving (or more so), but in addition charming, eloquent, and easy to love. Yet even on his deathbed, the king seems unable to recognize Hal for what he is.

For Shakespeare's King Henry IV, as for so many other monarchs, executives, and leaders of all kinds, the hardest thing about grooming a successor is overcoming his own overpowering ego. Even the most adroit inheritor may never be able to please the incumbent, who suspects that no one can quite measure up to his (or her) standards.

Much like the princes in Cymbeline, Hal makes his way far from court, though he is no stranger to corruptions of a different sort. He hangs around Eastcheap, an area of London rife with taverns, brothels, and a semicriminal underclass. His compatriots are drunks, whores, and grifters. None are more colorful and egregious than one of Shakespeare's greatest characters, Falstaff. The prince makes merry with them, jokes with them, and even comes very close to committing crimes with them. Yet it is clear from the outset that this will be a story not of a prince's reformation but of his education.

That distinction is critical: Hal probably enjoys the seedy boozing and wenching life (at least up to a point); yet he also makes it clear that it is only a contrivance. If his father has been deceived by externals, Hal intends to make use of them, as he makes clear in the second scene of the play:

> Yet herein will I imitate the sun,
> Who doth permit the base contagious clouds,
> To smother up his beauty from the world,
> That, when he please again to be himself,
> Being wanted, he may be more wondered at
> . . .
> So when this loose behaviour I throw off
> And pay the debt I never promised,
> By how much better than my word I am,

By so much shall I falsify men's hopes;
And, like bright metal on a sullen ground,
My reformation, glittering o'er my fault,
Shall show more goodly and attract more eyes
Than that which hath no foil to set it off.
I'll so offend to make offence a skill,
Redeeming time when men think least I will.[11]

The speech stands out for multiple reasons. In the scene to this point Hal, Falstaff, and their disreputable set have spoken in prose; here Hal reverts to iambic pentameter—the classically Shakespearean line of ten syllables with every other one stressed. Hal speaks easygoing vernacular prose to the denizens of Eastcheap, but to us and to himself he takes a higher road, delivering elevated speech that befits a king in the making.

Speaking perhaps to the audience, perhaps to himself, he explains that he is arranging matters so that others will contrast his virtues as king with the deplorable qualities on display during his earlier life. He intends to succeed his father by using the stagecraft of power. He wants to "attract more eyes" and to that end will use his current bad behavior as a "foil to set it off." Though he will inherit power, he understands intuitively that he will also have to work for his birthright, and to do so by artifice, concealment, and deception, even if it incurs his father's displeasure and even contempt.

His deception has clearly worked on his father, though even Henry IV himself once played upon the misperceptions of others to his own benefit. When, as Henry Bolingbroke, he sought the throne and gained it from Richard II, he declared that he sought only to restore his stolen lands. When confronted by rebellious nobles, including Northumberland and his son Hotspur, Henry IV claims that the time has come for him to reveal his true and violent self:

My blood hath been too cold and temperate,
Unapt to stir at these indignities,

And you have found me, for accordingly
You tread upon my patience; but be sure
I will from henceforth rather be myself,
Mighty and to be feared, than my condition,
Which hath been smooth as oil, soft as young down,
And therefore lost that title of respect
Which the proud soul ne'er pays but to the proud.[12]

Henry IV, himself no bad hand at deception in his earlier days, now believes that the correct way to exercise power is by revealing his hard side. It is the Shakespearean equivalent of the frustrated bully smacking his fist on the table, saying, "No more Mr. Nice Guy."

Henry IV's preference for Hotspur over Hal may have something to do with this fondness not only for dashing deeds but for bold rhetoric. Hotspur appears to have no filters whatsoever. After King Henry has ordered him to hand over prisoners taken in battle, he says,

And if the devil come and roar for them
I will not send them. I will after straight
And tell him so, for I will ease my heart,
Albeit I make a hazard of my head.[13]

As Hotspur's lord, Henry IV bristles at this, but one suspects that as a man he rather likes it.

Shakespeare's most powerful kings are, to a man, calculating and careful, their hearts under control. Despite what Henry IV may think, Hotspur has none of these qualities. There is no prudence here and no interest other than in easing his heart. Hotspur is no fit heir for a king: he has a charm, to be sure, in his boyish enthusiasms and undoubted courage, but he has not learned, and probably could never learn, prudence, that consummate virtue of princes.

Hal, by contrast, is disingenuous, as he will be throughout his time on Shakespeare's stage. He lies to us when he says that his rascally early life has only to do with creating an artful debut on the public stage through the story of his reformation. In truth, Eastcheap is not merely a convenient place for Hal to bide his time until the moment comes to exhibit his talents to the world; nor is it merely a venue for him to sow his wild oats. It is, rather, the place where he learns about normal humanity, the kinds of people over whom he will eventually rule and whose services he will need alongside those of the nobles. Hal's rhetorical gifts—including his magnificent St. Crispin's Day speech in *Henry V*—stem in part from his understanding of the common folk. Indeed, his central appeal there is that the commoner can become his "brother"—"be he ne'er so vile this day shall gentle his condition."[14] He has decided to get himself an education in Eastcheap and from the wildest teacher imaginable, Falstaff.

Falstaff is neither a commoner nor truly a gentleman, although he might by courtesy be named such. He is witty, ironical, funny, and utterly unillusioned about the world, to include the world of the court. At no point is that clearer than in the play-within-a-play of *Henry IV, Part 1*, Act 2, in which Falstaff and Hal, nominally to prepare the latter for a meeting with his father, stage an amusing scene. First Falstaff plays Henry IV; then Hal plays his father, and Falstaff plays Hal. Referring to Falstaff as "that trunk of humours, that bolting-hutch of beastliness, that swollen parcel of dropsies, that huge bombard of sack," Hal, playing his father the king, indicts him as cunning, crafty, and villainous. Falstaff (playing Hal) defends himself: "If to be old and merry be a sin, then many an old host that I know is damned." And at the end, Falstaff, possibly suspecting how their relationship may end, says, "Banish not him thy Harry's company. Banish plump Jack and banish all the world." For Shakespeare's readers and audience, those words ring true: Falstaff is the wider figure, and not merely in girth. "The Falstaffian prose is suppler and ampler than Prince Hal's verse," Harold Bloom writes, "and far more of the vast range of human potentiality is contained in it than in Hal's formulations."[15]

And yet this charming scene ends not merely abruptly but icily. To Falstaff's humorous but wary plea not to be excluded from the prince's company, Hal responds simply, "I do: I will." On the stage this can be played in a variety of ways—wistfully, or out of Falstaff's hearing, or more properly as a moment when the mask slips and we see the calculating king lurking underneath the japing exterior of a wayward prince.

The coldest possible interpretation of the line is bolstered by Hal's behavior after ascending to the throne. At the end of *Henry IV, Part 2*, Falstaff approaches the newly crowned King Henry V looking for a job, or rather a sinecure. "I know thee not, old man," the new king responds. Callous as that dismissal is, it is just the beginning of the humiliation in store for Falstaff.

> Fall to thy prayers.
> How ill white hairs becomes a fool and jester!
> I have long dreamt of such a kind of man,
> So surfeit-swelled, so old and so profane;
> But being awaked, I do despise my dream . . .
> Presume not that I am the thing I was,
> For God doth know, so shall the world perceive,
> That I have turned away my former self;
> So will I those that kept me company.
> When thou dost hear I am as I have been,
> Approach me, and thou shalt be as thou wast,
> The tutor and the feeder of my riots.
> Till then, I banish thee on pain of death.[16]

It is a cruel dismissal of one whose affection is undoubted. It is ungrateful besides because Falstaff was not simply the "tutor and feeder of my riots" but a teacher of an altogether different kind. It is dishonest: we know that as Hal, Henry V was not dreaming but already calculating his ascent to the crown while he was yet a prince. The speech invokes piety when Henry V's only relationship with the Divine will be an attempt to buy out any lingering heavenly anger over the murder of Richard II. In banishing Falstaff "on pain of death," he goes so far as to threaten his old friend's life.

Unfortunately, this is also exactly what Henry needs to do now that he is king. Falstaff is not so much dispensable as a positive danger to the new monarch. He embodies values at odds with the aristocratic ethos the king must display and be seen to value. He will always be a visible reminder of Henry V's rascally youth and all the doubts that his escapades raised among the nobles of Henry IV's realm. If Hal's purpose in having such a louche boon companion was indeed, as Hal has told us, to serve as a foil against the exemplary uprightness of his ultimate kingship, the new king Henry V has no choice but to bury Falstaff in the past and banish him from court.

Undoubtedly Hal learned much in Falstaff's company. Falstaff embodied a kind of realism about human nature that will serve the future king well as he deals with reluctant soldiers, squabbling captains, and recalcitrant mayors. And that is, in part, because he sees clear through the thing that Hal will later declare to those around him is most precious: honor. On the field of battle Falstaff soliloquizes (in prose),

Honour pricks me on. Yea, but how if honour prick me off when I come on? How then? Can honour set to a leg? No. Or an arm? No. Or take away the grief of a wound? No. Honour hath no skill in surgery, then? No. What is honour? A word. What is in that word "honour"? What is that "honour"? Air. A trim reckoning. Who hath it? He that died o'Wednesday. Doth he feel it? No. Doth he hear it? No. 'Tis insensible then? Yea, to the dead. But will it not live with the living? No. Why? Detraction will not suffer it. Therefore I'll none of it. Honour is a mere scutcheon. And so ends my catechism.[17]

Hal/Henry V could not be more different. "If it be a sin to covet honour," he says to a fellow noble, "I am the most offending soul alive."[18] But from Falstaff he has learned that his motivations are different from those of most mortals and that to inherit his power with a lasting grip, he will have to appeal to *their* hopes and fears. At the same time, he cannot afford to openly acknowledge that reality, which is why he chooses not merely to reject Falstaff but to publicly humiliate and banish him from the court at the end of *Henry IV, Part 2*.

Falstaff has taught Hal that the people he leads have profoundly different interests and desires than he does. In so doing he has, unwittingly, taught the inheriting king how to manipulate them, how to play to their sympathies and their egos, how to make them serve his ends. He has made Hal acutely aware of how different he is from the population he will lead, or rather, use.

Kings—or executives—have to be driven men or women. Except in the sleepiest of organizations, they have to lead, not preside; to desire more than they seek to preserve. Avarice may drive some of them, but to consider personal greed their chief motive, even in the business world, is to adopt a shallow cynicism, all the more unrealistic for pretending to be hard-headed. The titans of industry have more money than they know what to do with. Rather, what motivates them and their key subordinates is honor, or if one prefers, glory or reputation. It may be denominated in dollars (or yachts or private airplanes), but it is still in the end about distinction and thus not all that different from that of Shakespeare's courts.

Most people are not built like that, or if they are, they exercise their ambitions more modestly. Falstaff undercuts honor in the most profound way possible; worse yet, he mocks it. It is one of the paradoxes of power, however, that Hal, later King Harry, must understand and motivate those who live in the world of Falstaffian reality while rejecting the man who most embodies it and who helped him understand it.

To the very end Henry IV doubts his son. While Hal indulges and learns from Falstaff, he continues to try to appease his father and is never entirely successful. At the end of *Henry IV, Part 2*, Hal has picked up the crown from the bedside of (as he believes) his dead father, but Henry is not dead and, waking, bitterly resents it. "I never thought to hear you speak again," Hal protests. His father snaps,

Thy wish was father, Harry, to that thought.
I stay too long by thee; I weary thee.

54

Dost thou so hunger for mine empty chair
That thou wilt needs invest thee with my honours
Before thy hour be ripe? O foolish youth,
Thou seek'st the greatness that will overwhelm thee![19]

Henry IV, Hal's actual father, sees his son's ambition as the true father of his thoughts—an ironic formulation if ever there was one. Despite Hal's battlefield successes Henry IV thinks him as yet unready for the responsibilities that will come his way. The two reconcile in this scene, but the gap between them remains. And Henry's dying wish is not that his son and heir will gain honor but that he may have tranquility.

How I came by the crown, O God forgive,
And grant it may with thee in true peace live.

Kings do not like sharing their glory and even begrudge their successors the opportunity to outshine them through some great achievement—which Hal, as Henry V, surely will. Henry IV, himself motivated by the desire for power, does not wish to bequeath to Hal what the prince most wants, namely, glory. He wishes him peace, which is, if anything, a consolation prize and perhaps a hint that he believes that his son is not his match.

We may guess that, left to his own devices, Henry IV would never have picked Hal as his successor. He would rather have chosen his youthful enemy Hotspur, whose uncontrolled temper would probably have blown up the kingdom. Henry IV, one of Shakespeare's canniest kings, thus exhibits a spectacular blind spot, one that he shares with many leaders poised to handpick their successors: an inability to accurately assess the prince that arises from his failure to fully understand himself. Henry IV senses his own deficiency as a leader. He recognizes that he is unable to inspire others but cannot see that, to succeed, a king must combine such inspiration with calculation and duplicity. He feels the weight of monarchy on his shoulders but doubts that anyone can really carry it as well as he can.

Inherited power is the norm and is always perilous. Unearned, it may be easily lost, and its glories may blind the new wielder to the grubby necessities of its effective exercise. Prince Hal became a successful king because he realized that inheritance would never be enough, that he had also to earn his right to wear the crown. Tutored by Jack Falstaff, he had come to understand the hearts of those who would serve him and, from that, deduced the dark arts of manipulating them. But not all leaders have the luxury of inheritance—some must first take hold of power themselves.

CHAPTER 3

Acquiring It

T HERE IS A HARDER BUT POSSIBLY A SURER PATH TO POWER, ONE that relies on neither inheritance nor brute seizure. One can acquire it. Whether through clever usurpation or winning election, this method depends on cunning and calculation and adroit maneuvering rather than force.

Shakespeare's view of how self-made men and women get to the top is not a pretty one. Those who are skillful mix soft manners and measured brutality, concealing what they can and revealing what they must. All the while they must be unceasingly wary. When Henry IV on his deathbed says, "Uneasy lies the head that wears a crown," he is referring less to the burdens of responsible rule than to the ever-gnawing awareness that someone would like to snatch the coronet for their own—including his own son.

Few Shakespearean figures are more complex than Henry IV, the man born Henry Bolingbroke who maneuvered a legitimate king out of the crown but could never be certain of his hold on power thereafter. He first appears in *Richard II* in the midst of his banishment from the court after proposing a duel to preserve the king's honor. When he returns, before the time of his exile is up, Henry insists that he is simply seeking to reclaim the lands and possessions that Richard has confiscated, taunting Henry's gallant and dying father, John of Gaunt, as he does so. His earlier claim to be the king's defender seems more and more dubious.

In that opening dispute, Henry accuses his rival, Thomas Mowbray, of high treason before Richard. Shakespeare has Henry finish his accusation with three rhyming couplets:

> Since the more fair and crystal is the sky,
> The uglier seem the clouds that in it fly.
> Once more, the more to aggravate the note,
> With a foul traitor's name stuff I thy throat,
> And wish—so please my sovereign—ere I move,
> What my tongue speaks my right-drawn sword may prove.[1]

From the first one senses that even when angry, Henry will not let himself be spontaneous. By deploying rhyming couplets rather than the more usual blank verse, Shakespeare often suggests contrivance on his speaker's part—in this case, a careful orchestration of outrage, no matter how sincerely felt.[2] There is also, moreover, more than a hint of brutality in reserve ("with a foul traitor's name stuff I thy throat"), which cannot but come across as overkill given that we are never entirely certain what the quarrel is about. The quarrel may be real: Bolingbroke says it results from Mowbray having stolen money that should have gone to soldiers' pay and, on top of that, having orchestrated the death of the Duke of Gloucester, Bolingbroke's uncle. But those putative causes seem to dwindle in the background as Bolingbroke rages about his offended honor and his contempt for Mowbray. In short, one can see here, at the very outset of the play, both Bolingbroke's manipulation of his image and some elements of it that he cannot control.

It is impossible for Henry to foresee the chain of events that will bring him to the crown. His duel with Mowbray is first scheduled by Richard and then called off as the king exiles both Bolingbroke and Mowbray. Relenting only somewhat—and that whimsically—as John of Gaunt pleads for his son, Richard reduces Henry's sentence by four years. And then we see in Bolingbroke's response the fascination with power that will eventually lead him to the throne:

> How long a time lies in one little word!
> Four lagging winters and four wanton springs
> End in a word: such is the breath of kings.[3]

One can imagine the gleam in his eye, evoked by neither relief nor gratitude but by marvel at what it is that a king can do with just a few carelessly uttered words. It is at this point, one may surmise, that Henry begins to think about taking the crown from an indecisive and arbitrary king. Like many an ambitious courtier, he is at once enchanted by what supreme power can do and contemptuous of its current holder.

He eventually returns in arms, but nominally only to reclaim what is rightfully his. He rallies around himself other nobles who have either been damaged by Richard or merely despise him and, in a sequence of confrontations with the despairing king, wrests the throne from him. Yet he does not openly express his desire to be king. He is discretion personified, content to let the mercurial Richard crumple under pressure and, indeed, without violence. In the climactic scene in which he wins the crown, he orders his subordinates to negotiate with Richard. The speech is extraordinary in its shift of emotional tones. He begins by instructing his emissaries to convey to the king that

> Henry Bolingbroke
> On both his knees doth kiss King Richard's hand
> And sends allegiance and true faith of heart
> To his most royal person, hither come

Even at his feet to lay my arms and power,
Provided that my banishment repeal'd
And lands restored again be freely granted.

Thus far, moderation. And then the bloody threat:

If not, I'll use the advantage of my power
And lay the summer's dust with showers of blood
Rain'd from the wounds of slaughter'd Englishmen.

And then moderation again, albeit with language designed to evoke slaughter should Richard fail to yield:

The which, how far off from the mind of Bolingbroke
It is, such crimson tempest should bedrench
The fresh green lap of fair King Richard's land,
My stooping duty tenderly shall show.[4]

It is a breathtaking combination of deference and brutal threat, coupled with the suggestion that there is still a way out. It is calculated to unsettle the high-strung Richard—and does so.

Bolingbroke further explains to the nobles how he will approach Richard:

Methinks King Richard and myself should meet
With no less terror than the elements
Of fire and water, when their thundering shock
At meeting tears the cloudy cheeks of heaven.
Be he the fire, I'll be the yielding water:
The rage be his, whilst on the earth I rain
My waters; on the earth, and not on him.

The passage could have come from the Taoist classic the *Tao Te Ching*, which celebrates the virtue of water over stone in achieving one's aims. Henry will always distort reality to some extent but can never do so completely. He may pretend to be a cooling and calming draught of water, but he holds in reserve an unlimited capacity for violence.

One acquires power by using people for one's own ends. Bolingbroke often does this directly, though he also works indirectly, through the much rougher Northumberland. Henry is superficially all deference to the toppling King Richard, instructing his followers, "Stand all apart, And show fair duty to his majesty." And when Richard, weeping and distraught, asks for a mirror to see "what a face I have, Since it is bankrupt of his majesty," Bolingbroke orders one for him. When Northumberland presses Richard to sign his abdication papers, causing the latter to lash out, "Fiend, thou torments me ere I come to hell!" Bolingbroke pulls Northumberland back. "Urge it no more, my Lord Northumberland."[5] Similarly, he can show clemency, to the Bishop of Carlisle, for example, who has remained loyal to Richard and reproached Henry and prophetically warns of the civil strife to follow. Yet that indulgence is measured, as with all of Bolingbroke's actions: he pardons the bishop while being careful to put him under a kind of house arrest.

> Carlisle, this is your doom:
> Choose out some secret place, some reverend room,
> More than thou hast, and with it joy thy life.
> So as thou liv'st in peace, die free from strife;
> For though mine enemy thou hast ever been,
> High sparks of honour in thee have I seen.[6]

This is staged, like so many of Bolingbroke's words and deeds. He is showing kingly magnanimity while neutering a potentially dangerous opponent by sending him to "some secret place."

None of this should be taken to suggest that Bolingbroke is in any way soft. Far from it: he orders the summary execution of two of Richard's key aides, dehumanizing them as "caterpillars of the commonwealth," and in the end he orders, by indirection, Richard's murder in the dungeon at Pomfret Castle. This he does not even do in our hearing. Rather, we learn it from the murderer Exton:

> Exton: Didst thou not mark the King, what words he spake:
> "Have I no friend will rid me of this living fear?"
> Was it not so?
> 1st Servant: These were his very words.
> Exton: "Have I no friend?" quoth he. He spake it twice,
> And urged it twice together, did he not?
> 2nd Servant: He did.
> Exton: and speaking it, he wishtly looked on me,
> As who should say, "I would thou wert the man
> That would divorce this terror from my heart,"
> Meaning the King at Pomfret. Come, let's go.
> I am the King's friend, and will rid his foe.[7]

The murder is ordered covertly, but once it becomes inescapably public, Henry bobs and weaves once again. When Exton appears to collect his reward, Henry turns on him. He does not deny that he had requested the murder, but he declares, with the ingratitude of a king,

> They love not poison that do poison need,
> Nor do I thee.

And with that he banishes the astonished Exton: "With Cain go wander through shades of night / And never show thy head by day nor light."

The ingratitude of princes is proverbial. It is also necessary: the people who do the dirty work of politics are often not the ones you want to have lingering around thereafter. It is one of the reasons that a favorite Washington pastime is watching a presidential transition, because it is quite certain that the advisers who helped during the campaign will find themselves shockingly displaced by others who are more needed. This is even true of politicians with much higher standards of ethics than Henry Bolingbroke.

Winston Churchill finally succeeded Neville Chamberlain as prime minister of Great Britain just as German panzer armies crashed through French lines in May 1940. He had been ably seconded by a courageous band of Conservative rebels who had, like him, criticized Chamberlain from the time of the disastrous September 1938 Munich conference and even before. Their fierce opposition helped topple Chamberlain and replace him with their hero and leader. Their considerable courage in defying their party elders was ill rewarded, however, by Churchill's decision to retain the old Tory establishment and profess a respect and even affection for the fallen prime minister. They were stunned.[8] Yet Churchill believed he had little choice: he needed experienced old hands to run the government, and even more importantly, he knew how shaky his hold on power was. The old barons of the Conservative Party may have distrusted him, and he may have disliked them, but he needed them, at least for the moment. Power did not simply fall into Churchill's lap. Indeed, he deserved as much blame as Chamberlain, or more, for the debacle of the Norwegian campaign that toppled his predecessor. Like Henry Bolingbroke he cultivated an image, accurate enough, of energy and enterprise; but he also outmaneuvered his rival Edward Halifax to succeed to the prime ministership. It was acquisition at work here, not inheritance.

At least Churchill was not sanctimonious. Henry IV, in Shakespeare's telling, certainly is. After banishing Richard II's murderers, he turns to his court and declares,

> Lords, I protest, my soul is full of woe
> That blood should sprinkle me to make me grow.
> Come, mourn with me for what I do lament
> And put on sullen black incontinent.
> I'll make a voyage to the Holy Land
> To wash this blood off from my guilty hand.
> March sadly after; grace my mournings here
> In weeping after this untimely bier.

Henry does very little that is not calculated, including making this confession. That he desired Richard's death and orchestrated it is too widely known to be denied—so he will admit to it. But he will put on a show of sorrow and declare his intention to atone by going on crusade against the infidel. He never does, although again in *Henry IV, Part 1* and *Part 2*, he avows his desire to go fight in the Holy Land only to die, in a calculated irony of Shakespeare's, in a room named "Jerusalem." Dissembling to the end, Henry celebrates this:

> Laud be to God, even there my life must end.
> It hath been prophesied to me many years
> I should not die but in Jerusalem,
> Which vainly I supposed the Holy Land.
> But bear me to that chamber: there I'll lie.
> In that Jerusalem shall Harry die.[9]

It is characteristic of Henry that he tries to have his interpretation of events perpetuated, even when it is, to put it mildly, implausible.

Henry's rise to power is artfully achieved. It is in some measure concealed, as he explains to his son, Prince Hal, in *Henry IV, Part 1*. Little wonder, then, that he would disapprove of Prince Hal's making a public spectacle of himself by keeping low company. His deceptions were as deep but different, and he cannot imagine acquiring power in such a fashion. He reprimands his son for his brazenness:

> Had I so lavish of my presence been,
> So common-hackneyed in the eyes of men,
> So stale and cheap to vulgar company,
> Opinion, that did help me to the crown,
> Had still kept loyal to possession
> And left me in reputeless banishment,
> A fellow of no mark nor likelihood.
> By being seldom seen, I could not stir
> But, like a comet, I was wondered at.

In his own telling, the mystery of remoteness was key to Henry Bolingbroke's acquisition of power. Charles de Gaulle employed a similar technique. As a little-known brigadier general in 1940, he assembled a motley group of resisters and adventurers in London following the defeat of France in a lightning war. Against the odds he became the leader of Free France, the liberator of Paris, and, until 1946, the effective leader of France. Falling from office he retreated to his Normandy home, Colombey-les-Deux-Églises, until in 1958 he was summoned to the leadership of a France rent by near civil war over the conflict in Algeria in the 1950s. From then until 1970 he created and presided over the Fifth French Republic. Few politicians have understood or wielded the power of calculated aloofness as he did.

De Gaulle kept a close eye on affairs during his self-imposed exile from Paris and from politics but was able to avoid the manipulation and deceptions upon which Bolingbroke had to rely. In Henry IV's speech to his son Hal he reveals more of how he wrested the throne from Richard:

> And then I stole all courtesy from heaven
> And dressed myself in such humility
> That I did pluck allegiance from men's hearts.[10]

Again, the mask slips: his humility was dressing, his courtesy stolen, and his allegiance snatched. It is a picture of an unlovely human being doing unlovely things to get power. He may have some pangs of conscience, but like most ambitious men who have cut their way to the top, he does not intend to dwell overmuch on how he got there, other than to give himself a sly pat on the back for having fooled his way to the crown.

Henry Bolingbroke outmaneuvers the hysterical Richard without causing outright civil war, at least initially. He wins the adherence (temporarily) of lords and chieftains who not unreasonably consider themselves his equals. He takes power, consolidates it, and in this play and the two that follow it (*Henry IV, Part 1* and *Part 2*) manages to pass it on intact to his son, Henry V. He does this through artifice, although never completely successful artifice, which explains the quarrels and fights that dog him throughout his reign. But complete concealment of political ploys is never really possible. As the adage goes, one cannot fool all of the people all of the time. Henry's success rests on fooling, or in some ways confusing, people just enough.

Henry climbs to power by means that are partly justified by Richard's incompetence, misrule, and, indeed, injustice. But Henry's hands are also stained with blood, and his pretense of merely seeking redress for wrongs convinces no one, not even himself. His desire for power and his calculated ruthlessness are softened, occasionally masked, but never completely invisible to an attentive observer.

Henry has acquired power through open struggle backed by subterfuge. He commits a crime to be sure, but he has not achieved power by pure, unsuspected conspiracy. And like most who get there, he seems to understand that he cannot simply conceal his ambition; rather, he must soften its edges, seduce as much as or more than he coerces, and, while always holding lethal measures in reserve, seek, wherever possible, to win power by acclaim rather than mere force. And yet, as masterful as he is, the whiff of illegitimacy never leaves Henry or even his son. At the same time, those who have brought him to power will think themselves aggrieved that they have not been allowed to share equally in it. By hiding some of his own control of the situation behind a masterful noble like Northumberland, whom he uses to great effect, Henry sets up his own continuing struggles.

Great democratic politicians, even the most successful ones and even the best of them, often have more than a whiff of Henry IV about them. Take Abraham Lincoln, who went from an obscure background as an ungainly, ill-dressed country lawyer to president. Like Henry IV, he had a talent for saying things that were largely, but not entirely, truthful. In his first great debate with Senator Stephen A. Douglas, for example, he insisted, "I have no purpose directly or indirectly to interfere with the institution of slavery in the States where it exists. I believe I have no lawful right to do so, and I have no inclination to do so."[11] Strictly speaking that may have been true—or not. As his acidic former law partner, William Herndon, once remarked, "Any man who took Lincoln for a simple-minded man would very soon wake up with his back in a ditch."[12]

Lincoln, like Henry, had an acute sense of the theatricality of politics. His calculated decision to grow a beard in 1860, making a craggy face older and more like that of the "Father Abraham" he would become in popular songs of the time, was but one of many theatrical gestures. He had selected the opportune moment to soften his image without weakening it. He, like Henry, thought timing everything in politics—a common theme in Shakespeare as well. When he decided that the moment was ripe to tackle the question of slavery, he rejected compromise, famously saying, "The tug has to come & better now than later."[13]

From the first, the aspiring politician faced challenges to his legitimacy. Lincoln was a new man from the rough West, who had to win Easterners over by careful speech, which he did in his famous Cooper's Union address of February 27, 1860. He thought of costuming for this occasion, and so, in a not entirely successful effort to dispel the image of a crude Westerner, went out and bought a new Brooks Brothers suit.[14] And he had to deal with potentially rivalrous nobles, of a kind, the leaders of the new Republican Party, who, with reason, considered themselves more experienced, better educated, and even more popular than him.

Most of all, Lincoln was, like Henry, deeply ambitious. His unillusioned law partner, Willy Herndon, captured it best: "He was always calculating, and always planning ahead. His ambition was a little engine that knew no rest."[15] And as with Henry, his aims and ambitions were not always on display.

Lincoln was, of course, an infinitely greater man than Shakespeare's Henry IV. He had the ability to genuinely win others over to his side in a way that Henry ultimately could not—there is no one comparable in Henry's court to William Seward, the secretary of state who had been a rival for the Republican Party nomination and initially attempted to arrogate to himself near-presidential powers, but whom Lincoln won over. Most importantly, of course, Lincoln's moral core and statesmanlike vision have no parallel in Henry, or indeed any other Shakespearean character. Henry may have wanted to be a good king, but preserving his kingdom was something different and lesser than Lincoln's desire to preserve the Union.

And yet Henry's story illuminates some aspect of Lincoln as well. Lincoln's power rested on artifice as much as on moral force. He contrived to ensure that the Southern states would fire the first shot of the war, thereby unifying the North; he appointed generals whom he knew to be incompetent because they would guarantee the support of their communities. In a discussion with Secretary of War Edwin Stanton over the appointment of Alexander Schimmelfennig, a Prussian-born soldier of doubtful skill, he reportedly declared, "The only point I make is, that there has got to be something done that will be unquestionably in the interest of the Dutch [German-Americans], and to that end, I want Schimmelfennig appointed." When the secretary protested that Schimmelfennig was not the best of the German Americans available, Lincoln replied, "No matter about that, his name will make up for any difference there may be, and I'll take the risk of his coming out all right."[16]

And so Schimmelfennig was appointed a general, despite his having spent most of the Battle of Gettysburg hiding in the town in which his men had gotten hopelessly disorganized. In a more serious vein, Lincoln ordered General Ulysses S. Grant to refrain from costly offensive operations in 1864 in order to secure his reelection. He repeatedly blocked potentially mutinous members of his cabinet by moving them at opportune moments. The statement oft attributed to Lincoln— "Honest statesmanship is the wise employment of individual meanness for the public good"—bespeaks a deeply cunning man who had no illusions about political figures or their motivations.

Both Shakespeare's Henry IV and Lincoln, to differing degrees, end as tragic figures, having achieved the preeminence they desired, accomplished what they sought—and paid an immense personal price to do so. Neither could be described as happy, and both were lonely. Both knew that their hands had necessarily been dipped in blood, and although they accepted that necessity, neither relished it. Both were profoundly realistic about the people around them.

Power may be acquired in ways other than Henry IV's or Lincoln's careful calculation and maneuvering. Sometimes it comes within reach because of some outstanding quality or achievement. But this often does not work out well, because the acquisition of power hinges on versatility and agility. Outstanding ability alone will not suffice, particularly when military heroes enter politics. Nowhere does Shakespeare make this clearer than in his telling of the tale of Martius, the triumphant Roman general who turns traitor to his country and meets a pitiful death at the hands of the enemies he has joined with the idea of punishing Rome for its treatment of him.

The setting of the tale in the play *Coriolanus* is a Rome riven between patricians and plebians. The play opens with famine and crowds protesting and complaining. One of the patricians, Menenius, does his best to soothe the mob; Martius, who is an eloquent if not a reflective speaker, baits them. Meeting the crowd he opens by saying,

> What's the matter, you dissentious rogues
> That, rubbing the poor itch of your opinion,
> Make yourselves scabs?[17]

He despises their cowardice and, even more so, their fickleness.

> He that depends
> Upon your favours, swims with fins of lead,
> And hews down oaks with rushes. Hang ye! Trust ye?
> With every minute you do change a mind,

> And call him noble that was now your hate,
> Him vile that was your garland.[18]

Shakespeare gives us nothing to make us think that Martius is wrong in this fundamental judgment, although he shows a crowd more divided in its opinion than perhaps the arrogant general believes.

But a military crisis calls forth all of Martius's talents, and he leads the Roman army in a victorious campaign against the city of Corioles, home of the Volscians. He is then honored with a new name, Coriolanus, and sets his sights on election to the consulship.

In a Rome that no longer has kings, the rank of consul is the greatest honor of all. Despite the reservations of some of the plebians and the worried opposition of their representatives, the tribunes, Coriolanus seems on the verge of achieving what he desires. A confused crowd of citizens is ready to confer the title he craves so long as he submits to one condition: that he show them the wounds he has received in Rome's service.

The pliable, well-fed, and often-liquored patrician Menenius attempts to counsel Coriolanus, advising him to speak in accommodating tones to the crowd. Coriolanus responds,

> What must I say?—
> "I pray sir,"—Plague upon't! I cannot bring
> My tongue to such a pace. "Look, sir, my wounds!
> I got them in my country's service, when
> Some certain of your brethren roar'd and ran
> From th'noise of our own drums."

Menenius pleads with his friend:

> O me, the gods!
> You must not speak of that; you must desire them
> To think upon you.[19]

But it is no use. Coriolanus makes the case that at least he does not flatter the crowd; they will have none of it. They want to see the wounds, and then the general cracks,

> Better it is to die, better to starve,
> Than crave the hire which first we do deserve.[20]

Matters go downhill from there, the two wily tribunes inciting Coriolanus to more outrageous statements and the plebians outraged by his insults. He narrowly escapes death and is instead banished from the city. He turns on them in wounded pride and a magnificent, vengeful fury:

> You common cry of curs! Whose breath I hate
> As reek o'th'rotten fens, whose loves I prize
> As the dead carcasses of unburied men
> That do corrupt my air: I banish you!
> And here remain with your uncertainty!
> Let every feeble rumour shake your hearts!
> Your enemies, with nodding of their plumes,
> Fan you into despair! Have the power still
> To banish your defenders, till at length
> Your ignorance—which finds not till it feels,
> Making but reservation of yourselves,
> Still your own foes—deliver you as most
> Abated captives to some nation
> That won you without blows! Despising
> For you the city, thus I turn my back.
> There is a world elsewhere![21]

And before very long Coriolanus has deserted to the Volscians, throwing himself on the mercy of an old enemy, Aufidius. He leads their armies against Rome but refrains from devastating the city at the pleading of his family; he is then in turn killed by the outraged army of his adopted city, egged on by Aufidius, who envies his prowess.

The story of Coriolanus is of a brilliant leader—there can be little doubt that he is the general one would want in any fight—but one who is unidimensional in his leadership. Fighting men admire him, and indeed one of Aufidius's lingering grudges is that his own soldiers rhapsodize about the Roman general. He is courageous, eloquent, and—in war—shrewd. As a political leader, however, he is a failure, and that is entirely predictable from Act 1 of the play, not just because of his temper but because his values are at odds with those of a republic. He aspires to the highest political office but has no political skills, and the qualities that serve him so well as a battlefield commander hinder him from understanding, let alone playing, the game of popular politics.

The crowd wants Coriolanus to show them his wounds. In the play's context that is meant quite literally: they want to see the scars. They want this not to verify Coriolanus's record but rather to gawk—and perhaps to bring him down to their level. They want to strip him naked and see where the sword has bitten into human flesh. It is a very democratic sentiment to which democratic societies today are equally prone. Citizens of the United States in the twenty-first century also clamor to see their leaders' wounds—their marks of personal suffering or, to use a cant word of the time, their "vulnerability." They wish to celebrate not their heroism but the frailness of their humanity. The Franklin Delano Roosevelt Memorial, dedicated by President Bill Clinton in 1997, shows that aesthetic. The thirty-second president, who led his country through World War II, is shown in a wheelchair. In real life he went to great lengths to conceal the disability, resulting from polio, that had left him confined to it, and he would not have wished to be portrayed that way.

The popular clamor for the showing of wounds exhibits itself in the contemporary treatment of veterans as victims rather than heroes. It is unquestionably the case that America's wars in Iraq and Afghanistan, as in Vietnam before them, included many examples of the traditional martial virtues of bravery, coolness under fire, perseverance, and decisiveness in a crisis. Yet those receive much less attention than post-combat stress in all its many forms. Rather than focusing on true acts of bravery, the thing to do is to thank soldiers for their service, and to do so indiscriminately, for example, by giving first rights in boarding an airplane to those who have worn their uniform, even if their service has consisted entirely of repairing tanks in Fort Hood, Texas, a duty for which they are well compensated.

Earlier generations celebrated sergeants Alvin York or Audie Murphy, who displayed the soldierly virtues in combat to astonishing degrees. This was true of generations in which a mass military was mobilized from the male population, with virtually all families touched by conscription and military service. In such a world celebration of traditional martial virtues came easier than it does today, when civilians are distant from the world of military service.

Most Americans today would be hard-pressed to name any recipients of the Medal of Honor for service in Iraq or Afghanistan. But they are curious about the psychological wounds of American service personnel and often wish to gaze at those. When teaching a course on Shakespeare to a class that included at least half a dozen veterans of these recent wars, I asked whether any of them had been asked, in effect, to show their wounds. What ensued was a set of uncomfortable and even bitter reminiscences from men and women who had served honorably, even with distinction, and asked neither to be pitied nor to have their psyches probed by those for whom war was a kind of spectator sport.

Yet, quite apart from the particularly painful indignity that Coriolanus refuses to endure and some contemporary soldiers must, we easily see that he is doomed to fail in winning, as he wishes, the consulship. His violent and uncontrolled temper is just one flaw among many. Although soldiers sometimes rise to high political office, many try and fail, lacking as Coriolanus does (if to a lesser degree) the wiles and flexibility that democratic politicians need. After America's wars some generals have made it: Zachary Taylor and Ulysses S. Grant come to mind following the nineteenth-century Mexican-American and Civil Wars, respectively, as does Dwight D. Eisenhower, who won two terms in office as president in the mid-twentieth century. Yet, for the most part, generals have failed when they tried their hands at electoral politics: Leonard Wood, for example, the towering military figure of the early twentieth century, is today barely remembered but ran for president; William Westmoreland, America's Vietnam commander, could not gain a Senate seat in conservative South Carolina; Wesley Clark, a brilliant and compelling general in the late twentieth century, failed thoroughly in his run for supreme office.

America is not alone in generating talented generals who are hopeless politicians. In Israel, which has been at war ever since its inception, some generals have come to the top: Ariel Sharon, most notably, and before him Yitzhak Rabin. But most others, whose names are now obscure, have failed utterly. They have done so despite the genuine and profound admiration of most Israelis for their military. And the reason is that they are unfit to navigate what Coriolanus, in a rare moment of insight, calls the world's "slippery turns." Ariel Sharon captured this best in his autobiography. After describing military experience at the top as one in which a leader experiences "great victories and also terrible defeats," moments of "exultation and of deepest grief," fear and horror, and the experience of life and death decisions, he captures his astonishment at the world of politics:

> The same person enters the political world and finds that he has one mouth to speak with and one hand to vote with, exactly like the man sitting next to him. And that man perhaps has never witnessed or experienced anything profound or anything dramatic in his life. He does not know either the heights or the depths. He has never tested himself or made crucial decisions or taken responsibility for his life or the lives of his fellows. And this man—it seems incredible—but this man too has one mouth and one hand.[22]

While there are those like Sharon or de Gaulle who can bridge the gap—although de Gaulle himself reflected at length on the profound differences between soldier and politician—for the most part the temperaments of the two are well-nigh unbridgeable.[23]

Coriolanus reminds us of the truth that different forms of excellence in leadership are often not fungible. The hero of the play does not understand this, because he is singularly unreflective—his emotions and his views are transparent, and interestingly, he seems incapable of a set-piece soliloquy. And he is crippled as a political leader in one other way. In the climactic scene at the end of the play, when he is about to be killed, his nemesis Aufidius taunts him. Martius has called on the god of war, Mars, and Aufidius sneers at him, "Name not the god, thou boy of tears!" It is a shocking moment. Coriolanus, in almost his last words before the mob falls upon him, calling up as they do memories of slain sons and daughters, fathers and cousins, shouts,

> Cut me to pieces, Volsces, men and lads,
> Stain all your edges on me. Boy! False hound!
> If you have writ your annals true, 'tis there,
> That like an eagle in a dove-cote, I
> Flutter'd your Volscians in Corioles.
> Alone I did it. Boy![24]

Yet this scream—it is not really a speech—proves Aufidius's point. Coriolanus is, in fact, a boy. He has a boy's pride, a boy's lack of judgment, a boy's soaring self-image (he imagines himself an eagle, when he is at least as much a butcher), a boy's generosity, and a boy's foolish self-absorption. Like a boy he cannot see himself as others see him, and like a boy he is astonished and outraged by craftiness and duplicity.

Coriolanus's boyishness is not unique. In his poem "The March into Virginia," Herman Melville wrote,

> All wars are boyish, and are fought by boys
> The champions and enthusiasts of the state.

He was right. There is often in the military character something of boyishness in its admirable sense: generosity, bravery, innocence, and straightforwardness. But those very qualities are at odds with those required in politics, which is why Aufidius consistently loses to Coriolanus on the battlefield and yet deftly does him in on the field of politics.

In the end, however, Coriolanus has succumbed not only to his own simplicity in matters political but to his sense of honor—that pride that forbade him to exhibit his scars to the people of Rome and caused him to boast to the Volscians of his exploits in killing large numbers of them rather than make the case that he had just saved them from yet another ruinous war. He is a traitor done in, paradoxically, by his sense of honor.

The same story can be told of Benedict Arnold, who became the archetypal American traitor, racking up an extraordinary series of military successes in the war for American independence before switching sides with the hope of leading British armies against his erstwhile countrymen. A self-taught soldier, he helped seize the critical outpost of Fort Ticonderoga in upstate New York from a British garrison, led an extraordinary march to Quebec from Boston in 1775, very nearly taking the city, conducted a brilliant rearguard action as the rebels were forced to retreat from Canada, built and led an American fleet that successfully delayed a British invasion in 1776, and in 1777 was singularly responsible for the battles that would ultimately doom a second British invasion and lead to the surrender of a British-German army under Major General John Burgoyne—an event that in turn smoothed the way for French intervention in the American Revolution and eventual American independence. During that time as well, Arnold received at Quebec and again at Saratoga crippling leg wounds; in earlier campaigns he lost most of his considerable personal fortune as well as his first wife, who died while he was at the front.

And yet he turned traitor, compromising American defensive plans for West Point on the Hudson, nearly entrapping George Washington and his official party, and when his cover was blown by the arrest of his handler, Major John André in 1779, he fled to the British garrison in New York. Nor did his treason end there: receiving the rank of brigadier general in the British army, he led two destructive raids into American territory, burning his hometown of Norwalk, Connecticut, in one and very nearly capturing Thomas Jefferson in Virginia in the other. He cautioned Lord Cornwallis about the folly of letting himself get backed into the Yorktown peninsula and wrote a sensible memorandum to King George III on what it would take to mobilize Loyalists to fight against the American rebels.

Contemporaries before and after have long wondered what drove Arnold to treason. Prior to switching sides, he had served as military governor of Philadelphia, where he was at odds with local politicians intent on persecuting Loyalist sympathizers. Accused of peculation he received a relatively mild reprimand from George Washington, who was not, in truth, particularly concerned by Arnold's behavior. Up to the very moment the treason was revealed, Washington believed that Arnold was his most capable and devoted subordinate. Arnold had been passed over earlier for promotion, but he was nevertheless one of only a handful of major generals by the time he reached out to the British; he had been hounded by those who had, in his view, failed in the field, but he had nevertheless earned himself a secure place in the American revolutionary pantheon.

Later generations contented themselves by viewing Arnold as a cruel, malevolent, and even cowardly figure. None of these square with the facts as known or with the documented admiration and respect that he had from his most capable subordinates, peers, and superiors. Difficult as it is to reconstruct the motivation of historical figures, one has to think that like Coriolanus, Arnold fell victim to an outraged sense of honor. Convalescing from his second wound, received at the Battle of Saratoga in 1777, when he played the leading role in defeating the British invasion from Canada, he came to the conclusion that "having so fervently given so much to the cause of liberty," he had been "utterly betrayed."[25]

Arnold, like Coriolanus, felt that he had been treated extraordinarily shabbily by those whom he had saved from disaster. He too had his wounds—there is on the battlefield of Saratoga a monument to the leg that bore them—which he disdained showing to the congressional committees probing his conduct. Perhaps, like Coriolanus, he had seen too much war, and it had left him psychologically scarred. But it is not difficult to imagine him delivering a speech like Coriolanus's at the end of Act 3:

> Despising
> For you the city, thus I turn my back.
> There is a world elsewhere!

He too had fallen victim to outraged pride.

Neither Coriolanus nor Arnold ever found a way back to power. Both discovered that traitors to one side are very rarely trusted by those who have welcomed their treachery. Neither had the possibility of political success in gaining or retaining power. Neither could empathize, let alone sympathize, with the politicians who tormented them, much less figure out how to outwit them. Both were splendid military leaders, whose leadership could not survive in the world of political power, much less reach the heights there.

The acquisition of power by maneuver and cunning requires aptitudes and skills unlike those of military leadership. The Arnolds and Coriolanuses and other generals who would not dream of turning traitor never quite understand that the qualities that have given them success in war will unfit them for success in politics. Allowing for differences, it is a surprising discovery for other accomplished men and women who learn that what got you to your current position of eminence will not take you to the very top.

In the world as it is, the Henry Bolingbrokes (and in the best case, the Abraham Lincolns) are the ones who can achieve power, cloaking, if not entirely concealing, their ambition and their artifices, adjusting their methods and appearance to circumstances, using both clemency and punishment without sentiment and often without personal animus. They have, above all, the supreme virtue of unillusioned realism about their fellow creatures and the overwhelming drive for power without which they could not succeed. The Coriolanuses and Arnolds, less calculating, more ardent, and in some ways more brilliant, can achieve success and earn glory, but only in one dimension. Yet neither tale is a happy one. The tragedy of a Bolingbroke or a Lincoln lies in the melancholy of their realism; the tragedy of a Coriolanus or an Arnold lies in their psychological fragility in the face of ingratitude from those they serve.

CHAPTER 4

Seizing It

H ENRY IV GAINED POWER USING ARTIFICE, BUT HE DID NOT SIMPLY take it. He arranged things so well that it was offered to him by Richard II, the king he would later order killed after donning the crown himself. Yet even with the acclaim of most of the other political figures of the realm—lords like Northumberland—and the acquiescence of the rest, his reign was haunted by his knowledge that all around him realized that he had not succeeded legitimately to the throne that Richard possessed by right. It is the fate of a successful aspirant to power to fear that others will take the same path. Still, Henry IV, though he has blood on his hands, does not simply take the crown by force; it is given to him by the psychologically broken man who unworthily wore it.

Very different is the path to power of those who openly wrest it from the hands of those who currently hold it, and who do so by real or metaphorical murder. Taking power in this way requires some kind of coup. Such things happen all the time in institutions and corporations as well as in politics, and Shakespeare explores their manifestations across numerous plays.

At their most incisive, Shakespeare's portraits of power open for us the minds of those who climb to the top over the bodies—real or metaphorical—of the previous incumbents. He does this nowhere more powerfully than in *Julius Caesar* and *Macbeth*. Among Shakespeare's many insights is that the first murder invariably leads to others and that Macbeth's hope that "this blow / Might be the be-all and the end-all" is vain—as indeed the murderous noble suspects.[1] One killing will lead to another, and another, with little hope for a peaceful outcome at the end of it all, bringing at best a reign haunted by the fear of assassins as talented as oneself.

Shakespeare shows us that this naive hope flows from the complex motives of those who conspire against a king. That very complexity often helps undo the successful plotters in ways that he explores. His rendering of the assassination of Julius Caesar and the eventual defeat of the conspirators by Caesar's nephew Octavius (later Augustus Caesar), his friend Mark Antony, and General Marcus Aemilius Lepidus is a study in the complexity of motives for taking power in this bloodiest of ways. When the play begins, Caesar is at the height of his popularity. He has been offered a crown, which he declines, but his rise motivates a group of conspirators to turn against him and eventually kill him in the Senate.

Why do they do it? At the very end of the play, Mark Antony, Caesar's devoted friend and eventual avenger, condemns them as having acted out of jealousy. Perhaps it is easier that way, because admitting the complexity of their motives might require a comparable look at his own and those of Caesar's avengers. Gazing at the corpse of Brutus, the leader of the conspiracy, he declares,

> All the conspirators save only he
> Did that they did in envy of great Caesar
> He only, in general honest thought
> And common good to all, made one of them.[2]

As is often the case, Shakespeare has one of his characters offer a comfortable and plausible judgment that falls apart on close scrutiny. It would be simpler for all concerned if the conspirators consisted only of an envious and deplorable gang led by a misguided but honest patriot. That would make it easier to knit back together the fabric of Roman elite politics. But that is not the reality as Shakespeare depicts it.

From the outset of the play the variety of the motives that lead to the conspiracy against Caesar are on display. In the opening scene two senators, Marullus and Flavius, chase away the commoners celebrating Caesar's triumphs, offering as they do so two expressions of resentment of Caesar. The senators are angry at Caesar's defeat of Pompey the Great, whom he is causing the Romans to forget. They worry too that if Caesar becomes king, he will "keep us all in servile fearfulness." These emotions are not envy but resentment of a certain kind of injustice to Pompey and anxiety about their own futures.

The most complex motivations are those of Cassius, the close friend of Brutus, who eventually lures and manipulates him into leading the conspiracy. Cassius's initial argument to Brutus for the conspiracy does not suggest that he envies Caesar's reputation, power, or wealth. Rather, he says,

> Why man, he doth bestride the narrow world
> Like a Colossus, and we petty men
> Walk under his huge legs and peep about
> To find ourselves dishonorable graves.[3]

The issue for Cassius and those like him—ambitious, capable men—is not that they want what Caesar has but that they fear he will prevent them from getting what *they* desire most, namely, honor. As Cassius tells Brutus, "Well, honor is the subject of my story."

Cassius's craving for honor could not survive under a protracted Caesarean dictatorship. A Rome in which members of their class jostle for office and military success would, under Caesar's domination, become one in which one man alone would hold the former and get all credit for the latter. It galls Cassius to think about that, particularly since he knows Caesar to be but a frail human being like the rest of us—who feels the cold and once needed Cassius's help to swim across a rushing river. Moreover, Cassius sees in Caesar's rise not merely the ascendancy of an unworthy competitor but a sign of the decline of a republic that, in his own way, he cherishes.

> Poor man, I know he would not be a wolf
> But that he sees the Romans are but sheep.[4]

No one envies a wolf, and most certainly no Roman ever admired a sheep. Cassius's conspiracy is the product of a dark view of his political predicament, that of a man of strength and vision in a decadent society. He craves power, to be sure, but as an opportunity both to display and make use of his own considerable talents and to stop the decline of a political order that allowed men like him to rise and distinguish themselves. One of the other conspirators, Caska, puts it starkly:

> Indeed, they say the senators tomorrow
> Mean to establish Caesar as a king,
> And he shall wear his crown by sea and land
> In every place save here in Italy.[5]

Still other conspirators have more personal motives. The setup for the actual killing of Caesar falls to Metellus Cimber, who comes to plead for Caesar to rescind the banishment of his brother, Publius Cimber. Caesar's haughty dismissal of the plea—which both Brutus and Cassius have seconded—is the signal for Caska to plunge the first knife into Caesar's body.

As for Brutus, despite Mark Antony's encomium at the end of the play, it is far from clear that envy does *not* play a role in shaping his decision to turn on his benefactor. He is won over to the conspiracy in part by the flattery orchestrated by Cassius, who forges messages from citizens calling upon Brutus to be true to his ancestors who drove the

Tarquin kings from Rome. And indeed, Cassius is more direct than that.

> The fault, dear Brutus, is not in our stars
> But in ourselves, that we are underlings.
> "Brutus" and "Caesar": what should be in that "Caesar"?
> Why should that name be sounded more than yours?[6]

Cassius, the keenest student of human nature in the play, has appealed directly to Brutus's envy, and not without effect.

In the end, however, it is not just envy that brings Brutus to the point of assassination but fear that Julius Caesar is like "a serpent's egg / Which hatched, would as his kind grow mischievous." If Caesar is indeed "a serpent's egg," Brutus must "kill him in the shell."[7] In this, as in other respects, the conspirators' motives for getting rid of Caesar do not lack foundation. He is a man who clearly yearns to be king and who will endanger not only their positions in society but their very understanding of who they are.

Brutus will have his way throughout the play. He brooks little opposition in his direction of the conspiracy and no rivalry, deflecting the participation of Cicero with the excuse that the great orator and statesman—his only real peer in Rome—would "never follow anything / That other men begin."[8] In truth, neither would Brutus. He has been Caesar's friend, and Caesar his benefactor. In some fundamental ways he resembles him, because he too is determined to lead, not follow. Nor does he lack a high opinion of his own virtues. When he later quarrels with Cassius, he says,

> There is no terror, Cassius, in your threats:
> For I am armed so strong in honesty
> That they pass by me as the idle wind.[9]

In this Brutus resembles Caesar, who makes a great show of his fearlessness. There are in both the leader of the conspiracy and its victim similar veins of arrogance and hubris, the assumption of superiority over their fellows and raw vanity. And it is indeed Brutus's overweening self-confidence that leads the conspirators to make their biggest mistakes, leaving Mark Antony alive and allowing him to make an unconstrained speech to the Roman mob over the corpse of Caesar.

Like so many other conspirators, the plotters against Caesar are divided by differing motives. They quarrel, they do not entirely trust one another, and in the end they lose decisively to Caesar's heir Octavius and Mark Antony. Yet they are not without dignity, captured best in the farewells of a reconciled Brutus and Cassius on the eve of the fatal Battle of Philippi:

> Brutus: And whether we shall meet again, I know not:
> Therefore our everlasting farewell take:
> For ever and for ever farewell, Cassius.
> If we do meet again, why, we shall smile;
> If not, why then this parting was well made.
> Cassius: For ever and for ever farewell, Brutus:
> If we do meet again, we'll smile indeed;
> If not, 'tis true this parting was well made.

The mirrored language here reflects a deeper harmony between Cassius and Brutus. They are different, but not quite as different as one might think; theirs is a real friendship, again analogous to that on the other side between Mark Antony and Caesar, but with greater fellow feeling. Whereas Antony worships Caesar and sees himself as a devoted follower, Cassius knows that Brutus is his superior, but only by a margin. In all the things that matter, their farewell language says that they are equals. They are comrades in a way that Antony and Caesar never could be.

Conspirators often have complicated motives. In American politics the most fascinating and ambiguous conspirator of all was Aaron Burr, killer of Alexander Hamilton, unwanted and unscrupulous vice president under Thomas Jefferson, would-be architect of a western independent country hived off from the United States, serial philanderer, devoted father, and traitor who got off on a misdemeanor and died in obscure poverty. Henry Adams, describing the inauguration of Thomas Jefferson as president and Burr as vice president, wrote, "An aristocrat imbued in the morality of Lord Chesterfield and Napoleon Bonaparte, Colonel Burr was the chosen head of Northern democracy, idol of the wards of New York city, and aspirant to the highest offices he could reach by means legal or beyond the law; for as he pleased himself with saying, after the manner of the First Consul of the French Republic, 'Great souls care little for small morals.'"[10]

Burr is as much a study for novelists as for biographers, and indeed Gore Vidal did a fine, if excessively sympathetic, job of capturing the twists and turns of his character in his fictional treatment of Burr's side of the tale.[11] His aging Burr is charming and, despite his numerous misdeeds, not a monster. Vidal is right in showing that Burr was not simply a scoundrel and a killer, even if he was a traitor and is most famous for a lethal duel with his chief rival. As Jefferson and other contemporaries understood, to defend the new republic against the likes of Burr and his plots, one had to reckon with that complexity.

When asked why public figures leak damaging national security information, one of the top reporters at the *Washington Post*, Thomas Ricks, said to me, "You would have to be Shakespeare to explain the motivations." True enough. Mark Felt, one of the most famous leakers of all time—the man who was chiefly responsible for the resignation of Richard M. Nixon from the presidency—turns out in retrospect to have been one of the most complicated conspirators of American history. He was the FBI deputy director who, as the source code-named Deep Throat, provided Bob Woodward and Carl Bernstein the raw materials for their exposés of election wrongdoings by Nixon's reelection campaign, beginning with the break-ins at the Watergate hotel complex. In retrospect, Woodward recalls, he and Bernstein had little time (or perhaps inclination) to inquire into Felt's motives. Decades later, Woodward concluded that the motives were profoundly mixed:

Felt wanted to protect the FBI, he disliked being at the beck and call of obnoxious White House staffers, he was furious at being passed over to succeed founding FBI director Edgar J. Hoover, and finally, "Felt liked the game." He enjoyed running Woodward as his agent.[12] In the name of integrity, Felt lied repeatedly about his role in Watergate, and he died a conflicted and probably an embittered man.

Conspirators alone do not make a successful conspiracy, however. It takes a willing or at least a complacent victim for that. Shakespeare's Henry IV, one can be quite certain, would not have exposed himself to his dangerous fellow nobles in the reckless way that Caesar does; nor would he have indulged in Caesar's many illusions. Cassius notes that Caesar is

> superstitious grown of late,
> Quite apart from the main opinion he held once
> Of fantasy, of dreams and ceremonies.[13]

Decius Brutus diagnoses the leader's weaknesses most accurately:

> When I tell him he hates flatterers,
> He says he does, being then most flattered.

Caesar has fallen into the trap of most dictators, past and present. He surrounds himself with those who feed his ego and openly and repeatedly avow his superiority to all others. He becomes impervious to bad news, to caution, and even to good sense. Caesar can be manipulated through these weaknesses, but there are others in addition that set him up for death. The first is his fatalism, and the second is his monstrous ego, which work together to pave the way for his fatal encounter in the Senate House on the Ides of March.

> Cowards die many times before their deaths;
> The valiant never taste of death but once.

And then, on his way to the Forum, when told of an ill omen (the augurs having opened up an animal offering without a heart), he says,

> Caesar should be a beast without a heart
> If he should stay at home today for fear.
> No, Caesar shall not. Danger knows full well
> That Caesar is more dangerous than he.
> We are two lions littered in one day,
> And I the elder and more terrible,
> And Caesar shall go forth.[14]

This personification of danger is preposterous. These are the words of a man who has lost touch with reality. Here, as on other occasions, Caesar speaks of himself in the third person, no mean indication of an ego out of control. One can hardly imagine a Winston Churchill or a Franklin D. Roosevelt, two men with powerful egos, speaking in such a way, although an Adolf Hitler might.

In his final speech rejecting Cassius's plea to pardon Publius Cimber, Caesar speaks with willful arrogance. Caesar cannot just turn down the request but has to insult the man making it.

> I could be well moved if I were as you:
> If I could pray to move, prayers would move me.
> But I am constant as the northern star,
> Of whose true-fixed and resting quality
> There is no fellow in the firmament.
> The skies are painted with unnumbered sparks:
> They are all fire, and every one doth shine;
> But there's but one in all doth hold his place.
> So in the world: 'tis furnished well with men,
> And men are flesh and blood, and apprehensive.
> Yet in the number I do know but one
> That unassailable holds on his rank

Unshaked of motion. And that I am he
Let me a little show it even in this.[15]

This is hubris, but it is more than that. The dictator begins by insulting a suppliant and continues by priding himself on a literally unearthly constancy, which those around him do not in fact believe he possesses. This is not mere stubbornness but a kind of intoxication with power and self, blinding Caesar to the fate that awaits him. A subtler man might have chosen selective clemency (and indeed, in historical fact, Caesar was skilled in that way). But Shakespeare's Caesar has lost all sense of proportion about himself, and with it the kind of wariness needed to preserve himself.

The success of a conspiracy, then, depends as much on the weakness of those conspired against as the skill of those who are plotting. Indeed, in some ways more so, because Brutus, disregarding the sound advice of Cassius, proceeds to set up his own political failure even once the assassination is done. It is not the murder of Caesar that dooms Brutus to his own death on the battlefield of Philippi. Rather, it is his failure to understand and accept the logic of the violent act that he has endorsed and led.

Cassius sees this early on. He says that Mark Antony, "so well beloved of Caesar," should not outlive him. He counsels, prudently, that Antony, "a shrewd contriver," should join Caesar in his bloody fate. But Brutus turns this down, declaring that such a course "will seem too bloody":

> Like wrath in death and envy afterwards—
> For Antony is but a limb of Caesar.
> Let's be sacrificers but not butchers, Caius . . .
> Let's kill him boldly, but not wrathfully:
> Let's carve him as a dish fit for the gods,
> Not hew him as a carcass fit for hounds.

Brutus too suffers from delusions, or rather, a fatal lack of realism. Murder is murder; the assassination is, and must of necessity be, butchery. Caesar cannot be "carved as a dish fit for the gods," and it is folly to think so. Cassius fully understands this, but his warnings go unheeded.

Brutus is keen that others will consider

> Our purpose necessary and not envious,
> Which so appearing to the common eyes,
> We shall be called purgers, not murderers.[16]

He cannot bear the thought of aspersions being cast on his motives; unable to think ill of himself, he, in his vanity, finds it intolerable that others will do so. Nor can he, in the strength of his self-understanding, realistically assess how others will view this bloody deed. His misconception of how others will see him and his clemency to Antony are fatal, because Cassius is right. Mark Antony is indeed "a shrewd contriver," a master manipulator and formidable soldier, and he will seek revenge.

Brutus refuses to accept the inevitable logic of violence, which is that one murderous, illegal act will require others in its train. He is, in his way, as vain as Caesar in wanting no one to think that he envies Caesar or that his motives are any but the purest. His speech over Caesar's corpse begins, "Believe me for mine honour and have respect to mine honour, that you may believe" and goes downhill from there. It is stilted, self-obsessed (he uses a personal pronoun more than a dozen times in one short paragraph and speaks in prose rather than the more compelling iambic pentameter suited to such an occasion), fixated on the purity of his own motives, and silent on Caesar's real or projected misdeeds. He refers to the other conspirators not at all.

Brutus has, moreover, made two gross errors in the stagecraft of coup. The first comes when he orders his fellows to

> Bathe our hands in Caesar's blood
> Up to the elbows and besmear our swords.
> Then walk we forth even to the market-place,

And waving our red weapons o'er our heads
Let's all cry, "Peace, Freedom and Liberty."[17]

It is an appeal that must ring hollow, because after a long period of civil war, Rome had been at internal peace under Caesar's dictatorship. Freedom and liberty mean less to the masses than they do to the patrician conspirators. And the sight of the bloodstained conspirators serves not to diminish the shock of Caesar's killing but rather to enhance it, not to create a sense of normalcy but to arouse a variety of passions, none of them good. If he had hoped to avoid their appearing as butchers, Brutus has chosen the visual display most likely to convince the Roman public that that is exactly what he and the others are.

His biggest mistake, however, is his rejection of Cassius's advice not to let Mark Antony speak at the funeral, a piece of folly made even worse by his decision to march the conspirators away as he does so. It is a piece of foolish generosity merited neither by Antony himself— who is raging for revenge and willing to "cry havoc and let slip the dogs of war," as he says in a soliloquy by Caesar's corpse—or by the febrile condition of the Roman populace. And so the way is paved for Antony's superb speech turning the people of Rome against the conspirators.

A foolish ruler is killed by a conspiracy that has let itself be guided by a vain, incompetent, and naive leader who fails to accept and act on the logic of what he and his comrades have done. There is something to learn from the fates of both men, but also from Caesar's friends and avengers, who do not make the same mistakes but some of whom make different, if equally instructive, ones. Their actions too will breed more violence that extends well beyond the horizons of a play that ends with the deaths of Brutus and Cassius.

The three leaders of the countercoup, Antony, Octavius, and Lepidus, having driven the conspirators out of Rome and now preparing to launch a war against them, make no such mistakes. At the opening of

Act 4, they are coolly ticking off a list of Roman notables to be murdered in order to consolidate their power:

> Antony: These many, then, shall die; their names are pricked.
> Octavius: Your brother too must die; consent you, Lepidus?
> Lepidus: I do consent.
> Octavius: Prick him down Antony.
> Lepidus: Upon condition Publius shall not live,
> Who is your sister's son, Mark Antony.
> Antony: He shall not live. Look, with a spot I damn him.[18]

It is a marvelously compact scene. The conspirators show no mercy even to kith and kin; yet an undercurrent of resentment in the byplay between Lepidus and Mark Antony bodes poorly for their future relationship. Once Lepidus leaves the room, Antony coolly remarks to Octavius that their colleague "is a slight unmeritable man, / Meet to be sent on errands." He proceeds to tell Octavius that Lepidus should not share in their tripartite power. When Octavius (who has quietly dominated the initial decisions to kill off opponents) mildly observes that Lepidus is a "tried and valiant soldier," Antony responds,

> So is my horse, Octavius, and for that
> I do appoint him store of provender.
> It is a creature that I teach to fight,
> To wind, to stop, to run directly on,
> His corporal motion governed by my spirit,
> And, in some taste, is Lepidus but so:
> He must be taught, and trained, and bid go forth;
> A barren-spirited fellow; one that feeds
> On objects, arts and imitations
> Which, out of use and staled by other men
> Begin his fashion. Do not talk of him
> But as a property.

Octavius gently suggests that Antony may be getting ahead of himself. The play moves on, but there is a larger lesson here.

The triumvirate are, unlike the conspirators against Caesar, ruthless enough to see their task through. But they are at least as divided by temperament and ambition as their foes. Lepidus is indeed a plodding figure, easily outmaneuvered. Antony, for his part, cannot refrain from showing off his brilliance and his superior experience ("Octavius, I have seen more days than you"—never the kind of thing a younger man likes to hear from an older one). Octavius alone in the play calculates shrewdly and keeps his counsel, willing to be underestimated by his partners as an inexperienced youth. He is, in Shakespeare's telling as well as that of historians, utterly ruthless but able to mask it, as well as his ambition and his cunning, better than any of his older and more experienced rivals. Like many a successful conspirator, he succeeds in large part by being underrated.

Without Antony's brilliant oratory and stage management, however, Octavius would never have had a chance. Octavius is a behind-the-scenes type, a bloodless operator, whereas Antony is a gifted demagogue who shrewdly gauges and appeals to his audience. If Octavius is Stalin, Antony is Trotsky. In possibly the most powerful scene in the play (Act 3, Scene 2), he makes the most of the opportunity that Brutus has provided him to deliver a eulogy for Caesar to the Roman populace, unrestrained by the presence of the conspirators who have left the scene, influenced by a Brutus who has foolishly taken Antony's gesture of goodwill following the assassination at face value.

Brutus, with the naiveté of the high-bred aristocrat, assumes that the crowd merely needs to be assured of his sincerity and his personal rightness. Antony from the outset takes a very different approach. He intends to address the emotions and the concerns of the populace. Unlike the self-obsessed Brutus, he figures in his own speech only as a foil to stimulate the anger of the mob. He famously begins by saying that he comes "to bury Caesar, not to praise him," although of course he will do just that. He deploys a heavy-handed irony that comes to partake of a biting sarcasm as he repeats it more than half a dozen times:

> For Brutus is an honourable man;
> So are they all, all honourable men.[19]

Where Brutus spoke in prose about himself, Antony speaks in iambic pentameter about Caesar, Brutus, and the people of Rome, putting himself forward only to discuss his overpowering grief at the loss of his friend and mentor.

Antony's oratorical tricks are sometimes hackneyed, but they work:

> I am no orator, as Brutus is,
> But, as you know me all, a plain blunt man
> That love my friend, and that they know full well
> That gave me public leave to speak of him.
> For I have neither wit, nor words, nor worth,
> Action, nor utterance, nor the power of speech
> To stir men's blood.

For such an obviously eloquent and rhetorically adroit political leader, this is a whopping lie. There is no more transparent calculator than the general who begins a remark with "Well, I'm just a broken down old cavalry man, but . . . " And yet the crowd always falls for it.

They fall too for Antony's appeal to their cupidity (his reading of Caesar's will and his reminders of Caesar's financial generosity). They are taken in by the theatrical gesture of Antony choking up by Caesar's corpse, which he uses as the ultimate prop in a political drama:

> Bear with me.
> My heart is in the coffin there with Caesar,
> And I must pause till it comes back to me.

In point of fact, he has chosen an apt moment to break up his speech, which had thus far consisted of increasingly ironic tributes to Brutus's honor, calculated to instill doubt among the plebians. He will then move to enrage them, turning them into a violent mob once they have begun murmuring among themselves, wondering whether Caesar was wronged, and expressing sympathy for Antony's grief.

Antony is a superb stage director too: as he has inflamed the mob he pauses:

> You will compel me then to read the will?
> Then make a ring about the corpse of Caesar,
> And let me show you him that made the will.
> Shall I descend? And will you give me leave?

He has made the audience into active participants, minimizing his own role while causing them to become collaborators in his ultimate purpose of turning them against the conspirators. He will come down to their level, physically as well as metaphorically, and he will seem to act only with their permission when in fact he is manipulating them in accordance with his desires. The conspirators acted on their own, thinking only of pacifying the crowd, not mobilizing it. Antony's approach is just the opposite.

Antony succeeds because he knows how to speak to the mob, which is the gift of the most dangerous populist politicians. He has, as successful demagogues always do, a feral instinct for their fears, their lusts, their resentments, and their willingness to suspend judgment. And he knows exactly what he is doing. He has built his appeal to the mob systematically, creating a series of increasingly intense emotional climaxes, until they explode into riot. The weeping, mournful, reluctant inciter to mayhem watches the plebians leave. The mask falls, and the cold calculator replaces the impassioned demagogue:

> Now let it work. Mischief, thou art afoot:
> Take thou what course thou wilt.

And in the very next scene the crowd comes across the poet Cinna, who is going to Caesar's funeral. When one of the plebeians confuses him with one of the conspirators of the same name, he protests, "I am Cinna the poet, I am Cinna the poet," but the mob does not care. One of the plebeians declares, "It is no matter, his name's Cinna. Pluck but his name out of his heart and turn him going." And so they kill him.

Antony's grief is no doubt real; so too is his calculated use of it and his artful whipping up of mob violence. Demagoguery works only when its purveyor believes some of what he is saying—or can make himself believe it for a time. Like most unscrupulous leaders, Antony taps his own anger and resentments while focusing on manipulating a much less sophisticated audience. He is an astonishingly dangerous man, who can unleash mayhem and upheaval. Yet, in the end, he too will fail, as we see foreshadowed in the very last scene of the play.

Cassius and Brutus are both dead, having fallen on their own swords rather than surrender to their enemies. Brutus's body is discovered, and Antony and Octavius stand over it. Antony, a complicated man capable of generosity as well as malice, gives an eloquent tribute to their fallen foe, "the noblest Roman of them all." The other conspirators, he declares, acted in envy of great Caesar.

> He only in a general honest thought
> And common good to all, made one of them.
> His life was gentle, and the elements
> So mixed in him that nature might stand up
> And say to all the world, "This was a man!"[20]

It is a touching tribute, albeit one quite at odds with the accusations that he leveled at Brutus in the speech over Caesar's corpse.

One might have concluded the play with these lines, a fitting tribute to a Roman senator who may or may not have made the right choice, we feel, but who was a decent man. Indeed, despite Antony's sarcasm about Brutus being an honorable man when speaking to the mob, clearly he really does believe that Brutus was honorable. Shakespeare does not, however, permit this uplifting ending. Octavius gets the last word, not Antony:

> According to his virtue let us use him,
> With all respect and rites of burial.
> Within my tent his bones tonight shall lie,
> Most like a soldier, ordered honourably.
> So call the field to rest, and let's away,
> To part the glories of this happy day.

And then, *exeunt omnes*—all the actors depart the stage. Octavius's tribute is, like the man himself, chilly, formalistic, and distant. It is trite and artificial, as the rhyming couplet at the end suggests. And it suggests a power grab: Antony may have provided the motor force that brought Brutus down, but it is in Octavius's tent that Brutus's bones will lie. One competition for power has ended, and another has immediately begun. This final scene foreshadows the outcome—the noble, eloquent, heroic, and human (though not humane) Antony will fall victim to the cold-blooded politician with whom he has allied. Antony becomes, like Brutus, a quester for supreme power, and as is foreshadowed here, he eventually succumbs to a clever and far more colorless rival. Those who defeat one kind of treachery, in other words, may end by begetting new forms of treachery.

Shakespeare's historical figures do not always match historians' judgments, but in this case they do. Octavius, who as Augustus inherits Caesar's rule, building the institutions and practices of an empire over an uninterrupted thirty years, was not a particularly brilliant soldier (though a conscientious one), not an inspiring orator (although a competent one), but a brilliant behind-the-scenes manipulator. He kept old forms of republican governance while undermining them. Like Viktor Orban, the cunning prime minister of Hungary since 2010, who gradually undermined institutions like the judiciary and the press by indirect means while consolidating his own rule, Octavius kept the appearance of a republic while substituting one-man rule for domination by the Senate. Caesar may have yearned to be crowned king, as the play suggests; Augustus insisted on a far more modest title, *princeps*, first citizen. He wanted the substance of power, not its appearance, which would have been dangerously provocative to lingering adherents of the old republic. As Niccolò Machiavelli suggests that princes ought, he put men to sleep by his apparent mildness. Antony, on the other hand, ended a suicide, defeated by his erstwhile colleague at the Battle of Actium, having besotted himself with Cleopatra and cast aside his talents and the opportunity they provided him—a subject Shakespeare explores at length in *Antony and Cleopatra*. It is, rather, the cold, calculating, enigmatic Augustus who triumphs. Demagogues, Shakespeare suggests, may be able to seize power, but personal flaws often prevent them from effectively using it.

Conspiracy is one way of seizing power, but there is another that is more straightforward yet: murder. And this Shakespeare explores in the tragedy of Macbeth, the nobleman who murders his liege, seizes the throne, and is in turn slain by the husband and father of some of his victims, Macduff. Unlike Brutus and Cassius, Macbeth does not defend his actions with lofty condemnations of tyranny; unlike Antony and Octavius, he is not delivering the masses a righteous act of revenge. The king is legitimate, and Macbeth has been treated well, prior to his act of regicide.

What makes the matter all the more puzzling is not only that Macbeth has no grievance against the king but that he is not portrayed from the outset as particularly evil or even indecent. He is no Iago or Richard III, telegraphing his thirst for betrayal and murder from the moment he steps on stage. He is, however, primed for violence. A wounded officer reports to Duncan the defeat and death of the rebel Macdonald, who had come to the battlefield with a formidable army. Macbeth, he reports,

> Disdaining Fortune, with his brandished steel,
> Which smoked with bloody execution,

Like Valour's minion, carved out his passage,
Till he faced the slave,
Which ne'er shook hands, nor bade farewell to him,
Till he unseamed him from the nave to th' chops,
And fixed his head upon our battlements.[21]

From this we discover a number of things about Macbeth. We learn about his reckless courage (the odds seem to have been against him), his disdain for the formalities of chivalric warfare, even in dealing with a noble adversary, and his capacity for bloody deeds. The phrase "unseamed him from the nave to th' chops" conveys a particularly brutal image, evoking as it does a sword stroke that disembowels a man by cutting him open in one blow from the navel (possibly the crotch) up to the jaws. In this one phrase alone, Shakespeare evokes the decisive, shocking violence of which Macbeth is capable. The question is what will unleash that innate quality.

Macbeth's willingness to murder his king (who is also his cousin) only emerges gradually. Unlike Richard III's murderous ambition, it has to be fanned by external forces, of which there are two: the three witches, to whom we are introduced in the very first scene of the play, and the formidable Lady Macbeth. The witches, whose prophecies haunt Macbeth and us, only predict and tempt; they do not force Macbeth to do anything against his will. But they find a willing target nonetheless. They hail Macbeth by his proper title (Thane of Glamis), predicting a yet higher honor (Thane of Cawdor), and then say that he will be "king hereafter." And when he indeed becomes Thane of Cawdor in the same scene, his reaction is ambivalent:

This supernatural soliciting
Cannot be ill; cannot be good. If ill,
Why hath it given me earnest of success,
Commencing in a truth? I am Thane of Cawdor.
If good, why do I yield to that suggestion
Whose horrid image doth unfix my hair,

And make my seated heart knock at my ribs,
Against the use of nature?[22]

Macbeth understands that he probably would come by kingship not through succession—Duncan has a son, though he can select his heir—but rather through crime. And he admits to himself that the thought of Duncan's murder, which "yet is but fantastical," disturbs him. He does not, however, simply reject it.

Macbeth's companion Banquo (whom he will cause to be murdered) cautions,

And oftentimes, to win us to our harm,
The instruments of darkness tell us truths,
Win us with honest trifles, to betray's
In deepest consequence.

This is one of the themes of the play. The witches do not lie to Macbeth, and they do not use occult powers to make him do their will (it is not entirely clear that they even have independent wills). Rather they present partial truths, and an ambitious man impulsively seizes on those without reflecting too deeply upon them. In a similar vein, Adolf Hitler, who judged the Western statesmen whom he encountered in Munich in 1938 as "worms," failed to realize that a year later, in September 1939, they had evolved. The British prime minister who celebrated the Munich Agreement, which in effect handed Czechoslovakia over to the German dictator in September 1938, had, over the next year, evolved into a committed if ineffective enemy of the Nazi regime. It is the kind of error dictators often make.

Macbeth is egged on by his wife as well, who is his "dearest partner of greatness" and becomes his coconspirator in the great enterprise of murder and usurpation.[23] Like many formidable leaders, he depends in many ways on a spouse, whose influence, be it benign or malign, is often only partly visible. Mikhail Gorbachev, Anwar Sadat, and Franklin Delano Roosevelt were all supported and often subtly influenced by life partners, for good or for ill. And if Lady Macbeth plays to the stereotype of the evil partner, there are plenty of examples of the exact contrary, the wife who restrains, encourages, and tempers—the role Clementine Churchill played in reining in her occasionally splenetic husband.

That role is often invisible to contemporaries. Indeed Macduff, whose family will fall victim to Macbeth later in the play, when first he hears of the murder of Duncan, declines to tell her of the crime that she helped incite:

> O gentle lady,
> 'Tis not for you to hear what I can speak:
> The repetition in a woman's ear
> Would murder as it fell.[24]

For the various nobles in this play, Lady Macbeth is present but not particularly important; for Macbeth himself, however, she is critical in stripping away his last compunctions about the murder of King Duncan. Indeed, she nearly commits the murder herself, stopped by one heartbreaking qualm: "Had he not resembled / My father as he slept, I had done't."[25] Lady Macbeth motivates her husband, but he is not her puppet; she encourages murder but still has some lingering compunctions. As Shakespeare continually reminds us, even villains are complicated, and few are simply the instruments of others.

On occasion, contemporaries denounce spouses or other intimate counselors as the hidden hand manipulating a weak leader—the profound antipathy to Marie Antoinette, the wife of Louis XVI of France, played an important role in facilitating the French Revolution. But *Macbeth* shows us that it is Macbeth's "vaulting ambition" that drives him to murder, not the incomplete prophecies of the witches or the alternating persuasion and taunting of his wife.[26] Often counselors merely help leaders unlock the better or worse parts of their natures, enhancing native ruthlessness or prudence.

Macbeth, like Brutus in *Julius Caesar*, will undertake a murder. Unlike Brutus, however, he realizes that what begins with one dagger stroke may not end there.

> If it were done, when 'tis done, then 'twere well
> It were done quickly. If th'assassination
> Could trammel up the consequence, and catch
> With surcease success: that but this blow
> Might be the be-all and the end-all, here,
> But here, upon this bank and shoal of time,
> We'd jump the life to come.[27]

He would be willing to take his chances on damnation if the slaying of the sleeping king would be the end of it.

> But in these cases,
> We still have judgment here, that we but teach
> Bloody instructions, which being taught, return
> To plague th'inventor.

He knows, in other words, that it may not end with one murder, and indeed it does not. Before the play is over, he will have ordered the deaths of his companion Banquo, the family of Macduff, and others. He has been trapped in the logic of violence that Brutus refused to acknowledge, that Cassius understood, and with which Mark Antony played. And remarkably, he is trapped by the logic of violence even though he has seen it coming.

Macbeth's apprehensions are correct, but not entirely in the way he may have expected. His continued killings and oppression do indeed stimulate revolt and lead to his eventual downfall and death. But a more profound consequence of rising to power through crime is made clear when, at the end of the play, he learns of the death of his wife, possibly through suicide. We have learned that Lady Macbeth has gone mad, recognizing her guilt and that of her husband. Yet her husband's response reveals how numb his actions have left him.

> She should have died hereafter;
> There would have been a time for such a word.
> Tomorrow, and tomorrow, and tomorrow,
> Creeps in this petty pace from day to day,
> To the last syllable of recorded time;
> And all our yesterdays have lighted fools
> The way to dusty death. Out, out, brief candle,
> Life's but a walking shadow, a poor player
> That struts and frets his hour upon the stage,
> And then is heard no more. It is a tale
> Told by an idiot, full of sound and fury
> Signifying nothing.[28]

There is no grief here, no self-examination, no regret. Macbeth's soul has died long before his body will receive the fatal blow from Macduff. He is capable of decisive action, of brutality and great energy, but as a human being, he does not have much left.

And that may be *Macbeth*'s greatest lesson for the student of power. Those who have risen by murder find themselves bound by its inevitable consequences. They lose human sympathies and bonds, and although they may still function, and even function effectively, they have lost some of what made them human, and that is in many ways the true tragedy of the man for whom the play is named. A look into the dead eyes of a Vladimir Putin ordering the invasion, ravaging, and rape of Ukraine is but one contemporary example.

Parallels can also be seen in the case of Paul Kagame, the unquestioned ruler of Rwanda since 2000. He was born into a prominent minority Tutsi family that fled a violent majority Hutu rebellion to Uganda. There, after serving in a rebel Ugandan army, he rose through the ranks before switching to become a founder of the Rwandan Patriotic Army (RPA). A talented soldier like Macbeth, he emerged as his country was gripped by a ferocious civil war, including a slaughter of Tutsi by the Hutu-led government. Then a student at the US Army Command and General Staff College at Fort Leavenworth, he hastily returned home. He gathered a rebel army and reconquered his country. Leading the outnumbered RPA against a Rwandan government force twice as strong, he overthrew the Hutu government.

Kagame brought peace to Rwanda and even a measure of justice, rebuilding a country that had experienced extraordinary acts of brutality. For a time the country became one of the success stories of Africa, capable of reconciliation despite a war and genocide that had cost eight hundred thousand lives. While the upbeat stories concealed darker truths, to include revenge killings and torture, Kagame became celebrated as a hero, welcomed at Harvard and celebrated by American presidents. One journalist recalls,

> Many of the diplomats and analysts I talked to weren't entirely bothered by Kagame's authoritarian streak. Some even told me—and maybe this has something to do with the low expectations for Africa—that this is exactly what the continent needs: more Kagames, more highly skilled strongmen who can turn around messy, conflict-prone societies and get medicine in the hospitals and police officers on the street and plastic bags out of the trees. Liberties aren't so important in these places, the argument goes, because who can enjoy freedom of speech or freedom of the press when everyone is killing one another?[29]

The hard edges seemed an acceptable price to pay for order, improved medical care, safety, and a degree of prosperity in a traumatized and overcrowded country.

But as time went on, Kagame became a dictator, probably ordering the assassination of his own Banquo, Patrick Karegaya, the former head of external intelligence murdered in his hotel room in South Africa in January 2014. Nor was he the only former close associate of Kagame who needed to fear assassination. The former chief of staff of the Rwandan army, General Kayumba Nyamwasa, similarly fled to

South Africa and narrowly escaped an assassin's bullet and knife as well.[30]

In one interpretation, Kagame's is the story of a man who was always ready to commit murder and successfully deceived sympathetic Westerners for many years. But perhaps *Macbeth* reveals to us another possibility: that Kagame was a soldier with a capacity for ruthlessness, an aptitude for decisive action, and an opportunity. We prefer our villains straight—and Kagame may be one such. But perhaps the truth is more complex. Shakespeare helps us see that, like the rest of us, those who seize power are often caught up by the unforeseen consequences of their own actions. They may dimly anticipate these consequences but choose to ignore them until it is too late, and this transforms them from whatever they may have been into pitiless—and isolated—killers. As one review of the best book on the death of Karegaya and Kagame's war against his rivals puts it, "Less 'the Switzerland of Africa,' Kagame's Rwanda, when seen through [author Michela] Wrong's retributive lens, more closely resembles the blood-soaked Scotland of *Macbeth*."[31]

Once again, Shakespeare got there first.

PART II

EXERCISING POWER

Power, having been gained, may be maintained and exercised through inspiration, which sounds kinder than it often is. But it also requires manipulation of others in a variety of ways, and in some cases it is built—figuratively or in sober fact—on murder.

CHAPTER 5

Inspiration

Paul Kagame was a clever tactician and a ruthless commander, but he also had to rouse a country rent by a hideous civil war and cultivate the admiration of foreign donors and supporters. In other words, he had to inspire.

Leading anything—whether a country, a university, or a club—requires a blend of these skills. One cannot lead well without management, that is, the skilled coordination of the activities of groups of people; command, the giving of authoritative direction to subordinates; and hardest of all, inspiration, getting others to do things they would not do otherwise or to do them better than they normally would. One can learn management (staff colleges and business schools teach that) and, with a bit more effort, the art of command. Inspiration, however, is an altogether subtler art. As Shakespeare shows us, it is more gift than skill and often eludes otherwise talented statesmen.

In *Julius Caesar*, for example, Shakespeare shows us that Cassius can manage. He can coordinate the activities of the conspirators to persuade Brutus to step forward, then conduct the actual attack on Caesar with not a little contrivance and cunning. But to the extent he leads, he has to lead from behind. Julius Caesar assesses him accurately:

> He reads much,
> He is a great observer, and he looks
> Quite through the deeds of men. He loves no plays
> As thou dost, Antony; he hears no music.
> Seldom he smiles, and smiles in such a sort
> As if he mocked himself and scorned his spirit
> That could be moved to smile at anything.[1]

It is a wary and shrewd judgment, and an accurate one. The inspirational leader, whether of good or evil character, loves a kind of theater, can use words, and hears their music.

Caesar does not describe Cassius as an eloquent public speaker, for he is nothing of the sort. He is the quintessential behind-the-scenes operator, persuasive with individuals and small groups, but not someone to stand before an irresolute throng and rally them to action. For that, other attributes are needed—foremost among them, the ability to inspire through speech and small, symbolic acts.

Henry Bolingbroke is a talented commander, though he also lacks the gift of inspiration. This doesn't prevent him from being a capable leader, sizing up situations and telling people what to do. He can order killings calmly, showing exemplary restraint when required. When Northumberland bullies the newly deposed Richard II into reading a paper containing accusations of "grievous crimes" committed by him and his followers

> Against the state and profit of this land;
> That by confessing them, the souls of men
> May deem that you are worthily depos'd

Richard practically breaks down, shouting, "Fiend, thou torments me ere I come to hell!" Henry then says, "Urge it no more, my Lord Northumberland."[2] With equal calm Henry indirectly orders Richard's murder. There is never a doubt of what he wants done and whom he expects to do it.

But although initially a popular figure, Henry is not an inspirational one. He does not rouse his fellow nobles to rise up against Richard—they are already discontented with the feckless king. He is popular for a time with the masses, but there too he is chiefly seen as a ready replacement for the despised Richard. No one acts out of love for him as either Henry Bolingbroke or Henry IV. He gives no memorable speech, and he stirs no emotion beyond a kind of satisfied self-interest and relief. People respect him, and some most certainly fear him, but he excites no affection or emulation once Richard has been deposed; he cannot appeal to the imagination, pointing people beyond themselves or making them think that great deeds are within their grasp.

That inspiration deficit helps explain the uneasiness of his reign. Begun under the shadow of a usurpation and murder, it is rife with the revolts of envious nobles and rival chieftains. The deposed Richard II warns Northumberland of this, calling him "the ladder" by which Bolingbroke rose, and prophesies, correctly, that in a short time

Thou shalt think
Though he divide the realm and give thee half
It is too little, helping him to all.
He shall think that thou, which knowst the way
To plant unrightful kings, wilt know again,
Being ne'er so little urged, another way
To pluck him headlong from the usurped throne.[3]

Richard was a dreadful leader but, particularly after his fall, a keen observer, as some defeated and dispossessed leaders can be. He sees very clearly that Henry IV uses people as ladders, as instruments for his own ambition. Richard knows too that eventually those around him will recognize this and resent it.

That is, to some extent, the nature of all those who exert power: they use people because they must, even at the price of what it does to their souls. In his classic novel about the Battle of Gettysburg, Michael Shaara describes Confederate general James Longstreet looking at the division commanded by General George Pickett showing up on the battlefield: "It was like being handed a bright new shiny gun."[4] Shaara depicts Longstreet as a humane and even compassionate leader—and yet his immediate thought about these five thousand soldiers is, and must be, instrumental. By the end of the novel, Shaara's hero, the civilized and idealistic Colonel Joshua Lawrence Chamberlain, also accepts that view of war and his role in it.

Great leaders generally attempt to conceal their coldly utilitarian view of other human beings, even from themselves. They know that they must to some extent mask it and proceed to use people while inspiring others to efforts out of the norms of human behavior—as Pickett's ill-fated charge against Union lines at Gettysburg proved to be. That can occasionally be done by fear, but fear has its limits. Even the towering totalitarian leaders of the twentieth century—Vladimir Lenin, Adolf Hitler, Joseph Stalin, and Mao Zedong—sooner or later encountered the limits of fear and had to inspire. In less fraught times and places, no organization run primarily by fear can be lastingly successful. Dictators require willing compliance, even at times initiative, on the part of those they rule, which is why they spend as much effort as they do in motivating them. Leaders of free peoples and states do this to an even greater extent.

Inspiration, in turn, depends on speech. At a certain point, a leader must look his followers in the eye and describe not only what must be done but why they must do it. Most often in politics, but in other settings as well, it involves binding together past, present, and future; it provides an imagined picture from the future looking back at this time and place, when what we do—and it must be we, not I—matters.

It provides reassurance of ultimate rewards—which may be entirely intangible, such as honor or revenge, fame or prestige—for the sacrifices and effort of the moment. It requires, finally, elevated speech—language that one would not use around the kitchen table or in a bowling alley—that will be memorable, capturing the gravity of the moment and the magnitude of what is at stake.

In our own time, we see this kind of leadership but rarely, though Winston Churchill offers as good an example as the twentieth century can provide. In the words of John F. Kennedy, Churchill mobilized the English language and sent it into battle. Churchill's curiously self-deprecating remarks about his wartime speeches underestimate their importance as historian John Lukacs, in his superb account of 1940, shows.[5] And yet Lukacs also notes that, for some of his more refined listeners, they seemed "too grandiloquent, sham-Augustan, for their taste," and he quotes approvingly George Orwell's shrewd diary entry from June 24 stating that "uneducated people are often moved by a speech in solemn language that they don't actually understand but feel to be impressive."[6] An inspiring speech is no simple thing: what will ring false to some will stir others.

Kennedy himself inspired a generation in his presidential inaugural speech of 1961, evoking as he did the transition of leadership, at a critical moment in the Cold War, from the leaders of World War II to the subalterns who fought it.[7] Kennedy's speech, the most powerful since Abraham Lincoln's Second Inaugural, used many of the devices that one finds first in Shakespeare. The product of a long process of collaboration and rewriting with his counselor, Theodore Sorenson, it was carefully crafted to meet specific purposes. "JFK knew," Sorenson recalled, "that an inaugural address stamps a brand on a new president that can last for years, both nationally and globally, as either a warrior or a peacemaker, a bore or a source of inspiration, as first-rate or mediocre."[8] It made his succession as president, elected in an extremely close (and possibly even fraudulently enabled) election against an opponent with whom he largely agreed, something of much larger significance and consequence:

Let the word go forth from this time and place, to friend and foe alike, that the torch has been passed to a new generation of Americans—born in this century, tempered by war, disciplined by a hard and bitter peace, proud of our ancient heritage—and unwilling to witness or permit the slow undoing of those human rights to which this nation has always been committed, and to which we are committed today at home and around the world.[9]

It was elevated speech that some later regretted as opening the way to the Vietnam embroilment. Consequences aside, its effect was tremendous, bearing the hallmarks of a lot of inspirational rhetoric—the individual recedes into the background (Sorenson describes Kennedy's deliberate avoidance of the first person)—and placing the current moment in a long historical context. While American politicians since then have striven to hit those heights, they have rarely succeeded, while his challenge—"And so my fellow Americans ask not what your country can do for you—ask what you can do for your country"—still echoes. It had more than a touch of Shakespeare about it.

Of all Shakespeare's inspiring leaders, there is none more so than Henry V. Many aspects of his character are deeply unsavory, as we shall see in later chapters, and one may, in fact, conclude from Shakespeare's portrayal that he is cynical, self-pitying, exploitative, and brutal. But he is also unquestionably an inspirational leader. If Shakespeare gives us one speech that echoes through the centuries, it is Henry V's call to the embattled British (not English—a Scot, an Irishman, and a Welshman have all been given minor voices) on the eve of the Battle of Agincourt. He gives it after a sleepless night in the camp, during which he has discovered that many of his men are brooding about the difference between the responsibilities and penalties that fall on kings, on the one hand, and commoners on the other.

The great speech begins almost in impromptu fashion, as if developing naturally out of a private conversation. Henry is conversing with one of his nobles, Westmoreland, who acknowledges the fact known to all in the camp that the army is outnumbered by the French. In a shrewd preemptive stroke, Henry makes a virtue of what is, in any reasonable view of the matter, a terrible predicament.

> No, faith, my coz, wish not a man from England:
> God's peace! I would not lose so great an honour
> As one man more, methinks, would share from me
> For the best hope I have. O, do not wish one more![10]

What may seem to be a private remark to Westmoreland leads into a speech clearly intended for the ears of Henry's soldiers. From his disguised rambles around the sleeping camp the night before, he knows that his men are dispirited, doubtful about their cause, uncertain about their leader, and fearful of their prospects. To Westmoreland, he has confessed that he is driven by honor—personal honor—which is why he uses the personal pronoun three times in four lines. That makes sense to a fellow noble like Westmoreland. But the king's personal honor is of little concern to the yeomen he must rouse for combat, and so he addresses them very differently, tapping the motivations that will hearten them for a desperate battle. Part of Henry's brilliance lies in his ability to speak to both audiences, a problem that even Churchill struggled with, if George Orwell is to be believed.

Henry begins by issuing an order, clearly designed for the ears of the rank and file, not those of their officers.

> Rather proclaim it, Westmoreland, through my host,
> That he which hath no stomach to this fight,
> Let him depart; his passport shall be made
> And crowns for convoy put into his purse:
> We would not die in that man's company
> That fears his fellowship to die with us.

Henry has shifted now to the royal we; he speaks not as an aristocratic seeker of glory but as a king, though the first-person plural

115

has begun to lay the groundwork for eliciting from his men a bond that transcends class. He has proclaimed a grand gesture, worthy of a king's magnanimity, while at the same time affirming the soldier's cardinal virtue, courage. It is an offer intended to appear sincerely made, perhaps, but one may doubt that even the most timid of his men would consider losing face by taking it. Like many such offers, it is rhetorical, made for theatrical effect, not actual consequence. Henry will inspire by both celebrating the soldier's virtues and using the most powerful of negative incentives: shame.

It is now the moment for Henry to begin placing the upcoming battle in a historical context: he will appeal to his soldiers to act not just in the moment but in the knowledge of a future that will see them successful and, most importantly, honored in ways that are meaningful to any veteran of any rank.

> This day is called the feast of Crispian:
> He that outlives this day, and comes safe home,
> Will stand a tip-toe when the day is named,
> And rouse him at the name of Crispian.

Henry tacitly acknowledges the risks inherent in battle, stipulating that the celebrations will belong to the soldier who "outlives this day," which implies that some will not. He knows that to paint too rosy a picture of his army's prospects would undermine his purpose. But by accepting the fact that some will not, in fact, outlive this day and return safely home, he magnifies the glory that awaits the surviving majority. He has connected the day with a familiar holiday, commemorating the memories of two martyred Christians, Crispin and Crispian, but makes clear that henceforth the name will be associated not with the martyrs but with the soldiers' deeds— or more truthfully, with his speech. Indeed, a quick internet search for St. Crispin's Day elicits far more material on Shakespeare's rendition of the speech than on the holiday or the martyrs whom it commemorates.

This is not deception per se: Henry's words produce a victory that validates his speech. He promises that the excitement and pride of this special moment will not abate:

> He that shall live this day, and see old age,
> Will yearly on the vigil feast his neighbours,
> And say "To-morrow is Saint Crispian."

Unlike Coriolanus, who would have considered showing his wounds to his fellow citizens vulgar and humiliating, the privates in Henry's army will not.

> Then will he strip his sleeve and show his scars.
> And say "These wounds I had on Crispin's day."

More cynically, or perhaps just more realistically than Coriolanus, Henry accepts the values and mores of his soldiers. He does not hold them to his standards of behavior: he, after all, would not be one to show off his wounds. But not only does he not begrudge them doing the same, he in fact encourages them to do so. Because of his unusual self-education as a prince, he knows that he must appeal to them in a way that would never work with his nobles.

He puts his soldiers decades into the future, imagining themselves as veterans looking back on this moment in time and the exploits of their youth:

> Old men forget: yet all shall be forgot,
> But he'll remember with advantages
> What feats he did that day:

There is also a bit of soldierly humor here: the veterans will tell their stories "with advantages." In other words, he knows that veterans tell war stories in which their deeds grow with the telling. He winks at that pardonable failing, promising even greater glories:

Then shall our names,
Familiar in his mouth as household words—
Harry the king, Bedford and Exeter,
Warwick and Talbot, Salisbury and Gloucester—
Be in their flowing cups freshly remember'd.

He is not King Henry, as his father would have been, but "Harry the king," a foreshadowing of the promise of reputational equality that he will repeat further on. He is appealing as well to the common desire to drop names, particularly of those who have dared and done great things. That pardonable bit of bragging will, moreover, extend beyond his soldiers' lifetimes, to their children's and even beyond.

This story shall the good man teach his son;
And Crispin Crispian shall ne'er go by,
From this day to the ending of the world,
But we in it shall be remember'd.

And now for the punchline:

We few, we happy few, we band of brothers;
For he to-day that sheds his blood with me
Shall be my brother; be he ne'er so vile,
This day shall gentle his condition.

The we has ceased to be royal, transforming into an expression of fellowship. His men understand and accept the reality of social distinctions, but he offers a transcendence of them that goes beyond mere equality to kinship.

There is one more element to promise them:

And gentlemen in England now a-bed
Shall think themselves accursed they were not here,

And hold their manhoods cheap whiles any speaks
That fought with us upon Saint Crispin's day.

It is not enough that they will have become the good king's brethren: they will also be able to look down not just on their peers, other villagers who can draw a longbow, but on gentlemen. They will be, henceforth and forever, a breed apart. It is an appeal evoked time and again to call soldiers to the colors: the belief that service in war will make them not merely the equals of others but in some ways their moral superiors.

This is a perfect speech. It is no coincidence that *Henry V* was made into a film during World War II with the support of the British government and Churchill's personal backing. The more troubling aspects of the play were omitted—Henry's ordering of the execution of plotters against him, the ferocious threats of pillage and rape at the siege of Harfleur, and the slaughter of French prisoners at Agincourt. Rather, the focus was on Laurence Olivier's rendition of the St. Crispin's Day speech, which had, in turn, found its echo in Churchill's own August 20, 1940, speech: "Never in the field of human conflict was so much owed by so many to so few."[11]

Outstanding as it is, the St. Crispin's Day speech does not stand alone in the play as a moment of inspiration—Harry's words are always calculated for maximum effect on his chosen audience. When the French herald, Mountjoy, speaks to him for the last time before the battle, Henry says,

Let me speak proudly. Tell the Constable
We are but warriors for the working-day;
Our gayness and our gilt are all besmirched
With rainy marching in the painful field.
. . .
But by the mass, our hearts are in the trim.[12]

The audience is not only Mountjoy but his nobles and any who overhear him. One aspect of Harry's genius is his ability to make adversity into a source of pride and strength. His men might be disheartened by the gaudy display of the well-outfitted French—but they will take a perverse pride in being "but warriors for the working-day." Their tattered and stained clothing is a mark of soldierly prowess rather than evidence of the misery of an arduous campaign.

The king plays on comradeship and vanity, all the while acknowledging and even celebrating the hazards of war. At the siege of Harfleur he launches a desperate attack:

> Once more unto the breach, dear friends, once more,
> Or close the wall up with our English dead.[13]

He appeals to ancestral pride and patriotism:

> On, on you noble English,
> Whose blood is fet from fathers of war-proof . . .
> Dishonour not your mothers; now attest
> That those whom you called fathers did beget you.
> Be copy now to men of grosser blood
> And teach them how to war. And you good yeomen,
> Whose limbs were made in England, show us here
> The mettle of your pasture; let us swear
> That you are worth your breeding—which I doubt not,
> For there is none of you so mean and base
> That hath not noble lustre in your eyes.

And he ascribes them qualities that some of them clearly do not possess:

> I see you stand like greyhounds in the slips,
> Straining upon the start.[14]

He turns war into a violent sport rather than an instrument of statecraft, a not-uncommon motif in speeches given during battle. And once again he promises, as he will much more vividly at Agincourt, personal fellowship with the king himself, describing himself not as Henry but rather as "Harry."

> The game's afoot
> Follow your spirit, and upon this charge
> Cry "God for Harry! England and Saint George!"

Blood-quickening stuff to be sure. But Shakespeare is careful to provide the counterpoint that shows how difficult (or if one prefers, how manipulative and calculating) the task of inspiration is. At Harfleur his exhortations are followed by his erstwhile companions Nym and the Boy wishing they were somewhere else: "Would I were in an alehouse in London! I would give all my fame for a pot of ale and safety," and it is up to Captain Fluellen to appear and, emphasizing his commands with blows, say, "Up to the breach, you dogs! Avaunt you cullions!"[15] Even with Fluellen beating his men into soldierly behavior, they clearly do not storm the town. What compels surrender is instead Henry's terrifying speech in Act 3, Scene 3, in which he threatens,

> I will not leave the half-achieved Harfleur
> Till in her ashes she lies buried.

And worse besides.

Shakespeare denies the reality of neither the inspiration (one cannot read or hear Harry's speeches without feeling their power) nor the underlying reluctance, apprehension, and hesitancy they are intended to address. Inspirational speech necessarily masks unromantic realities and attitudes and seeks to make them abate, at least for some critical time. Henry is an exceptional leader not because he is intoxicated by his own rhetoric but because he uses it to drive his men onward in a cause that is desperate and possibly illegitimate.

Nor does Henry inspire by formal speech alone. The evening before Agincourt, he walks among his soldiers' bivouacs, chatting with them. In a prologue to Act 4 of *Henry V*, the Chorus paints a word picture of an uneasy camp, attempting at once to rest and to prepare itself for the trials of the morrow. The soldiers are not the eager greyhounds of Harfleur, nor yet the sturdy yeomen of Harry's speech on the morrow, but rather "the poor condemned English" who

> Like sacrifices, by their watchful fires
> Sit patiently and inly ruminate
> The morning's danger; and their gesture sad,
> Investing lank-lean cheeks and war-worn coats,
> Presenteth them unto the gazing moon
> So many horrid ghosts.

At this moment no rousing speech is possible—the men are scattered around their campfires; and night is, in any case, the moment when courage and self-confidence usually ebb away. And then,

> O now, who will behold
> The royal captain of this ruined band
> Walking from watch to watch, from tent to tent,
> Let him cry "Praise and glory on his head!"
> For forth he goes and visits all his host,
> Bids them good morrow with a modest smile,
> And calls them brothers, friends and countrymen.

Harry wears what military historian John Keegan calls "the mask of command," a cheerfulness and calm that is in some measure feigned or at least assumed. In private, generals may sob, nurse splitting headaches, or erupt in temper: the good ones hide that reality from those they lead. And yet this assumed cheerful self-confidence cannot be unearthly; the trick, which Henry has mastered, is retaining the human connection.

A largess universal, like the sun,
His liberal eye doth give to every one,
Thawing cold fear, that mean and gentle all
Behold, as may unworthiness define
A little touch of Harry in the night.

Henry inspires not only by the set-piece speech but by the small touches, the slap on the back, the few words about nothing in particular, the moment of comradeship around a campfire.

A very similar scene occurred before the Battle of Cowpens in 1781, when Daniel Morgan, leading a force composed chiefly of American militia with but a handful of state and Continental troops, took on a slightly larger, considerably better-trained and -disciplined, and arguably better-officered force of Loyalist regulars commanded by a ruthless and talented commander, Banastre Tarleton. Morgan too walked around the campfires at night, reassuring the jumpy militia, connecting with them as a scarred veteran and as both their leader and a peer. One militiaman recalled, "He went among the volunteers, helped them fix their swords, joked with them about their sweet-hearts, told them to keep in good spirits, and the day would be ours. . . . 'Just hold up your heads, boys, three fires,' he would say, 'and you are free, and then when you return to your homes, how the old folks will bless you, and the girls kiss you, for your gallant conduct!' I don't believe he slept a wink that night."[16]

Perhaps the greatest British general of World War II, William Slim, used a similar technique as he rebuilt his 14th Army after it had been driven out of Burma by the Japanese in 1942, an operational debacle in the most difficult geographical setting of the war. In addition to implementing reorganization, training, and logistical improvements, he went into the field, meeting with small groups of soldiers from every unit: "I often did three or four of these stump speeches in a day. . . . Two things only were necessary: first to know what you were talking about, and, second and most important, to believe it yourself.

I found that if one kept the bulk of one's talk to the material things the men were interested in, food, pay, leave, beer, mails, and the progress of operations, it was safe to end on a higher note—the spiritual foundations—and I always did."[17] Small wonder that Slim's troops, whom he led through some of the most difficult campaigns of World War II, referred to him affectionately as "Uncle Bill."

Many leaders rely on these moments of informal chat with their followers before some great enterprise. For the ones to whom this comes naturally, it usually works. Curiously, we have only the Chorus's word to describe Harry's effect. Given his rapport with average soldiers, it is not surprising that Henry V could engage in the easygoing talk that came naturally to Daniel Morgan and William Slim. But Shakespeare seems intent on making a different point. When the play continues and we overhear Henry's actual conversations with the troops, we realize that their views of him and the predicament in which he has placed them are mixed. Some are deeply loyal and faithful to him; others are preoccupied with their fears. He will not convince all of them, and he wanders off afterward filled not with satisfaction at having motivated his men for the day ahead but resentful that some of them are quite prepared to blame the king if all goes poorly on the morrow. Shakespeare shows us that inspiration is necessary because the common run of humanity knows, as Falstaff does, that the underlying motives of kings are selfish and crass, that the men are being used in service of their leaders' ambition and errors.

"A touch of Harry in the night" is powerful, but it is on his great speeches, above all the St. Crispin's Day speech, that Shakespeare's Harry's success as an inspirational leader depends. Close scrutiny of this and other Shakespearean speeches reveals a mastery of the techniques of rhetoric with which Shakespeare was probably familiar from his classical reading and which are effective to this day.[18] For example, Aristotle asserts that an effective speech has at least three elements: *ethos*, the establishment of a credible character; *logos*, rational argument; and *pathos*, proportionate emotion. Henry V excels in all of these, particularly *ethos* and *pathos*. Brutus's speech over Caesar's body, by contrast, is long on *ethos* (he shows that he is a serious man) but short on both *logos* (his rationale for killing Caesar rested on what the dictator might do, not what he had done) and *pathos* (he was more preoccupied with proving his own worthiness than with exciting fear of Caesar's tyrannical propensities). Mark Antony's speech, by contrast, which unleashes a civil war, has all three: he manages to portray himself as a loyal friend of Caesar who is (initially at least) generous to his enemies; he gives the Roman people rational explanations for why they should be grateful to Caesar; and he is extraordinarily powerful, if somewhat contrived, in his portrayal of his emotions.

Shakespeare uses many other rhetorical devices: *chiasmus*, for example, the inversion of words or phrases, as in Kennedy's "Ask not what your country can do for you—ask what you can do for your country"; *antithesis*, as when Harry contrasts the gaudy French with the haggard English; and *caesura* and *enjambment*, the artful use of stops and run-on sentences in a formal speech, breaking the rhythm to calculated effect. When one reads these speeches, even the briefest, carefully, one realizes just how much artifice went into their preparation.

A close study of Shakespeare's techniques, devices, and presentation has nurtured some of the best inspirational speakers of our era. Winston Churchill's use of elevated and occasionally archaic speech (*foe* for *enemy*, for example) was as artificial and yet as necessary as Shakespeare's iambic pentameter. Indeed, the very texts that he used were occasionally formatted for reading as a kind of blank verse. Thus, in a secret session of Parliament on June 20, 1940, the day before France signed an armistice taking it out of the war, he read,

> If Hitler fails to invade
>   or destroy Britain
>   he has lost the war.[19]

Churchill was not trained as an actor, but when he prepared his speeches, he chose his words, to include matters of timing and emphasis, with care. He leaned heavily on *anaphora*, the use of repeated words or phrases. In the greatest paean to English patriotism in Shakespeare, John of Gaunt, Henry Bolingbroke's dying father, speaks of "this blessed plot, this earth, this realm, this England." Churchill's equivalent was his June 4, 1940, speech to the House of Commons: "We shall go on to the end, we shall fight in France, we shall fight on the seas and oceans, we shall fight with growing confidence and growing strength in the air, we shall defend our Island, whatever the cost may be, we shall fight on the beaches, we shall fight on the landing grounds, we shall fight in the fields and in the streets, we shall fight in the hills; we shall never surrender."[20] The hammering away at "we shall fight" is classic Churchillian rhetoric. And indeed there were even more direct borrowings, as noted before in Churchill's tribute to the fighter pilots of the Royal Air Force: "Never in the field of human conflict was so much owed by so many to so few." It was not far from Henry V's celebration of "we few, we happy few."

Isaiah Berlin, the Oxford philosopher and wartime diplomat, reviewed the first volume of the statesman's memoirs, using that as an opportunity to reflect on Churchill's rhetoric. He speaks of Churchill's poetry and continues the metaphor:

> The units out of which his world is constructed are simpler and larger than life, the patterns vivid and repetitive like those of an epic poet, or at times like those of a dramatist who sees persons and situations as timeless symbols and embodiments of eternal, shining principles. . . . The archaisms of style to which Mr. Churchill's wartime speeches accustomed us are indispensable ingredients of the heightened tone, the formal chronicler's attire, for which the solemnity of the occasion called. Mr. Churchill is fully conscious of this.[21]

Like most of his generation, Berlin admired Churchill intensely and was profoundly grateful for his wartime leadership in a way almost incomprehensible to a more cynical and disillusioned age.[22]

Berlin also saw in Churchill's theatricality a quality essential to his success as a statesman:

There are those who, inhibited by the furniture of the ordinary world, come to life only when they feel themselves actors upon a stage, and thus emancipated, speak out for the first time, and are then found to have much to say. There are those who can function freely only in uniform or armour or court dress, see only through certain kinds of spectacles, act fearlessly only in situations which in some way are formalized for them, see life as a kind of play in which they and others are assigned certain lines which they must speak.[23]

Perhaps Henry V too only comes fully to life when rallying his embattled soldiers for the climactic effort at Agincourt.

It is, however, a common mistake in the romanticization of Churchill after the war to place sole emphasis on the inspiring passages of his speeches. To be sure, those words had a profound effect, particularly in the darkest days of 1940, following Dunkirk, the surrender of France, and the Blitz. But it is often forgotten that most of these speeches were devoted not to rousing motivational appeals but to careful descriptions of how the war had gone to that point and how his various publics should understand the situation.[24] The elevated rhetoric was deployed carefully and selectively, because it was not appropriate to the more mundane but equally necessary persuasive speech of reporting on the progress of the war.

Heightened rhetoric has its place, a point less understood today than it once was. Literary critic Joseph Wood Krutch once said, "To Shakespeare, robes and crowns and jewels are the garments most appropriate to man because they are the fitting outward manifestation of his inward majesty, but to us they seem absurd because the man who bears them has, in our estimation, so pitifully shrunk."[25] One might say the same of elevated speech, such as Henry V's rallying of his troops before Agincourt or Churchill's incandescent speeches of the summer of 1940. Americans will occasionally hear presidents strain for such effect at their inaugural addresses, with mixed success. At other times the informal style—influenced, possibly, by the false intimacy of the television or computer screen—is the one to which we can relate easiest. But in the theater at least, we can recapture the power of formal address when we see Henry rally his men, outnumbered as they are, five to one, and doomed as they have conceived themselves.

If there is a contemporary leader who—to the surprise of those who observed him and perhaps to himself—embodies Shakespearean qualities of inspirational leadership, it is Volodymyr Zelensky, president of Ukraine during Russia's 2022 invasion.[26] It is no coincidence that he was an actor before becoming a businessman and a politician. Although his field was comedy, his theatrical training surely stood him in good stead when, against his expectations, the Russian military launched an unprovoked onslaught against his country on February 24, 2022. It began, among other strikes, with an attempt to kill him, his staff, and his family.

Before entering politics he had played an accidental president in a successful comic series, *Servant of the People*. For many observers that was enough to discredit his real-life term as president. In truth, however, Zelensky's theatrical talents proved essential in rallying not only his own people but, no less important, the array of Western nations that would come to provide indispensable weaponry and intelligence support to the embattled Ukrainians.

James Glossman, an experienced director, playwright, and teacher of drama, remarked once to my students that he commences his thinking about a new staging of a Shakespeare play by thinking about the set and the costumes; from those physical elements of the drama, everything else flows. The insight applies to the theater of politics as well. Zelensky chose his set at the outset: on the first shocking night of war, he would not move to a secure bunker or out of Kyiv, even as bombs and missiles fell and as Russian murder squads came looking for him. Rather, he would stay in his presidential office and venture into the capital's streets. On the second night of the war, cell phone in hand, he took that most twenty-first-century of all art forms, a selfie. "'We're all here,' Zelensky said after doing a roll call of the officials by his side. They were dressed in the army green T-shirts and jackets that would become their war-time uniforms. 'Defending our independence, our country.'"He later explained to a journalist why he did that: "You understand that they're watching. . . . You're a symbol. You need to act the way the head of state must act."[27]

Zelensky's seemingly impromptu speech that night was brief, and all the more powerful for that. Its central feature was Shakespearean anaphora, or repetition. After naming each of his subordinates with the phrase "is here," he continued,

> We are all here.
>
> Our soldiers are here. The citizens are here and we are all here. We will defend our independence. That's how it will go.
>
> Glory to our defenders, both male and female. Glory to Ukraine![28]

Intentionally or not, Zelensky echoed Churchill's June 4, 1940, speech, not in its soaring peroration but in its matter-of-fact determination to fight "if necessary for years, if necessary alone. At any rate, that is what we are going to try to do. That is the resolve of His Majesty's Government—every man of them. That is the will of Parliament and the nation."

There was also a theatrical quality in the contrast between Zelensky's band of brothers, who looked like one, and the weird, remote staging of Russian president Vladimir Putin's meeting with his security council on February 21, three days before the attack. Where Zelensky's subordinates stand close by him, grim faced but resolute, Putin's are kept thirty or forty feet away; where Zelensky has chosen as his set an embattled street in Kyiv, the Russians are meeting in a gaudy palace; where Zelensky is holding the camera that captures the moment, Putin is hunched over a desk, glaring out at stony-faced and discomfited advisers. As theater alone, the contrasts, often noted, were striking.

Zelensky's costuming was equally brilliant. He wore an olive-drab T-shirt or fleece pullover—not quite a military uniform but enough like one to show that he was a wartime leader who yet did not pretend to be a soldier. A closely trimmed but scraggly beard replaced the smooth face of a boyish-looking political neophyte, making him seem older and, dare one say it, more conventionally manly. As the former style critic of the *Washington Post* noted, here was Everyman as wartime leader.[29]

Zelensky's theater of inspirational leadership extended well beyond Ukraine. With a good actor's sensitivity to his audience, he tuned the pleas for help that he addressed to the world, often speaking every day by video to distant parliaments and assemblies. To the British Parliament, he invoked Shakespeare and Churchill:

> The question for us now is to be or not to be. Oh no, this Shakespearean question. For 13 days this question could have been asked but now I can give you a definitive answer. It's definitely yes, to be.
>
> And I would like to remind you the words that the United Kingdom have already heard, which are important again. We will not give up and we will not lose.
>
> We will fight until the end, at sea, in the air. We will continue fighting for our land, whatever the cost.
>
> We will fight in the forests, in the fields, on the shores, in the streets.
>
> I'd like to add that we will fight on the banks of different rivers and we're looking for your help, for the help of the civilised countries.[30]

The message to the United States was related but appropriate:

> Ladies and gentlemen, friends, Americans, in your great history, you have pages that would allow you to understand Ukrainians, understand us now when we need you, right now. Remember Pearl Harbor, terrible morning of Dec. 7, 1941, when your sky was black from the planes attacking you. Just remember it. Remember September the 11th, a terrible day in 2001 when evil tried to turn your cities, independent territories, into battlefields, when innocent people were attacked, attacked from air, yes. Just like no one else expected it, you could not stop it.[31]

To Germany, the tone was altogether different, playing on German guilt—an emotion to which his audience was, he knew, susceptible: "You must do what you can so that you will not be ashamed of yourselves after this war, after this destruction for the second time in 80 years, after the city of Chernihiv was bombed to pieces and destroyed. . . . You said this could never be repeated. Once again, there is an attempt in Europe to destroy an entire people."[32] Coming from a Jew who lost family members in the Holocaust, it was a visceral blow—but then, theater, including political theater, works on all emotions, including those that make spectators wince and cringe.

Zelensky seems to have played a less active role in the management of the war than did Churchill, which is hardly surprising: unlike the British prime minister, he had had scant experience of military matters before the war. But like Churchill he found occasions to walk the bombed-out streets and talk to soldiers on the front lines, to visibly console and encourage. For both of them, the "touch of Harry in the night" remained an essential part of wartime leadership.

Still, the power of rhetoric should not be underestimated. It could not have been predicted in 1940 that Britain would continue the war after the disaster of France's defeat; it equally could not have been predicted that the Ukrainian government would hold together and that Europe and the United States would rally, within months, to pour tens of billions of dollars' worth of munitions of ever-increasing lethality into a cause about which many had had reservations before the war. Churchill famously said after World War II that it was the British people who had had the lion's heart and that he had merely been privileged to give the roar. The truth is rather different: inspiring rhetoric was critical in sustaining Britain in 1940 and beyond, and inspiring rhetoric gave Ukraine an astonishing chance at self-preservation in 2022.

Still, rhetoric without competence in governance takes a leader only so far. Most of Churchill's wartime work consisted of chairing meetings at 10 Downing Street or in his bunker beneath it, reading and reacting to memoranda from a sprawling bureaucracy, communicating and negotiating with foreign leaders. Zelensky too has spent most of his days in meetings, negotiations, diplomacy, and management of Ukrainian domestic politics. Shakespeare too does not pretend that the heart of Henry V's leadership ability lay solely in his speech making. Indeed he makes a point of repeatedly contrasting the glowing words with brutal realities. Lines deleted from some movie versions of *Henry V* capture the king's brutality as well:

> But hark, what new alarum is this same?
> The French have reinforced their scattered men.
> Then every soldier kill his prisoners!
> Give the word through.[33]

Note that in the play this precedes the news that the French have raided the English baggage trains and massacred the boys left behind to guard them.

Part of Henry V's genius is his ability to shift from a commoner's chat to soaring evocations of glory. This is true as well of Churchill and Zelensky. More to the point, however, Henry could not successfully lead his kingdom through a difficult war to a lucrative peace without many other skills in bending others to his will. And it is to that darker set of skills that we turn next.

CHAPTER 6

Manipulation

Manipulation—the shadowy side of politics—is indispensable, even to the great inspirers.

Novelists capture this better than scholars, as James Gould Cozzens did in *Guard of Honor*, a story that draws heavily on his experiences working as an aide to the head of the US Army Air Forces during World War II:

> A public man had a front, a face; and then, perforce, he had a back, a backside, and in the nature of things it was so ordered that the one was associated with high professions and pronouncements and the other with that euphemistically denoted end-product. They were both always there. Which you saw best would depend on where you stood; but if you let yourself imagine that the one (no matter which) invalidated or made nugatory the other, that was the measure of your simplicity.[1]

Political manipulation resembles conjuring. Magicians (the stage kind, not those possessing or claiming truly occult powers) know that often their trickery, from card sleights to gimmicked contraptions, operate in plain view. The key to mystifying an audience lies to some extent in mastering technical skills in surreptitious actions but far more in understanding and then exploiting the psychology of the audience, which sees everything but hopefully understands very little of what it sees. The key is less concealment than misdirection, or rather, as conjurors more often think of it, control of the audience's attention. The nominal story in the trick is important and needs to be delivered dramatically, but the real work lies in the shadows.

Manipulation in politics takes many forms—think, for example, of old-time political bosses in American cities who amassed power in back rooms while carefully doling out favors and making deals. It occurs in Zhongnanhai, in the former imperial quarter of Beijing, when Xi Jinping launches campaigns against corruption (as widespread among his adherents as among his enemies) that will bring down particularly dangerous rivals. It occurs every time a politician holds a baby or pretends to enjoy a local delicacy that he or she actually finds revolting. It is the stuff of politics, winning associates and allies, lulling observers, laying traps for enemies, paying off favors, and neutralizing opponents. It is why ardent Democrats will pour money into the political campaigns of right-wing Republicans they loathe, seeking to prevent moderate, more competitive candidates from emerging; it is why Republicans may proclaim the sanctity of elections, then hire expensive consultants to draw electoral districts so that politicians can select the voters rather than the other way around.

Shakespeare's *Henry V* offers a master class in these occult political arts. He demonstrates for us why inspiration, for which Henry has talent in abundance, is never adequate for the exercise of power. There is simply too much dirty work that needs doing that a rousing speech alone cannot accomplish. For Henry, that includes launching an unjust war of conquest, suppressing conspiracy, maintaining discipline, compelling an enemy's surrender, and locking up a marital alliance that will ensure his possession not just of a wife but of a royal domain. Moreover, Henry will accomplish these things in ways which not only his nominal contemporaries but we as the audience will fail to understand unless we pay scrupulous attention to his words and the setting in which he utters them. It happens before our very eyes on stage, but we can easily miss what is going on.

Shakespeare shows us that successful political manipulation requires theatrical skills even more advanced than those involved in achieving the right look and tone and selecting the best rhetorical devices for inspirational speech. It requires acting skills, which Henry has in abundance. But he is also a master playwright and director. He stages scenes for the benefit of others. Like many top actors, he even on occasion will write the script and direct the action for a scene in which he has the acting lead. There is a hint of this in the prologue offered by the Chorus, a device that Shakespeare uses sparingly elsewhere. The Chorus begins by asking the audience to imagine large armies, "the vasty fields of France," and much else besides. The Chorus will, until the very end of the play, inflate Henry's accomplishments and celebrate them. But it also advertises, at the very outset, that this involves some measure of deception, asking the audience to go along with it, suspending disbelief—and we do. Thus, Shakespeare's artifice duplicates real life. We see, but we do not observe, although the evidence is clear enough, and often because we choose not to.

In the first scene of *Henry V*, the Archbishop of Canterbury and the Bishop of Ely open the play with words that have nothing to do with heroism or statecraft. They are instead preoccupied with a bill that, if passed, would cause the church to lose "the better half of our possessions." The question is how to prevent that, which leads Canterbury to suggest offering a donation to the king and urging him to launch a war in France. The play begins, in other words, with a manipulation in the form of the church attempting to lure Henry into a war in order to deflect him from seizing more church property. The two men sense that they will be pushing on an open door, and indeed so it proves.

The manipulators, however, soon find themselves manipulated in turn. Henry invites the clerics to expound on the question of whether he has a legitimate claim to the throne of France. And he warns them to be careful:

> For God doth know how many now in health
> Shall drop their blood in approbation
> Of what your reverence shall incite us to.
> Therefore take heed how you impawn our person,
> How you awake our sleeping sword of war.[2]

Henry acknowledges the moral weightiness of launching a war, which will involve

> much fall of blood, whose guiltless drops
> Are every one a woe, a sore complaint
> 'Gainst him whose wrongs gives edge unto the swords
> That make such waste in brief mortality.[3]

Henry then mildly claims that he knows in his heart

> That what you speak is in your conscience wash'd
> As pure as sin with baptism.

Of course the audience knows, and Henry surely does as well, that the clerics have anything but clean hands and pure consciences. They are out to save the church's possessions, and so they obligingly provide a long-winded, well-nigh incomprehensible explanation of his rights in France. This prompts Henry to ask a straightforward question: "May I with right and conscience make this claim?"

This scene is usually played for comic effect, as the baffled and impatient king tries to cut to the conclusion of a convoluted lecture on the Salic law. As conjurors know too, a good chuckle is the best way of distracting an audience, because it prevents them from seeing the magician's manipulative skill. In this case, Henry has achieved one of his constant background goals—that blame for any action, no matter how cruel or unjust, will fall not on him but on those around him—so he charges Canterbury with a faithful and accurate reading of the Salic law, which would give him a claim to France. Knowing, as Henry almost surely does, that the church has every reason to wish to see him go off to conquer France rather than shake the institution down for more money, he is satisfied when Canterbury complies. The archbishop responds, "The sin upon my head, dread sovereign!" And with these words Henry is free, in the public eye, from any complicity in the deed. Better yet, he can respond to the French ambassador who has, foolishly, come to bait him with a gift of tennis balls.

Tell him he hath made a match with such a wrangler
That all the courts of Franx will be disturb'd
With chaces.

And as will occur again, he resorts to blood-curdling threats:

For many a thousand widows
Shall this his mock mock out of their dear husbands;
Mock mothers from their sons, mock castles down.

He is, however, at pains to make clear that the fault for this impending slaughter lies not with him:

But this lies all within the will of God,
To whom I do appeal, and in whose name
Tell you the Dauphin I am coming on
To venge me as I may, and to put forth
My rightful hand in a well-hallow'd cause.

Courteous as ever, he sends the Dauphin's messenger on his way under safe conduct, with the prediction that "thousands [will] weep more than did laugh at" this jest.[4] The effect on the audience is a stir-ring premonition of the brilliance of Henry's later speeches—and not one of revulsion at his clever engineering of an unjust war of conquest. He has successfully manipulated not only the bishops but us, his audi-ence, as well.

Manipulation plays a part in far better causes than Henry's. Abra-ham Lincoln and Franklin D. Roosevelt both manipulated their way into wars that were just and necessary but not self-evidently popular. Lincoln, disregarding military advice, decided to keep a garrison at Fort Sumter in Charleston harbor, knowing that its presence would eventually prompt the new Confederacy to fire the first shots of the Civil War, as he wished. He could (and did) blame the South for initi-ating a war of brother against brother. In 1940 FDR assured his listen-ers that he would not send American boys to fight in foreign wars. In 1941, however, he gradually pushed American naval patrols operating under liberal rules of engagement out into the North Atlantic while proclaiming his intention of keeping America out of the European conflict. This undeclared campaign against the German U-boats that were threatening the shipping of war supplies to Britain might well have brought the United States into the European war even absent Pearl Harbor.

Henry has an easier task than Lincoln or Roosevelt—it can be better to be a king than a president—but the task before him is far from trivial. Political calculator that he is, Henry knows that before he launches the war, he must crush the one remaining plot against him being concocted by three nobles, Scroop, Cambridge, and Grey. Yet it is not enough to merely discover the plot: the miscreants must, like the accused in Joseph Stalin's show trials, be shown wicked beyond belief, incriminating themselves in a public spectacle, then engag-ing in abject confession of crimes so heinous that mercy is impossi-ble. And so Henry makes a show of pardoning a drunken man who had denounced him a few days earlier. The three conspirators, hoping to show an extravagant devotion they do not feel for the king whom they wish to overthrow, urge him not to do so, while the king faintly, almost whimsically, expresses a preference for mercy. Henry teases this out, luring them into protestations of commitment to his person and the need for harshness against all who would conspire against him.

And then comes the dramatic stroke. Henry distributes papers to each of the conspirators that reveal their guilt. They are caught; their situation is hopeless. And having been exposed, they confess and plead for mercy. The king is ready with his reply, which was, after all, the point of the setup pardon of the drunken critic of the king:

> The mercy that was quick in us but late
> By your own counsel is suppressed and killed:
> You must not dare, for shame, to talk of mercy,
> For your own reasons turn into your bosoms
> As dogs upon their masters, worrying you.[5]

This not only silences the guilty three: it hangs around their necks, not Henry's, the king's lack of clemency. Indeed, to make sure that no one watching misunderstands—and this is a public event, contrived as such by Henry—he proceeds to comment on them to the assembled nobles:

> See you, my princes and my noble peers,
> These English monsters!

They are not courtiers engaged in intrigue, who might be pardoned, but monsters, who must be disposed of. Nor will Henry let the crimes go without commentary. It is necessary for his purposes that the conspirators be publicly exposed not merely as traitors but as ingrates, not just as opponents of the king but as men whose lives have been characterized by duplicity and who have betrayed not only their king but their entire upbringing and presumed values.

> Show men dutiful?
> Why, so didst thou. Seem they grave and learned?

Why, so didst thou. Come they of noble family?
Why, so didst thou. Seem they religious?
Why, so didst thou.

Henry's role here is that of the inflexible prosecutor, and his use of anaphora—repeated phrases—hammers home their appalling guilt. There remains one last task for Henry in this powerful speech. He has not only to damn the traitors but show himself merciful and kind, even though he is actually unforgiving and ruthless.

He begins by making clear that the punishments he will dole out have nothing to do with his own feelings—in the phrase made famous in the movie *The Godfather*, this is not personal: it is business.

Touching our person seek we no revenge,
But we our kingdom's safety must so tender,
Whose ruin you have sought, that to her laws
We do deliver you.

Of course, we may suppose that is just as much a lie as it is in *The Godfather*. It's always personal. Still, Henry lays his own righteousness on thick by underscoring that he is handing the traitors over to the law rather than taking vengeance himself. And even this is not quite enough. He has to exhibit before all his personal grief at the moral collapse of Lord Scroop:

I will weep for thee,
For this revolt of thine, methinks, is like
Another fall of man.

From stern prosecutor he has shifted effortlessly to the role of grieving and bewildered friend and patron. It is another of Henry's perfect performances, in which he manages to have the best of both worlds: three traitors confessing their crime and being sent speedily to the block, while the king seems at once generous and noble, public-spirited and law-abiding, saddened and mournful rather than, as he really is, calculating, angry, and vengeful.

In fact, this was an abbreviated show trial, complete with the confessions of the guilty and their prompt executions. Henry does not rule through terror, as Stalin did, and he kills on a far smaller scale, with better reason and more control, but the principle is much the same as in the Soviet purges of the 1930s. Opposition, or even potential opposition, needs to be crushed publicly. The convicted need to appear not merely in the wrong but morally loathsome; the light shining on the leader has to find its contrast in the deep black of his disgraced followers' crimes. The ensuing death sentences must not appear to result from personal vengeance or vendetta. And above all, the doomed conspirators must confess their crimes and accept their fate—and even insist that they deserve it.

Henry V's success as a king rests on manipulation in many ways. He is, for example, capable of getting what he wants not only by appealing to the desire for reputation and prestige but by using fear. This is particularly apparent early on in *Henry V*, at the siege of Harfleur. Henry has urged his men on, crying "once more into the breach, dear friends, once more," but the town has not yet surrendered. Later in the play the king will insist that he will have "none of the French upbraided or abus'd in disdainful language; for when lenity and cruelty play for a kingdom, the gentler gamester is the soonest winner."[6] Yet here he summons the governor of the besieged town to the walls and unleashes a brutal threat.

Henry declares that if he has to resume the bombardment of Harfleur, he will leave the town buried in ashes, but that is not the worst of it. "The gates of mercy shall be all shut up," he says, then issues the real threat:

> And the fleshed soldier, rough and hard of heart,
> In liberty of bloody hand shall range
> With conscience wide as hell, mowing like grass
> Your fresh fair virgins and your flowering infants.[7]

The threat, to which he will recur, is of mass and unconstrained massacre and rape. And he reinforces that threat in several, calculated ways. He repeats it, choosing the most vivid possible language to do so:

> If not, why in a moment look to see
> The blind and bloody soldier with foul hand
> Defile the locks of your shrill-shrieking daughters,
> Your fathers taken by the silver beards,
> And their most reverend heads dashed to the walls,
> Your naked infants spitted upon pikes.

Meanwhile, in a way that is entirely characteristic of him, he detaches himself from any personal responsibility for the actions he unleashes. He does so by feigning indifference to the outcome while (again) reminding his listeners of what a licentious soldiery can do:

> What is't to me, when you yourselves are cause,
> If your pure maidens fall into the hand
> Of hot and forcing violation?

He conveys not only his indifference to the rape of the virgins of Harfleur but also his lack of control of his own men:

> What rein can hold licentious wickedness
> When down the hill he holds his fierce career?

As ever, Henry avoids all responsibility for what his men may do. But in fact, we see that he has a firm grip on them, and once the town surrenders, he orders his uncle Exeter, who will govern the town, to "use mercy to them all." We will see later the harshness of the discipline that he uses to enforce mildness toward the occupied French population.

To some extent Henry's threats simply reflect the realities of siege warfare in the early modern period, when it was indeed difficult to restrain soldiers from sacking a town, itself sometimes considered perfectly permissible. But there is a deeper game here as well. If he has to engage in slaughter, Henry will do so, but he prefers throughout the play to get what he wants by playing on the emotions of those around him. He wants glory and power, and he will spill blood to get those things, with no squeamish compunctions. And yet he does not relish violence either and understands its limits and its counterproductive potential.

Through it all, there is the touch of the master actor in Henry's behavior. He hints as much when in the Harfleur speech he describes a role that he often adopts: that of the simple soldier ("for as I am a soldier, / A name that in my thoughts becomes me best"). Throughout his career, however, Henry will play many roles, as those closest to him note. At the very outset of the play, the Archbishop of Canterbury says,

> Hear him but reason in divinity
> And, all-admiring, with an inward wish
> You would desire the King were made a prelate.
> Hear him debate of commonwealth affairs,
> You would say it hath been all in all his study.[8]

Henry is a chameleon. He has a favorite role, to be sure, that of a bluff soldier, and he will return to that again and again. But he will also play other roles—the generous king, the honor-seeking aristocrat, the stern judge—as he had earlier played at the role of the madcap prince and the reformed prodigal son. He is even more versatile than one of Shakespeare's greatest villains, Richard III, but he does not boast as much as Richard does about his ability to pretend to be things that he is not. He just does what he considers needful without talking about it to the audience or to anyone else.

Henry's manipulations extend beyond the use or threat of force in ways that make him look good, or at least innocent. They appear as well in his wooing of Katherine, the French princess, in the final part of the play, which is often rendered (particularly in the Kenneth

Branagh film version) amusingly and tenderly. In it, Henry stumbles through his schoolboy French and once again plays the simple soldier:

> But before God, Kate, I cannot look greenly nor gasp out my eloquence, nor I have no cunning in protestation, only downright oaths, which I never use till urged, nor never break for urging. If thou canst love a fellow of this temper, Kate, whose face is not worth sunburning, that never looks in his glass for love of anything he sees there, let thine eye be thy cook. I speak to thee plain soldier. If thou canst love me for this, take me; if not, to say to thee that I shall die is true; but for thy love, by the Lord, no; yet I love thee too.[9]

For this role Shakespeare has chosen to depict Henry as reverting to prose rather than verse. It is a consciously informal tone. His artfully rambling words (from a man who in every other context in the play has chosen them carefully) are designed to both charm and confuse a young woman, many of whose relatives were slaughtered the other day by the English archers and knights. In the end, she succumbs, and the crowns of England and France are united.

A closer look reveals, however, that this is no mere wooing by a love-smitten, rough-hewn warrior. Just before he goes to Katherine, Henry has conducted a steely negotiation with the king of France through the Duke of Burgundy, which will strip France of both possessions and sovereignty. After Burgundy has described a France brutalized and in mourning, Henry responds,

> If, Duke of Burgundy, you would the peace
> Whose want gives growth to th'imperfections
> Which you have cited, you must buy that peace
> With full accord to all our just demands,
> Whose tenors and particular effects
> You have, enscheduled briefly, in your hands.[10]

"Imperfections" is a cold-blooded way of referring to the ruin of his country that the French negotiator has described. In this case, however, Henry need not resort to the kinds of threats he used at Harfleur. He has the whip hand and can afford to use tranquil euphemisms rather than threaten more slaughter, but the threat is no less real.

As for the wooing of Katherine, it is rife with sexual innuendo: "If I could win a lady at leapfrog, or by vaunting into my saddle with my armour on my back, under the correction of bragging be it spoken, I should quickly leap into a wife."[11] And if there is not talk of rape, there is no question but that he means to bed her: "I get thee with scambling, and thou must therefore needs prove a good soldier-breeder." When she asks whether it is possible for her to love an enemy of France, Henry speaks in terms of possession: "In loving me you should love the friend of France; for I love France so well that I will not part with a village of it; I will have it all mine: and Kate, when France is mine, and I am yours, then yours is France, and you are mine." There is charm in this, but the meaning is clear to the audience, although not to Katherine, who is bewildered by the torrent of words. "I cannot tell vat is dat."

The final part of the seduction of Katherine comes when Henry declares that he will kiss her. She protests that that is not the French custom, to which Henry replies, "O Kate, nice customs curtsy to great kings." He kisses her, assuring her, "You have witchcraft in your lips," and slyly promising her power in return for her favors: "There is more eloquence in a sugar touch of them than in the tongues of the French Council, and they should sooner persuade Harry of England than a general petition of monarchs."

It is a master class in seduction, but underlying it is coercion, the lure of power, and the confusion of a woman who will be given away as part of a political deal to her country's conqueror. It is usually staged as a lighthearted romantic conclusion to the play, with an attractive young actress. The lines, and more importantly Henry's purposes, would be the same, however, if she were homely. He means to have her as a way of having France.

Much of politics is seduction, and many of the greatest wielders of power show skills similar to Henry's in convincing their auditors that they are in love with them. FDR was notorious for his ability to make people believe that he was on their side, only to be equally convincing to a rival or an opponent. It was maddening for his subordinates once they caught on—the diaries of Harold Ickes, secretary of the interior, offer ample proof of that—but it was necessary for the politician who built the greatest coalition of disparate domestic elements in American history.

Henry must use all of his theatrical skills, as playwright, director, and actor, even though he is king. Katherine has no choice, but he wants her to think she does. The conspirators have to be not only crushed but exposed, humiliated, and induced to voluntarily confess their corruption. The governor of Harfleur has to be shaken by fears of massacre and rape, even though, as we know, Henry intends to win France with the gentle arts more than through sheer violence. His soldiers have to believe that battle will make them brothers of the dashing young king, which they can never really be. He must always be seen as one whose good nature has been practiced upon; never as responsible for the mayhem he threatens or actually unleashes; always as generous, perhaps a bit clumsy, but open-handed and giving. One has to ask why Henry is so relentless in his deceptions, even when he clearly has the upper hand.

The answer lies in Henry's realization that his eminence is fraught. In a moment alone (the only occasion when one can expect him to be frank) before the Battle of Agincourt, he drops to his knees. He acknowledges that his men have every reason to be terrified by the odds against them, and for once he prays.

> Not today, O Lord,
> O not today, think not upon the fault
> My father made in compassing the crown.
> I Richard's body have interred new,
> And on it have bestowed more contrite tears
> Than from it issued forced drops of blood.[12]

And more: he has paid five hundred indigent commoners to pray for pardon for the murder of Richard, and if successful, he will do more yet. Henry thinks he can manipulate God as well as human beings, or at least cut a beneficial deal with him.

He understands very well that his crown is not entirely legitimate. On his deathbed his father, Henry IV, had promised him that it would come down to him

> with better quiet,
> Better opinion, better confirmation,
> For all the soil of the achievement goes
> With me into the earth.[13]

Better quiet, opinion, and confirmation perhaps, but not complete assuredness. From the beginning of *Henry V*, we see that his power is not entirely secure: the church fears his confiscations, there are nobles ready to plot against him, and his playboy reputation from his days as prince has not yet disappeared.

Even more importantly, Henry knows something many leaders never fully realize: that having received an office or title, be it king, president, or chief executive officer, the holder must continue to win it day in, day out. The great politicians are always aware that power can slip through their fingers, that they can be toppled in an election or simply by others failing to take them seriously. The trickling away of authority at the end of a presidential administration, which I have seen firsthand, is a very good example of that. Phone calls are returned less quickly, important decisions are pushed off, and behind courteous faces and polite conversation one knows that foreign diplomats are simply waiting you out.[14]

Throughout the play Henry will never let down his guard, never stop using other people, never cease burnishing his reputation, less out of ego than perceived political necessity. Richard II, whom Henry's father had overthrown, had believed that legitimacy was enough to cement his authority; Coriolanus may have believed that sheer reputation, the charisma of a conquering general, would carry him forward. Henry V shows us that the wise, or at least the successful, leader never rests.

To his manipulativeness one must add Henry's ruthless streak, apparent very early on in his days as Prince Hal, when he and his teacher, friend, and tempter, Falstaff, are playing at an interview between Henry IV and his wayward son. It is one of Shakespeare's great comic moments, but it ends jarringly as Falstaff, playing Hal (who is having fun with a comic rendition of his father), makes a plea for himself: "No, my good lord, banish Peto, banish Bardoll, banish Poins, but for sweet Jack Falstaff, kind Jack Falstaff, true Jack Falstaff, valiant Jack Falstaff, and therefore more valiant being as he is old Jack Falstaff, banish not him thy Harry's company, banish not him thy Harry's company. Banish plump Jack and banish all the world."[15] Numerous critics have dwelt on that last line, because Falstaff is, indeed, a representation of normal humanity, and because without him the lights of humor and fun are much dimmer. More important, however, is Hal's four-word response, spoken as himself, not in the role of his father the king: "I do; I will."

Shakespeare turns a brilliant strobe light for just a few seconds on Henry's true character. True to form, Henry does not expand on why or when he will banish Falstaff: there is only that flash of heartless calculation. There are other flashes later on—at the end of Henry IV, for example, when Henry V has just been crowned and Falstaff comes to him for favors: "I know thee not, old man. Fall to thy prayers."[16] The first repudiation was promised in private; the second is, like the indictment of the conspirators in Henry V, conducted on a public stage, so that others will see of what stuff the new king is made. To tie up the loose ends of Falstaff's life, there is one more repudiation, offstage, at the very beginning of Henry V. We do not see Falstaff's death, but it is reported to us by his comrades. The hostess reports, "The King has killed his heart."[17] In three plays, then, we have seen how Henry will break with the most beloved of Shakespeare's characters, one who has taught him much—and he even manages to persuade us that, unfortunately perhaps, he is right to do so. Power is a ruthless business, as deposed prime ministers, presidents, and kings discover. Confidants who are no longer useful may be dropped and long-standing friends abandoned, new alliances of convenience struck up.

Beneath Henry's charm and assumed confidence lie a set of much darker emotions. He has his father's realism and willingness to make hard decisions; he would agree with Henry IV's declaration "Are these things then necessities? Let us meet them like necessities."[18] But whereas that approach to power is on the surface with Henry IV, and with it, accompanying anger and grief, the same mindset is more artfully and misleadingly presented by Henry V, which is why audiences and critics wrestle with the jarring moments. One of these is when one of his old companions, Bardolph (whose "face is all bubuncles, and whelks, and knobs, and flames o'fire") has been caught stealing from a church. He has been sentenced to death, but the case is brought to Henry. His response is curt (and delivered in prose): "We would have all such offenders so cut off; and we give express charge that in our marches through the country there be nothing compelled from the villages, nothing taken but paid for."[19]

One might not realize at this moment that Henry is speaking of one of the companions of his louche days as Prince Hal. One can attempt to soften the scene by having Henry look with an expression of regret, or at least sorrow, at the sight of Bardolph being hanged, and so it is often staged. But the words are the words. And they are a bit strange coming from the man who dwelt, almost pornographically, on the scenes of rape that would ensue if the governor of Harfleur did not surrender.

An even more straightforward moment of this kind comes in the middle of the Battle of Agincourt. Henry learns of the deaths of York and Suffolk from his distraught uncle Exeter. He says that he will wipe his own eyes so that they will not fill with tears; then suddenly,

> But hark, what new alarum is this same?
> The French have reinforced their scattered men.

Then every soldier kill his prisoners!
Give the word through.[20]

This curt order precedes the news that the French have raided the baggage wagons and slaughtered the boys guarding them, which produces outrage on the part of the semicomic Welsh captain Fluellen. Nothing is made of it—and yet it is another strobe light flashing on Henry's character. He sees a necessity—securing the army's rear from a French raid—and gives a brutal order that is, as Fluellen notes, against the law of war understood even in that crueler time.

Henry's political cunning is brilliant. But the toll on Henry's character is immense. One cannot imagine him having any true friends; his mercy and gentleness are all calculated. And at the core there is an emptiness. Shakespearean characters reveal themselves in soliloquy. In *Henry V,* that comes just before the Battle of Agincourt, after Henry has made the rounds of the camp in disguise and had a jarring conversation with soldiers who are not convinced that the king's cause is "just and his quarrel honourable." And one, Williams, speaks for privates in armies at all times:

> But if the cause be not good, the King himself hath a heavy reckoning to make when all those legs and arms and heads chopped off in a battle shall join together at the latter day and cry all "We died at such a place," some swearing, some crying for a surgeon, some upon their wives left poor behind them, some upon the debts they owe, some upon their children rawly left. I am afeard there are few die well that die in a battle, for how can they charitably dispose of anything when blood is their argument? Now if these men do not die well it will be a black matter for the King, that led them to it, who to disobey were against all proportion of subjection.[21]

The disguised Henry attempts to rebut this—perhaps those that die in battle have other sins that caused them to suffer or die, and in any case they should spend their time contemplating the state of their own souls rather than that of the king.

When the soldiers have left the stage and Henry is alone, he finally shows us his true feelings:

Upon the King! "Let us our lives, our souls,
Our debts, our careful wives,
Our children and our sins lay on the King!"
We must bear all. O hard condition,
Twin-born with greatness, subject to the breath
Of every fool whose sense no more can feel
But his own wringing! What infinite heart's ease
Must kings neglect that private men enjoy?

It is a spectacularly ungrateful comment. His men are not the brothers of the next day's St. Crispin's speech—they are fools. Their entirely reasonable fears of wounds and death, of the suffering of loved ones, and of the contrived reasons for the war have been transmuted into "infinite heart's ease." Henry has not suffered, but this is a "hard condition" for him. He goes further yet, contending, ludicrously, that all kings have over commoners is "ceremony," or pomp. He thinks it unfair that "instead of homage sweet" (which presumably he deserves), he gets "poisoned flattery" (which disgusts him). And he returns to the abuse of his own men (he has used the word "lackey" as well as "fool"), at least by implication, culminating in the declaration

The slave, a member of the country's peace,
Enjoys it, but in gross brain little wots
What watch the King keeps to maintain the peace,
Whose hours the peasant best advantages.

The hypocrisy is truly astounding. He will celebrate the sturdy yeomen of England as free men, but he really thinks of them as slaves;

he will congratulate them on enjoying the country's peace, which he preserves—in the midst of an unnecessary war that he has launched, he has claimed that the king works to maintain the peace—when we know, because he will shortly tell Westmoreland, that a thirst for glory motivates him most; he thinks his subjects dull witted ("gross brain"), able only to enjoy the peace—after he has just spent time in the camp watching them prepare themselves, at his orders, for war.

It is, in short, a passage of stunning self-pity and self-delusion, an ugly egotism that shows a lack of real sympathy with those he leads. What he lacks in sympathy, however, he makes up in empathy: he understands his men, even if at some level he despises them. As unattractive as Henry shows himself to be, he is still a brilliant leader. In a moment of lonely truth, he has no feeling at all for the men who will pay the price for his quest for glory. On a public stage, however, he will make us feel that he is one with them. In this he is quite like other political leaders, particularly but not exclusively populists, who have a feral instinct for where their followers may be but have no real solicitude for any of them. Perhaps scariest yet, we as audience members find ourselves taken in by him.

In this respect the action of the Chorus in *Henry V* becomes particularly important. It begins each act and ends the play. It is Henry's relentless cheerleader, celebrating his triumphs, often describing virtues he does not have, urging us to admire the king unreservedly. It is like a sycophantic press corps or pundit class, refusing to acknowledge the dark deeds underlying the king's power and celebrating his achievements no matter what lies behind them.

The Chorus is an unusual device, one that Shakespeare does not use in his other history plays. One of its functions seems to be to dull our sensibilities. There are enough jagged edges to Henry's character, all of them discussed above, from his launching of the war, to his cat-and-mouse game with the conspirators, to the bloodcurdling threats at Harfleur, to the execution of Bardolph, and more. The Chorus distracts us from those unpleasant facts—even, one may say, as Henry V does himself. And perhaps that is the point of having it. Henry's genius lies in concealing the numerous ugly sides of his personality either by manipulating the presentation of them or by speeding through them, as in his order to kill all the prisoners. His callousness toward his own men the night before Agincourt is covered by the Chorus praising the "touch of Harry in the night," for example. And so, the great many, and possibly most, of us reading or seeing the play come away cheering for the king and setting aside the flaws of which we are aware but upon which we choose not to dwell.

But there is one final illuminating flash. When the Chorus sums up the play by celebrating the glory of "this star of England," it concludes,

> Fortune made his sword
> By which the world's best garden he achieved,
> And of it left his son imperial lord.
> Henry the Sixth, in infant bands crowned King
> Of France and England, did this king succeed,
> Whose state so many had the managing
> That they lost France and made his England bleed,
> Which oft our stage hath shown; and for their sake
> In your fair minds let this acceptance take.[22]

It is another surprisingly gloomy note, akin to Octavius's wresting of Brutus's corpse for his own ceremonial purposes at the end of *Julius Caesar*. And like that moment, it may provide the key to the political meaning of the entire play.

Henry attempted, on the eve of Agincourt, to manipulate God as well as men and women; his purpose in that case was to elicit forgiveness for his father's murder of Richard II with alms, reburial of the dead king, and even his own tears. But God, or if one prefers, Fortune, unlike mortal men and women, does not yield to manipulation, and even the most brilliant wielder of power cannot predict his own death. In his moment Henry has won glory, and deservedly so. But his achievements are ephemeral, and if we step back and do not allow the

Chorus and Henry's own artifices to blind us, we see that and ponder its significance.

All of politics, and indeed all leadership, involves to some extent the manipulation of human beings, appealing to their emotions as well as their reason, occasionally cloaking motives and distracting others from unworthy deeds. And *Henry V* teaches us that manipulation can in fact achieve great things, the acquisition of a kingdom and of glory. That profound lesson is often difficult for us to accept: we would rather that great results come from clean methods. But that is often not the case.

A good illustration of this can be found in the work of a master biographer, Robert Caro, tackling the story of Lyndon Baines Johnson, who rose from obscurity in the hill country of Texas to the presidency of the United States.[23] It is, as Caro has often acknowledged, the tale of a politician who, by the standards of most liberal or progressive observers, achieved a great deal—particularly by way of removing barriers for African Americans at the polling booth and beyond—but who was consumed by a hunger for power and a relentlessness in its pursuit.

In his lifetime no one doubted that Lyndon Baines Johnson, the thirty-sixth president of the United States, was a master manipulator, although it was not until the publication of Caro's massive, multivolume biography that the extent and nature of his use of the dark arts became clear. An uneven (though not incompetent) public speaker at best, he more often got his way by cajolery, flattery, bribery, intimidation, and, no less, persuasion. He could steal an election and woo the editor of the *New York Times*; he could humiliate his subordinates and, even so, elicit fierce loyalty. He displayed in his own way a form of political art.

Caro's fourth volume, *Master of the Senate*, best reveals LBJ's cunning and what it could accomplish. He had nothing of the charisma of John F. Kennedy—himself a bit of Prince Hal cum Henry V—but he had plenty of stagecraft, beginning with costuming. He dressed in big, expensive suits that concealed his expanding weight (Caro reports that he began "wearing a girdle in an attempt to conceal what was sometimes an enormous paunch") and buffed his shoes up to a dozen times a day. He worked on performance art as well, believing as he did that "what convinces is conviction." "He was big all right, but he got bigger as he talked to you," recalled one of his associates.[24]

Like any good actor, he used his body as an instrument. He would tower over friends and opponents alike, draping arms over shoulders or leaning over editors who had to tilt back to look him in the eye. Some he would wheedle or seduce; others he would intimidate, notoriously insisting that his subordinates show him complete devotion. One favorite test was making a new speechwriter or other staff member report to him as he sat on the toilet, "lowering his tone, forcing me to approach more closely," as Richard Goodwin later reported. Yet he also knew how to lure those for whom the proximity to power, real and potential, was the ultimate draw. He was an acute student of individuals, like Cassius in Julius Caesar but with better success in manipulating them:

Often, for long minutes, the only words Lyndon Johnson spoke were words to encourage the man on the other end of the wire to keep talking—so that he could better determine what might bend the man to his purpose, what arguments might work. . . . Lyndon Johnson would stand or sit that way for a long time, motionless, intent, listening—pouring himself into that listening, all his being focused on what the other man was saying, and what the man wasn't saying; on what he knew about the other man, and on what he didn't know and was trying to find out.[25]

Johnson chose his scenery and stage as well. To win the support of the oil interests that he needed to fund his rise to power, he arranged a Senate hearing that left the career of a liberal economist at the Federal Power Commission in ruins. He orchestrated hearings that left Leland Olds without a job, Johnson's future backers deeply gratified, and his reputation for power heightened. It was, his biographer says, a demonstration of the quality of "utter ruthlessness in destroying obstacles" in his path to power.[26]

Johnson had, as cunning manipulators do, a feral instinct for others' weaknesses, which he could exploit ruthlessly and coercively. But he was even more effective when employing it for the purposes of seduction. Caro's description of his courtship of Senator Richard Russell, one of the towering figures of his time, makes for an astonishing read. Russell was many things LBJ was not—deeply well-read, committed to policy thoughtfully made, modest, and somewhat introverted. And on his principles, be they good or bad, he could be inflexible. LBJ needed his support for the civil rights legislation of 1964 and 1965, and Russell was a resolute segregationist. So Johnson went about the seduction of Richard Russell. And Johnson soon realized "that Russell, who was no longer so young, was a bachelor and lonely."[27] And so he won Russell over with careful attention, constant invitations to dinner, and incessant flattery. It had worked on the crusty Speaker of the House, Sam Rayburn, who would tear up when Johnson publicly said, "[Rayburn] has been like a daddy to me." It worked here as well.[28] Eventually, through a series of maneuvers that Caro documents in exquisite and fascinating detail, Johnson was able to overcome the Southern Bloc's ability to stop civil rights legislation. The Civil Rights Acts of 1964 and 1965 were in many ways his finest achievements.

Many aspects of Johnson's personality are disagreeable, even vile. He seems to have been a sexual predator; he was content to lie to get his way; his manner could be coarse, and he was willing to be cruel. And yet he accomplished some great things. Great political skill is often like that: deep but limited. He transformed the American welfare system, but his greatest achievement was surely making the lasting cracks in America's formal system of racial segregation. It was a masterly accomplishment in the face of a political system designed more to obstruct than to facilitate change, and on an issue in which prejudice and bigotry were so deeply rooted.

LBJ undoubtedly deserves acclaim for his legislative accomplishments on civil rights. Yet, when he faced a different challenge, that of the Vietnam War, he failed. His own Shakespearean flaws, not least of them his fear of humiliation, of appearing weak, led him to go along with the steady escalation of a war that he was not willing to go all out to win (putting his domestic programs in jeopardy) or to walk away from (marking him as a failure of a far more personal sort). The tragedy of it all is that he knew better; he proceeded not out of delusion but out of an anguished inability to let go or act effectively.

Johnson was a great manipulative leader, until he encountered a problem that he could not manipulate his way through. Henry V was an extraordinary leader, who could both inspire (in a way that Johnson never could) and manipulate. For both men, Fortune had the final say, no matter what their talents, aspirations, or dreams. But until that point they accomplished much, winning fame and achieving great things through methods that those around them never fully grasped.

CHAPTER 7

Murder

I T IS ONE THING TO SECURE POWER BY MANIPULATION AND
intrigue—that is not only the norm: it is often a necessity. But what
of power not only gained by murder but sustained by it? Many dictators kill their way to the top, as we have seen. Of further interest, however, is why they continue to kill once they are there. Is it a necessity,
or has it become a habit? Or is it merely the mode in which they are
most comfortable? Do they believe it the most reliable way of exercis-
ing rule, or do they reluctantly conclude they have no choice?

Though such brutality may seem far removed from our everyday
experience, the reality is that leaders in the less blood-soaked reaches
of corporate, academic, and workaday life can learn much from the
anatomy of political murder. After all, what is a firing but a metaphorical murder? Loyal subordinates (or subversive ones) may find a
job-ending knife in their backs and, as their moment on stage ends,
be astounded at the name they find engraved on the handle. Such

executions may be done discreetly, masked by excuses or euphemisms, as in the academic world when the official statement declares that "department chair so-and-so has decided to return to her first love, teaching." Corporate communications similarly assure us that "vice president X has decided to seek exciting new opportunities," leaving the destination conveniently unstated. Those who are not so lucky may face terminal encounters openly, in a humiliating meeting or even, as was the case in a recent American presidential administration, by 240-word tweet. At a certain point, more than one British prime minister has found him- or herself awaiting the arrival of the "men in gray suits" to deliver a quietus to a political career. And sometimes these are not single events but bloodbaths, the organizational equivalents of the St. Valentine's Day massacre, with entire cadres turned into the street, warnings about nondisclosure agreements ringing in their ears. Elon Musk's takeover of social media company Twitter in 2022 is a good example, replete with a massive culling (some of it preemptive) of those who failed to swear fealty to him, his sleep-in-the-office work ethic, and his whimsical understanding of free speech.

The use of murder—of the nonmetaphorical variety—to secure rule is, unfortunately, a matter quite familiar to those who have witnessed the twentieth and early twenty-first centuries. Indeed, Polish literature professor and critic Jan Kott, writing in the early 1960s, says that a mid-twentieth-century spectator or reader of Shakespeare "is not terrified—or rather, not amazed—at Shakespeare's depiction of cruelty. He views the struggle for power and mutual slaughter of the characters far more calmly than did many generations of spectators and critics in the nineteenth century. . . . Violent deaths of the principal characters are now regarded rather as an historical necessity, or as something altogether natural."[1] Perhaps Kott—a veteran of World War II and a Stalinist who changed his view only in 1957, years after the dictator's death—could contemplate slaughter with such cold-blooded equanimity. Most of us cannot. But he had a point. According to *The Black Book of Communism*, a monumental French-led work of research published in 1999, communism was directly responsible for eighty-five million deaths, dwarfing the twenty-five million of Adolf Hitler's Nazi regime. Those murders must forever be associated with those who ordered them: Vladimir Lenin, Joseph Stalin, Mao Zedong, Pol Pot, Ho Chi Minh, Fidel Castro, and others.[2] Ideology provided the rationale and shaped the decision-making cultures, but rulers gave orders, and men like the secret police chiefs Lavrenti Beria (Stalin) and Kang Sheng (Mao) carried them out.

Shakespeare's killer kings thus have much to teach us about the consequences of rule through murder, its efficacy, and its limitations.

To begin with, there is a distinction between those who kill in a limited fashion and those who wallow in slaughter. Henry IV is the best example of the former, those who murder their way to the top and then exercise restraint and clemency in far greater proportion once they are there. He orders the execution of some of Richard II's courtiers and then of Richard himself. But thereafter, although he can be authoritarian and brutal in his demands, he does not quietly order the assassination of his enemies. He is a prudent, if limited, king. He resorts to murder because he believes he needs it, not because he necessarily likes it.

As he says to Exton, who has faithfully followed his thinly disguised request to kill Richard II, "They love not poison that do poison need, Nor do I thee."[3] Here, Henry is honest in acknowledging that he needed the poison, or rather believed that he did, and there is no reason to think that he speaks anything other than the truth when he says that he does not love it.

In this, we see in Henry IV a truth identified by Niccolò Machiavelli, when he speaks of "cruelties badly used or well used": "Those can be called well used (if it is permissible to speak well of evil) that are done at a stroke, out of the necessity to secure oneself, and then are not persisted in but are turned to as much utility for the subjects as one can. Those cruelties are badly used which, though few in the beginning, rather grow with time than are eliminated."[4] Henry is imperfect because although he could use cruelty when appropriate and, equally so, moderate amounts of clemency, he never was able to dole out the benefits of his rule in such a way as to disarm or pacify his support-ers, who, having helped him to power, were disgruntled by his lack of generosity. "For injuries must be done all together," Machiavelli writes, "so that, being tasted less, they offend less; and benefits should be done little by little that they may be tasted better."[5] Henry IV gained his throne by killing not only his predecessor but several of Richard II's key courtiers, as much to send a signal to others as because of any dan-ger they posed. He did not continue in a course of bloodshed, which may be why he could retain his crown, yet he failed to dole out benefits "little by little," which is why he faced revolts to the end of his days.

The ideal Machiavellian prince seeks power for its own sake and as a way of displaying virtù. This means something akin to, but rather dif-ferent from, the English word *virtue*; it is the combination of skills and desire for glory that Machiavelli celebrates. Virtù stems from ambition and from a desire for glory but also from possession of the skills that bring one to preeminence and the desire to use them. There is nothing neurotic or twisted about such motivations: they are straightforward. In reality, however, Machiavellian princes are few and far between, which is one reason for some scholars' regarding Machiavelli's treatise as a satire or a fantasy. Whether that is a correct reading or not, Shake-speare helps us understand the human limits on crime "well-used" as a way of maintaining power. What he describes, and Machiavelli does not, is the corrosive effect of repeated criminal behavior on those who resort to it routinely for the everyday practice of ruling.

Whereas Henry IV remains merely imperfect, slaughter corrodes Shakespeare's Richard III and Macbeth to the core. Act after act, scene after scene, they violate Machiavelli's dictum about doing all of one's injuries at once, ordering slayings or else committing them themselves. One proof of the inefficiency of ruling through crime is evident in the sheer quantity of bodies each leaves strewn about.

For Richard III, the failure to rule through crime efficiently has to do with motivation. In *Henry VI, Part 3*, the future Richard III says that he can "set the murderous Machiavel to school." Knowing him-self to be both ruthless and a great actor, he seems to believe,

162

I can smile, and murder whiles I smile,
And cry "Content" to that which grieves my heart,
And wet my cheeks with artificial tears,
And frame my face to all occasions.[6]

But these two qualities alone do not, in fact, make a Machiavellian prince, who can act the part of a lion or a fox, as the Florentine put it, as the occasion requires. The Machiavellian temperament is one of superb self-control and calculation, single-mindedness in the pursuit of power, and a kind of even temper in the face of good and bad fortune equally. It is rarely found in real life. Richard III, arguably the most Machiavellian of Shakespeare's kings, lacks that final quality of steely equanimity, and indeed, that deficiency eventually brings about his downfall.

Shakespeare's Richard III is driven to seek power not only by innate ambition but by a potent combination of self-pity and self-loathing, combined with a monumental self-confidence in his ability to deceive. His soliloquy in *Henry VI, Part 3* explores those feelings and beliefs in depth. But these aspects of his emotional makeup do not immediately explain how he behaves once he becomes king. For it is not just that the murdering continues once he has put on the crown in Act 4 of *Richard III*—a Machiavellian prince may regrettably have to kill a few more people after getting to the top—but how he does it.

Richard, it must be remembered, has served a long apprenticeship in killing to his brother and predecessor as king, Edward IV. Early on he speaks to his implacable enemy, Queen Margaret, the widow of Henry VI, whom he has murdered.

Ere you were queen, ay, or your husband king
I was a packhorse in his [Edward's] great affairs,
A weeder-out of his proud adversaries
A liberal rewarder of his friends.
To royalize his blood I spent mine own.[7]

There are clues to Richard's governance by murder in this brief passage from the very beginning of the play, when he is still climbing his way to the throne. He views himself as a "packhorse," a utilitarian kind of creature that does what needs to be done in a routine, unobtrusive, almost unnoticed way. And what needs to be done? The rewarding of friends, to be sure, but first and foremost, he is a "weeder-out" of "proud adversaries." To the extent that one views governance as a process of weeding out (rather than inspiring or controlling), murder seems simply the most direct way of doing business. It helps, moreover, that the adversaries are proud, which suggests both that they have it coming and that they are likely to be surprised by the moment when the knife slips between the ribs. And there is one further element: Richard's resentment. He enters his quest for kingship, and presumably his monarchical rule itself, displeased that he should have to spill his own blood in order to make someone else king. This grievance justifies his certainty that others should rightfully spill *their* blood to sustain *him* as king.

Richard III is a friendless man, not only unlovable but knowing himself to be so. The Machiavellian prince, by contrast, would prefer to be both loved and feared, although if forced to choose, he will choose fear. But it is a particular kind of fear: "The prince should nonetheless make himself feared in such a mode that if he does not acquire love, he escapes hatred, because being feared and not being hated can go together very well."[8] Indeed, Machiavelli describes such a use of fear in the story of Cesare Borgia's pacification of the Romagna, told in Chapter 7 of *The Prince*.

Borgia discovered that the Romagna, which had been weakly governed by exploitative and incapable rulers, was in a state of chaos. He installed Messer de Remirro de Orco, "a cruel and ready man," with full power to pacify the place, which he did in short order, albeit through harsh measures. The story did not end there.

And because he [Borgia] knew that past rigors had generated some hatred for Remirro, to purge the spirits of the people and to gain them entirely to himself, he wished to show that if any cruelty had been committed, this had not come from him but from the harsh nature of his minister. And having seized this opportunity, he had him placed one morning in the piazza at Cesena in two pieces, with a piece of wood and a bloody knife beside him. The ferocity of this spectacle left the people at once satisfied and stupefied.[9]

Here is cruelty well used, in Machiavelli's view: appreciated, staged but not flaunted, calculated both to reassure and to intimidate. It has its analogies in the hiring of an efficient executive or dean to turn around a failing business or school, then his or her speedy and wordless dismissal after the necessary cruelties have been committed.

Richard is very different, however, from Cesare Borgia. At times in *Richard III*, as previously in *Henry VI, Part 3*, he positively revels in being hated, as when he taunts Queen Margaret, whose husband and son he has slain. The full repercussions of the hatred he has elicited are felt not only in the eventual coming together of his enemies at the Battle of Bosworth but in the dreams that haunt him on the night of his last battle. One by one the ghosts of those he has murdered appear to him, saying, "Despair and die!" Cold-blooded as he is, he cannot shake off the consequences of knowing the depth and extent of the hatred that surrounds him. He awakes from his troubled sleep disoriented and desperate:

> I shall despair; there is no creature loves me,
> And if I die no soul will pity me.
> And wherefore should they, since that I myself
> Find in myself no pity to myself?[10]

The only people Richard seems to have a kind of affection for are the murderers he employs. The conversation with the two murderers (they are not identified by name) whom he dispatches to kill his brother Clarence is revealing:

But soft, here come my executioners.
—How now, my hardy, stout, resolved mates;
Are you now going to dispatch this thing?[11]

Henry IV would never have welcomed Exton as "my executioner," but Richard has no such qualms. He admires the qualities that murder requires, hence his description of them as "hardy" and "stout," attributes one might fairly ascribe to the king himself. Murder appeals to Richard because he has had to murder people himself, and he appreciates the emotional makeup it requires. For him, murder is not a necessity simply, although it is that: it is also a test of one's mettle and even, in some cases, a source of pleasure.

The murderers explain that they have come for a warrant, which will allow them access to the imprisoned Clarence. Richard warns them to act quickly, in order to prevent the "well-spoken" Clarence from causing them to pity him.

Tut, tut my lord, we will not stand to prate.
Talkers are no good doers; be assured
We go to use our hands and not our tongues.

Richard himself is marvelous at both talking and doing, but that is hardly the point.

Your eyes drop millstones when fools' eyes fall tears.
I like you lads. About your business straight.

His admiration is sincere: he genuinely likes them, and he likes them for their complete lack of sentimentality. Accustomed to murder as a way of preserving power, Richard approves of the qualities that it requires, and he likes the men who are capable of it. He thinks pity or sympathy signs of weakness.

His affinity for murder goes even further, however. The worst of his crimes, the one for which he is indicted even today, is the murder of his two nephews in the Tower of London. This time the murderer, Tyrrel, has a name, and he reports to Richard in Act 4, Scene 3. Richard questions him closely about whether he has killed the boys and where they are buried. After getting some of the details, Richard continues,

> Come to me, Tyrrel, soon at after-supper,
> When thou shalt tell the process of their death.[12]

There are the leaders who do not want to know exactly how the dirty deed was done. Henry IV certainly did not. But Richard has, at this point, an almost pornographic interest in the details of how two children were killed. And the thought of hearing the details puts him in a positively joyful mood. He tells Tyrrel,

> Meantime, but think how I may do thee good,
> And be inheritor of thy desire.
> Farewell till then.

And he ends the scene looking forward to seducing Elizabeth, his niece: "To her go I, a jolly thriving wooer." Richard is, in short, turned on by killing.

The murder of the nephews in the Tower is the most notorious and most heinous of Richard's crimes. But it has another significance as well, for it marks the moment when his subtlety and cunning fail him. Rule by murder is thus not static. Shakespeare shows how the combination of formal power and rule with a kind of habituation to illegitimate force has an effect on the souls of those who resort to it. The first, most noticeable consequence is that one ceases to disguise the commission of murder.

Shakespeare's other killer king, Macbeth, ends up falling into the same pattern, though he begins in a much different frame of mind. Unlike Richard, Macbeth is reluctant to seize power through murder, although he does so after protracted internal wrestling with his conscience, while also facing pressure from his wife. Once he has decided to act, however, he does so without further hesitation.

In an extraordinary speech Macbeth announces the murder (which he will blame on Duncan's guards) to his nobles:

> Had I but died an hour before this chance,
> I had lived a blessed time, for from this instant
> There's nothing serious in mortality;
> All is but toys; renown and grace is dead,
> The wine of life is drawn, and the mere lees
> Is left this vault to brag of.[13]

As Shakespearean scholar A. C. Bradley notes, "This is . . . meant to deceive, but it utters at the same time his profoundest feeling."[14] The killer, soon to become king himself, knows that he has crossed some boundary and will never return to what he was.

Unlike the sociopathic Richard, Macbeth is not fundamentally an evil man at odds with society because of real or imagined slights and flaws. He is, rather, a successful military leader who succumbs to the temptation of power that lies before him. He has a seemingly happy marriage and knows genuine friendship with Banquo—whom he kills nonetheless. Where Richard appears to us in the *Henry VI* plays and then in *Richard III* a fully formed and murderous sociopath, albeit one whom we can understand and empathize with, Macbeth, by contrast, descends into crime. The Macbeth of the first scene in that play would not, we suspect, be willing to murder his friend Banquo on mere suspicion about the future. By the play's middle he will do that and more.

Macbeth's path downward to rule by assassination is far more self-aware and complex than Richard's but equally certain in its psychological trajectory. He is already suspected by Duncan's heir and some of the lords, even his friend Banquo, who conceives that Macbeth has "played'st most foully" for the crown. No sooner is he crowned king than he sees plots where, at the moment, there is only fear and foreboding. His first royal murder will in fact be that of Banquo, who received an ambiguous but promising prophecy from the three witches at the beginning of the play.

> Our fears in Banquo stick deep,
> And in his royalty of nature reigns that
> Which would be feared. 'Tis much he dares,
> And to that dauntless temper of his mind,
> He hath a wisdom that doth guide his valour
> To act in safety.[15]

Unlike Richard III, Macbeth can appreciate the virtues of his rivals, or rather, his victims. This quality costs him not a little internal conflict, but he hardens quickly to the necessity of killing to sustain his kingdom and accelerates the pace of his killings. In the same scene he summons two murderers (again, we do not know their names), whom he convinces that they have been injured by Banquo. He makes use of their natures, which they reveal in turn, the one saying,

> I am one, my liege
> Whom the vile blows and buffets of the world
> Hath so incensed, that I am reckless what I do
> To spite the world.

The other declares,

> And I another
> So weary with disasters, tugged with fortune,
> That I would set my life on any chance,
> To mend it, or be rid on't.[16]

Macbeth does not have, nor does he claim, any sympathy or commonality of feeling with the murderers, as Richard III does. He understands them, and he uses them, but they murder for reasons very different from his. Their lives have been miserable, his most fortunate. Where Richard III presents himself as a fascinating and charming, if lethal and terrifying, sociopath, Macbeth seems altogether more normal. In the end, however, both are killers, who make use of other killers without reservation.

Having killed King Duncan, Macbeth now embarks on a course of murder that he does not know how to stop and, indeed, does not believe he can. "It will have blood, they say; blood will have blood."[17] He understands his predicament:

> I am in blood
> Stepped in so far that, should I wade no more,
> Returning were as tedious as go o'er.
> Strange things I have in head, that will to hand,
> Which must be acted, ere they may be scanned.

There is no particular joy in this, merely the resolution to plunge on. And interestingly enough, he knows that what he has in his head are "strange things." Perhaps he senses that a career of unrestrained murder entails a kind of madness. But he will proceed even so.

Many a tyrant has found himself thus, too saturated with crime to have a chance of coming back to respectability, and so they escalate their crimes. Vladimir Putin's odyssey during the course of the Russian invasion of Ukraine, which began in February 2022, is a good example. The indiscriminate bombing of cities, the kidnapping of children, and the torture and assassination of Ukrainian officials escalated over time. Whether he had an inclination to stop or not, he no longer could, and so he escalated a war with genocidal elements even as his armies collapsed, his international position crumbled, and his economy shrank. His rhetoric and that of his henchmen (and women) went from grievances against Western policies to rage about Nazis and Satanists. He reached for more self-destructive acts, such as press-ganging men off the streets for an army that could not train and equip them, offensives that merely carpeted Ukrainian fields with corpses, and apocalyptic threats that alarmed but did not intimidate his enemies.

The routine use of murder coarsens and blunts Macbeth's perceptions of those around him. He hears what he wants to hear from the witches, who he knows can play games with human desires and aspirations. Indeed, he says to Lennox after his second meeting with them,

> Infected be the air whereon they ride,
> And damned all those that trust them.[18]

He has started in a different psychological place, but as with Richard III, Macbeth's turn to criminality poisons his judgment. He chooses to trust the witches' words, assuming that his throne will be secure because Birnam Wood cannot possibly come to Dunsinane and he cannot be killed by a man "of woman born."

Macbeth will also attempt to forestall their prophecies by killing his friend Banquo, whom they have foretold will be the progenitor of kings after him. Immediately upon seeing the three weird sisters, he declares,

> The flighty purpose never is o'ertook
> Unless the deed go with it. From this moment
> The very firstlings of my heart shall be
> The firstlings of my hand. And even now,
> To crown my thoughts with acts, be it thought and done.

Macbeth, a leader previously capable of reflection and calculation, has now decided to cast aside rationality and, with it, prudence. Whereas the Machiavellian prince uses crime judiciously and in a controlled fashion, thinking about how and why, he has chosen to make "the very firstlings" of his heart the firstlings of his hand. He will murder by instinct, not after consideration.

The castle of Macduff I will surprise,
Seize upon Fife, give to th'edge o'th'sword
His wife, his babes and all unfortunate souls
That trace him in his line.

To this particular crime—the attempted murder not just of Macduff but of his wife and children—he is goaded by one of the apparitions conjured up by the witches, who has warned, "Beware Macduff." At one level, Macbeth knows that "none of woman born" can harm him, and therefore (he believes) he can disregard Macduff. But then he declares that he will "make assurance double sure / And take a bond of fate." He retains enough humanity to describe his future victims as "unfortunate souls," but not enough to hold him back from ordering the bloody deed.

Macbeth has declared that he will resort to murder on instinct and snap decision: he is no longer a murderer by careful calculation (as was the case with Duncan); rather, he has convinced himself that his intuitions should lead immediately to action—the firstlings of his heart becoming the firstlings of his hand. And so he does, failing to kill Macduff, who has escaped, but exterminating his family.

Macbeth, unlike Richard III, knows what is happening to him. He knows that as a killer by habit, he is cut off from humanity:

And that which should accompany old age,
As honour, love, obedience, troops of friends,
I must not look to have; but in their stead,
Curses not loud but deep, mouth-honour, breath
Which the poor heart would fain deny, and dare not.[19]

This deadening of the soul of the ruler by murder is apparent not only to us but to Macbeth himself. Two scenes later he utters one of his most famous soliloquies upon hearing of his wife's death:

And all our yesterdays have lighted fools
The way to dusty death. Out, out brief candle,

Life's but a walking shadow, a poor player,
That struts and frets his hour upon the stage,
And then is heard no more. It is a tale
Told by an idiot, full of sound and fury
Signifying nothing.[20]

This nihilism will not prevent him from acting decisively to the very end. It does not even completely extinguish the elements of humanity that once existed in him—he offers Macduff the opportunity of escape:

But get thee back, my soul is too much charged
With blood of thine already.[21]

Macduff, bent on vengeance, insists on a duel, which ends in Macbeth's death at the hands of the bereaved husband and father, who just before killing the king describes him as a monster. This, indeed, is what Macbeth has become. Precisely because Macbeth was once decent, because he does have a few twinges of conscience, and because in the end he knows that what he craves is an illusion and his efforts are futile, he seems to us even more of a monster than Richard.

Macbeth's proclivity for rule by murder has had practical effects that go beyond the killing of the king's soul before the slaying of his body. He rules by fear alone, and everyone knows it. As Angus, one of the rebelling nobles, puts it,

Those he commands move only in command,
Nothing in love. Now does he feel his title
Hang loose about him, like a giant's robe
Upon a dwarfish thief.[22]

It is the tyrant's fate: the more powerful he may seem, the less his title may mean, because the obedience he elicits is driven solely by fear.

Rule by murder is quite literally addictive: once embarked upon it, many leaders find themselves unable to act in any other way until the end finally comes upon them. They may start as sociopaths like Richard III, who simply has no conscience, or become monsters who let themselves become habituated to killing, like Macbeth. But once they start, they find it impossible to stop.

The course of modern tyrants reflects both paths. Adolf Hitler had many of the sociopath's strengths, most notably the ability to read personalities. Perhaps his greatest strength, like that of all great dictators, was his ability to ferret out weakness. "The secret to Hitler's success lay in the mutual identification between speaker and audience—in the exchange of individual and collective sensitivities and neuroses," writes his most perceptive biographer yet, Volker Ulrich.[23] Not coincidentally, Ulrich too uses the theatrical metaphor to understand Hitler, describing him as "a fairly gifted actor who had mastered the art of appearing in a variety of masks and roles." He notes that Albert Speer said that Charlie Chaplin, in his 1940 film *The Great Dictator*, understood Hitler's character better than any other contemporary.[24] Albert Speer is a fascinating example of a highly intelligent man who succumbed to the Führer's hypnotic appeal. On April 23, 1945, as Germany was in its death throes and Speer himself was deliberately undermining the leader's scorched-earth orders to destroy every material aspect of a German people he believed unworthy of him, the armaments czar flew in a light plane to Berlin to bid Hitler adieu. Speer, as we now know, was an opportunist and a deceiver who would make a postwar career out of playing the penitent Nazi. Yet, calculating as he was, Speer could not escape Hitler's psychological grip, and so he took a completely unnecessary risk to visit the Führer in his bunker one last time.

Hitler's empathy, like that of most tyrants, was relatively narrow but deep. Winston Churchill and Franklin Roosevelt, and the countries they led, he could never truly understand. But in his reading of his own people, he was a genius.[25] The cunning of Nazi propaganda played upon the fears of a German population battered by what seemed an inexplicable defeat, the loss of territory, hyperinflation, and economic chaos. He was a great stage director, or at least knew how to hire others who were. One of the great moviemakers of the twentieth century, Leni Riefenstahl, documented the spectacle of the brilliantly staged Nuremberg rallies of the 1930s. They captured the desires of the German people for unity, strength, and cohesiveness, as did so much else that the Nazi Party did.

Hitler's claim on power rested on much else in addition to killing, but killing was nonetheless at its heart. And there was more of it as time went on. The Nazi Party was always a band of roughnecks, hardened in some cases by the experiences of World War I and then by the incessant and brutal street fighting of the period that followed it. But the actual killing was a crescendo, not something embarked upon all at once. By the standards of the early 1940s, the initial bouts of murder were relatively modest. During the Night of the Long Knives—actually several days of violence at the beginning of July 1934—several hundred people were executed, chiefly members of the Sturmabteilung (SA) militia that had helped Hitler in his rise to power. It was a decisive moment in consolidating Hitler's control of a movement that included revolutionaries whose personal allegiance was suspect. But it was contained.

In a similar vein, initially, many enemies of the Third Reich were plundered, beaten, or driven out of the country rather than simply shot. Even the brutality of the *Kristallnacht* pogrom against Jews and their institutions on November 9–10, 1938, which killed hundreds and demolished thousands of businesses, was not genocidal. These events foreshadowed greater violence to come, but they were not the same thing as the mass exterminations of 1941 and beyond.[26]

The relative restraint, as was shown in the violence directed against the SA in 1934 and against the Jews in 1938, reflected not humanitarianism but rather milestones in the process of habituating oneself to killing. As time went on, there was more and more of it—quite apart from the genocidal plans of Hitler and the Nazis for European Jewry. It became apparent in military policy. Thus, for example, in October 1942 the high command of the Wehrmacht issued the *Kommandobefehl*, which ordered the summary execution of Allied soldiers, including those in uniform participating in special operations and raids. German harshness toward civilians, apparent in World War I, took a quantum leap in the invasion of Poland when between sixteen thousand and twenty-seven thousand civilians and prisoners were simply shot out of hand in the opening weeks.[27] It appeared in a policy of extreme ruthlessness in the infliction of death penalties in the German army. Whereas the British and American armies had nearly eliminated the death penalty for combat refusal by World War II, the German army executed at least fifteen thousand of its own for crimes including the nebulous crime of *Wehrkraftzersetzung*, or undermining the war effort.[28] And the killing continued to the very end of the Third Reich, on the largest scale, as prison camp inmates were marched to their deaths in order to prevent their liberation by the advancing Red Army.

Like Richard III, Hitler became interested in the details of killing. This was particularly true in the aftermath of the July 1944 plot against his life, which came close to killing him when a bomb went off in his command bunker. The actual plotters and others suspected of complicity were tortured and executed by slow hanging—and according to Speer, Hitler took a ghoulish delight in watching the movies of their deaths.[29]

Like Richard III and Macbeth as well, Hitler ended up as a nihilist, clinging to hope ("a horse, a horse, my kingdom for a horse!") until only a few days before the denouement in his Berlin bunker, then simply wishing for destruction. Ever the director as well as playwright, "Hitler devoted most of his remaining energy in the spring of 1945 to staging Germany's heroic demise."[30] Believing that the German people had proven themselves unworthy of him, he issued orders (subverted by Speer and other subordinates) to thoroughly destroy all German infrastructure.

Hitler's embrace of murder and destruction on such a titanic scale was thus a process, not a reality from the outset of his rule. Of course, Hitler is the extreme case. Most dictators do not engage in such levels of mass murder. Stalin and Mao are the twentieth century's exceptions, and they too showed a level of fascination with the actual killing of their enemies that mirrors Hitler's. But there are other cases as well, in which leaders come to rule more and more through murder—if not in the strictly literal sense, then by the disappearing of enemies.

Xi Jinping, China's leader in the early twenty-first century, is a good example. The product of a ruthless-enough system, he rose to power through the elimination of opponents and the use of ever greater amounts of force—to the point of near genocide directed against the Uighur population of Xinjiang province, the destruction of self-rule in Hong Kong, and the public humiliation and imprisonment of competitors like the Shanghai politician Bo Xilai. A Shakespearean dynamic infuses these acts: some repression requires more, for the simple reason that one's enemies accumulate over time.[31] And thus freedom of expression in China, never complete, became more and more restricted through censorship and harsh punishment of those who spoke out against an increasingly dictatorial ruler.

All forms of rule that rest not merely on personal authority but on some degree of murder broadly understood have similar dynamics. What starts as a modest amount of murder gradually spreads, because every homicide has the potential to increase one's roster of enemies. If political murder succeeds at first—and it often does—it seems an easy and reliable way of dealing with difficulties. Anatoli Rybakov, in his novel *Children of the Arbat*, has Stalin say, "Death solves all problems. No man, no problem."[32] It is the creed of anyone who holds on to power by murder.

Rule by killing—even if it takes the form of suppression, exile, imprisonment, or (as in business) mere dismissal—affects the sensibilities of those who do it. Unsurprisingly, they hear fewer and fewer dissenting opinions, and long though their reigns may be, their sense of reality becomes increasingly impaired. They become paranoid, not least because they have made themselves more and more enemies. Those around them, acting "only in command, never in love," may implement their orders mechanically—and on occasion foolishly, as they try to make sure that they will not be the tyrant's next victim. And the leader himself becomes less imaginative and clever.

And most importantly, they fail. They fail in the end not only because most forms of power are ephemeral but because their sense of reality has become impaired. That is the most striking lesson of *Richard III* and *Macbeth*. Two highly intelligent men, who had commenced their careers of rule with a sophisticated understanding of their circumstances, become blinded by what a career of killing has done to their sensibilities. They know fear and little else. They do not understand motives that are much more complicated than the quest for revenge. They can elicit compliance but not creative initiative, and in the end, they too fall.

PART III

LOSING POWER

Sooner or later those who wield power lose it. But they may do so in various ways—by folly, by mischance, and sometimes even by relinquishing it voluntarily. Some very few are even content (more or less) when they do so.

CHAPTER 8

Innocence and Arrogance

I T IS IN THE NATURE OF POWER THAT THOSE WHO POSSESS IT FIND themselves wrapped in a cocoon that muffles the sounds of approaching peril. As the chief of staff of one American president told me, pointing to the Oval Office, "I cannot tell you how many people go in there having told me that they were going to set the president straight on some point or another and end up meekly agreeing with him instead." Years later I learned that truth myself the first time I briefed President George W. Bush. I realized afterward, to my shame, that I had pulled my punches—he was, after all, the president.

The aura of power has that effect. In the hallways of the White House leading to the meeting rooms, one sees expertly taken photographs of the president speaking to adoring crowds, looking wise, or else chopping wood in a manly way. Every couple of weeks the photographs are replaced with another set. Such atmospheric touches create a barrier through which bad news often does not penetrate.

The deafening and dulling effects of power can be much cruder than that. A court case in Delaware gave the world a glimpse into the text messages and emails sent to Elon Musk, the brilliant but erratic founder of an electric car company and much else besides. "What is so illuminating about the Musk messages is just how unimpressive, unimaginative, and sycophantic the powerful men in Musk's contacts appear to be," a journalist writes.[1] Musk has not, as of this writing, been ruined by the adulation received by someone who was, in theory, the richest man in the world, but it is not entirely surprising that, shortly after this, his takeover of Twitter ran onto the rocks, and his electric car company, Tesla, experienced a stock price collapse.

August titles and extreme wealth breed their own innocence about the world. That ignorance is often joined with arrogance. "Surely," the president, or CEO, or dean must think, "I know best." One thing leads to another, and this becomes their undoing, as Cardinal Wolsey discovers in *Henry VIII*:

> I have touch'd the highest point of all my greatness;
> And, from that full meridian of my glory
> I haste now to my setting. I shall fall
> Like a bright exhalation in the evening,
> And no man see me more.[2]

For lessons on the ways that innocence and arrogance, naiveté and complacency can combine to bring catastrophe, there is no better study than Shakespeare's three *Henry VI* plays.

Shakespeare wrote these before he wrote *Henry V*, even though, in chronological order, Henry V necessarily preceded Henry VI. Though frequently and incorrectly accounted as some of his lesser works, together they are a profound study of court politics in an era of weak kingship. There is plenty of drama—the rise and fall of Joan of Arc in *Part 1*, a popular revolt led by the demagogue Jack Cade in *Part 2*, a gruesomely murderous civil war culminating in the murder of the feckless King Henry VI in *Part 3*, and the rise of the future Richard III. The three plays have some more or less admirable figures, but a large part of their interest lies in the lack of outstanding characters of the stature of a Lear, a Macbeth, or a Henry V. Instead they present us with normal political figures struggling for power who stumble and connive, plot, betray, and are betrayed in turn. We can recognize them. We can also recognize the weak king who presides but does not rule, who sees but does not understand, who is manipulated but cannot control.

The series begins with news of Henry V's untimely death at a time when Henry VI is still an infant. Bad news comes in batches: around the warrior king's bier, his nobles learn that large parts of his newly won French domains have fallen to a resurgent French monarchy. What is worse, the troops in the field know the reality of what is going on back home:

> Amongst the soldiers this is muttered:
> That here you maintain several factions,
> And whilst a field should be dispatched and fought
> You are disputing of your generals.[3]

The common soldiers apparently sense not only the lack of firm leadership following the death of Henry V but the selfishness of and divisions among the dead king's lieutenants. What we learn about leading characters later in the play vindicates the troops' instincts: the senior leaders seek their own advantages and fail to either recognize or grapple with the challenges their country faces.

The soldiers' complaint reveals the problem of a kingdom led by an innocent—in this case, a king who is still a child. The soldiers sense that the problem is not just internal disagreement but a fatal lack of realism, captured by the "disputing of your generals."

> One would have ling'ring wars with little cost;
> Another would fly swift, but wanteth wings;

183

A third thinks, without expense at all,
By guileful fair words peace may be obtain'd.[4]

A strong king needs advisers, but a strong king would also enforce discipline in practical thought on his subordinates. Henry V, in Shakespeare's rendition, does not seem to consult much with his advisers or do more than use them as pawns in his political maneuverings. But Henry V was a kind of genius, who could work it all out on his own: his son was not.

Therein lies the real tragedy of the *Henry VI* plays. The interests of England are ignored or subverted by a flawed elite consumed by their competition for power at the expense of their country's needs. The king does not understand them and cannot control them. The patriots, like Talbot or Gloucester, are carried off by the accidents of war or by their own naiveté in the face of wilier aristocratic rivals. As a result, throughout the serial, England slides into civil war and a decline that culminates in the rise of the tyrant Richard III.

One has to wonder why these pathologies set in so quickly after Henry V's death. The real Henry died after a brief illness following his campaign in France, so this state of affairs was not the result of an extended interregnum. In this respect Shakespeare does not depart from the facts. Possibly the glorious king whom Shakespeare would celebrate in the play named after him did nothing, or could do nothing, about the underlying problem of rivalrous nobles who hated each other even more than they did the French. Filled as Shakespeare's plays are with former allies turning on one another, one has to suspect that he viewed this as the norm. The "band of brothers" conjured up by Henry V at Agincourt was ever something of an illusion.

As the bad news from the front pours in, some of the nobles quickly set sail for France in hopes of retrieving their country's fortune (and perhaps their own reputations) on the battlefield. One, the scheming Bishop of Winchester, a bitter rival of the regent, the Duke of Gloucester, is left behind:

Each hath his place and function to attend.
I am left out; for me nothing remains.
But long I will not be Jack out of office.
The King from Eltham I intend to steal,
And sit at chiefest stern of public weal.[5]

His words reflect a decaying leadership class, concerned not for the country's welfare but with status and role. He regrets being excluded from a position of high responsibility not as a missed opportunity to serve but rather for leaving him "Jack out of office." He is the political ally or adviser who is furious at coming through a presidential transition empty-handed, not someone who wishes to accomplish something. The bishop will seek to leverage access to or control over Henry VI in order to gain the status he desires to no end other than self-aggrandizement.

Henry VI himself does not appear until the beginning of Act 3 of the first part of these plays. The rivalry between the Bishop of Winchester and the protector, the Duke of Gloucester, has erupted in ferocious enmity. The boy king, seeing it, is simply dismayed:

Uncles of Gloucester and of Winchester,
The special watchmen of our English weal,
I would prevail—if prayers might prevail—
To join your hearts in love and amity.
O what a scandal is it to our crown
That two such noble peers as ye should jar?
Believe me, lords—my tender years can tell—
Civil dissension is a viperous worm,
That gnaws the bowels of the commonwealth.[6]

Henry VI is not stupid. Indeed, throughout these three plays, he sees the outbreak of internal conflict as a terrible danger. But he will never grow in his ability to judge his subordinates correctly and to administer the discipline that alone could preserve his reign, and indeed his life. He would prevail, but through prayer, not by command; he views the mutual hatred of Gloucester and Winchester as a scandal rather than what it is: a mortal threat to his realm's peace and his own throne. He can see but cannot judge; he is aware but cannot lead. Henry fails to make distinctions: thus, Gloucester is indeed a watchman of the welfare of England, but Winchester, as we have seen, is merely a conniving and ambitious courtier.

Like many a weak leader, Henry VI has poor judgment about which of his subordinates are truly capable and trustworthy. He has not learned, and indeed will never learn, that one of the harder parts of executive leadership lies in removing or sidelining subordinates who are incapable or even disloyal. He relies not on authority but on prayer and hope. He yearns for hearts joined "in love and amity" when no such thing is possible, and he preaches at his elders about the horrors of civil war rather than bending them to his will.

Interestingly, throughout the three parts of Henry VI, this young king will make increasingly shrewd assessments of what is going on. Like Richard II, another failed king, he is intelligent and eloquent without being wise or prudent. In no matter is this clearer than in his disastrous marriage to Margaret, daughter of the king of France. Henry is maneuvered into this by the scheming Suffolk, one of the rising new men, who is consumed by, and may even have consummated, his own lust for the beautiful French princess. The price paid for this marriage will be very high, including the cession back to France of English conquests, but Henry accepts it without much reflection. He has never experienced "the passion of inflaming love" before, but the idea excites him:

> I feel such sharp dissension in my breast,
> Such fierce alarums both of hope and fear,
> As I am sick with working of my thoughts.
> Take therefore shipping post, my lord, to France.
> Agree to any covenants, and procure
> That lady Margaret do vouchsafe to come

To cross the seas to England and be crowned
King Henry's faithful and anointed queen.[7]

It is an appalling misjudgment. Guided only by his own heartsickness and exasperated with his ambivalent thoughts, he treats a royal marriage—a high affair of state—like a mere love match, with someone he has never met and yet has become infatuated with, whom he assumes will be faithful when she is, in fact, profoundly faithless. This is a decision made in the midst of an internal emotional storm, not, as a royal marriage should be, after cool calculation. In return for his impulsiveness Henry VI gets a wily, powerful, and quite likely adulterous queen, who has "a tiger's heart in a woman's hide," as one of her victims later puts it.

The better counselors around Henry are all too aware of his weaknesses. Some even recognize the ways in which unscrupulous courtiers are using him for their own ends. Unfortunately, the good Duke of Gloucester is outmaneuvered by his rivals, who succeed in luring his wife into the practice of witchcraft, which causes the pious king to order the execution of her fellow witches, her banishment, and Gloucester's deposition as protector.

As is usually the case in Shakespeare, leaders who put their faith in supernatural forces, be they divine or magical, prove themselves incompetent in human affairs. Henry falls victim to this folly himself, declaring,

Henry will to himself
Protector be; and God shall be my hope,
My stay, my guide and lantern to my feet.[8]

Try as he might to convince himself that Providence will provide what his own skills as a leader do not, Henry VI is fated to learn the hard way that it will not.

Henry makes terrible decisions in the hopes of keeping everyone around him—his courtiers and his wife, above all—happy. He can never accept the fact that, as any leader learns, one has to make some people unhappy and move on. Eventually Henry's wife and subordinates come to disregard him altogether, shunting him aside on the battlefield, so that he will not get in the way. The king himself comes to realize that he is unfit for office.

> Was never subject longed to be a king
> As I do long and wish to be a subject.[9]

As he sits upon a hill, watching a battle in which fathers kill sons, and sons their fathers, he laments,

> O God! Methinks it were a happy life
> To be no better than a homely swain,
> To sit upon a hill, as I do now,
> To carve out dials quaintly, point by point,
> Thereby to see the minutes how they run.[10]

Kings who wish they were carefree shepherds often end up as slaughtered sheep, and so it is with Henry VI, who ends up the victim of Richard of Gloucester, the future Richard III. Henry gets off a few good lines before Richard slips the knife in—

> Teeth hadst thou in thy head when thou wast born
> To signify thou cam'st to bite the world.[11]

But to the end Henry is a king who does not understand the world of politics. Shortly before his final captivity, he assures himself that the populace of London will rise to support him because he has been a reasonable ruler whose merit has won him a high reputation among the common folk:

> I have not stopped mine ears to their demands,
> Nor posted off their suits with slow delays.

My pity hath been balm to heal their wounds . . .
I have not been desirous of their wealth
Nor much oppressed them with great subsidies,
Not forward of revenge, though they much erred.
Then why should they love Edward more than me?[12]

Henry is here, as throughout the trilogy, a child, even though nominally an adult. "It's not fair!" one can practically hear him saying. He is in one sense right about the people of London, who are portrayed for the most part as hardheaded folk who wish the aristocracy would stop fighting with one another and leave them in peace. But he is mistaken to think that they will act out of gratitude rather than prudent judgment—because he does not really know what prudent judgment is. He believes that in matters of power, love follows kindness, which it rarely does. Believing, as did Brutus, in his own virtue—a subtle but real form of arrogance in this meekest of Shakespeare's kings—he cannot see that the pragmatic Londoners will prefer a winner who will give them peace from the violence and disruption of civil war. Few leaders ever receive the gratitude they think they deserve, and indulge themselves in childlike sulks when they do not get it.

Clueless to the end, Henry VI is a pitiful but not a much-pitied ruler. Watching or reading these plays, one feels only annoyance at this king who remains a boy even into manhood, pious, vain in his seeming humility, trusting in people and powers who will neither rescue nor support him, casting aside trusted counselors, and making decisions that increase rather than mitigate the bloody civil war that impends. We should not feel sorry for him, for his failures bring ruin not merely upon himself but upon those loyal to him and an entire kingdom. The only pitiable aspect of this tale is that the nature of kingship made resignation of one's office impossible.

Henry loses his throne because he is a terrible king, and he is a terrible king because he remains innocent about the dark realities of power right up to the end. He cannot believe that his wife is a scheming adulteress, that many of his nobles have their own selfish ambitions, and that his good deeds will mean nothing in the face of the surging strength of grasping rivals. He will let his most valiant and loyal supporter, Gloucester, be cut down by schemers, which he views as unfortunate rather than, as it is, a mortal danger. His weakness brings his kingdom by a quick and sure path to ruin. His enemies, including those who will in their turn be ruined, understand him well:

> That head of thine doth not become a crown;
> Thy hand is made to grasp a palmer's staff
> And not to grace an awful princely scepter.[13]

A king's intelligence lies in understanding the facts of power and the motivations and behavior of those around him, not in high intellectual achievement, which is no guarantee of success in actual politics. In two particularly penetrating essays, British philosopher Isaiah Berlin described political judgment as "an acute sense of what fits with what, what springs from what, what leads to what; how things seem to vary to different observers. . . . [I]t is a species of direct acquaintance, as distinct from a capacity for description or calculation or inference."[14] Henry VI, like Richard II, can describe political truths and draw inferences, but both lack the practical grip on reality that preservation of their thrones, and ultimately their lives, requires.

One should note that in the *Henry VI* plays, the denouement is not one in which the plotters against him do particularly well either. Suffolk is beheaded by patriotic pirates; the Duke of York, father of Richard of Gloucester, is tortured and killed by Margaret, who in turn sees her son killed by Richard. The alternative to weak rule is not necessarily rule by a successful strong man but rather conflict and chaos.

This chaos takes two forms: the murderous rivalries among the aristocracy, described above, and upheaval from below, in the form of a popular uprising. The Jack Cade revolt depicted in *Henry VI, Part 2*, Act 4, is, in a very Shakespearean way, both comic and terrifying. Cade, a populist if ever there was one, "vows reformation":

There shall be in England seven halfpenny loaves sold for a penny; the three-hoop'd pot shall have ten hoops, and I will make it felony to drink small beer. All the realm shall be in common, and in Cheapside shall my palfrey go to grass; and when I am king, as king I shall be—

God save your Majesty!

I thank you, good people—there shall be no money; all shall eat and drink on my score, and I will apparel them all in one livery, that they may agree like brothers, and worship me their lord.

Following this, one of his lieutenants gives the famous shout "The first thing we do, let's kill all the lawyers," and Cade then gives the order to hang a man for being able to read and write.[15] This insurrection is not directed at Henry, but it is a result of the king's weakness and the kingdom's general decay.

Another of Shakespeare's victim-kings, Duncan in *Macbeth*, mirrors Henry VI's piety, his naive belief in the power of his own goodness, and his heedlessness of the facts of power. Curiously, everyone, including even his murderer, Macbeth, praises him, and yet the terms of that praise show his incapacity as king. Macbeth says, when contemplating the king's murder, that Duncan

Hath borne his faculties so meek, hath been
So clear in his great office, that his virtues
Will plead like angels, trumpet-tongued, against
The deep damnation of his taking off.[16]

On reflection one has to wonder whether meekness and innocence (the meaning of the word *clear*) are really royal virtues. Judging by the way his reign ended, one may presume not.

In fact, from the outset Duncan has spoken and acted in ways that suggest that eliminating him will not be too difficult. He is, to begin with, a spectator to the revolt that threatens his crown, not someone who has taken charge of a desperate situation. He welcomes the messenger who describes Macbeth's duel with the rebel Macdonald and listens to the account, but issues no substantive orders other than that the wounded captain receive medical care and that Macbeth be honored by being named Thane of Cawdor. He asks his son Malcolm what the scene was like at the execution of the previous thane and is told, "Nothing in his life became him like the leaving it." Duncan muses,

> There's no art
> To find the mind's construction in the face:
> He was a gentleman on whom I built
> An absolute trust.[17]

This is the first hint we have of Duncan's fatal innocence. The irony is, of course, that he will now place equally absolute trust in Macbeth, who will kill him.

Duncan is, like many who have been in power a long time (and he is usually portrayed as old), careless. He tells Macbeth, "More is thy due, than more than all can pay." It is not entirely wise to say that to an ambitious man, who will think that if more cannot be given him, he might as well simply seize it. Duncan is also complacent. "I have begun to plant thee, and will labour to make thee full of growing." Like many leaders, Duncan thinks of his subordinates as his creations. He assumes not only their deference but their malleability—again, an attitude calculated to put off an ambitious man and to blind the one who expresses it to how things may turn against him.

No sooner has he said these things than he compounds his errors:

> My plenteous joys,
> Wanton in fullness, seek to hide themselves
> In drops of sorrow.[18]

In other words, he is weeping. It is hardly the behavior of a king in command of his emotions as well as his realm. Kings can rarely afford to weep, at least not in public. And then comes the ultimate mistake:

Sons, kinsmen, thanes,
And you whose places are the nearest, know:
We will establish our estate upon
Our eldest, Malcolm, whom we name
The Prince of Cumberland.

In the Scotland of Macbeth's time, the king could select his heir, but Duncan has chosen the worst possible moment to make his selection. Macbeth, not Duncan's own young son, has put down the rebellion that threatened the king's throne. It is Macbeth who killed his most dangerous enemy and has just been told that he can never be adequately recompensed for these achievements. Unsurprisingly, Macbeth immediately mutters in an aside,

The Prince of Cumberland: that is a step
On which I must fall down, or else o'er-leap,
For in my way it lies. Stars, hide your fires,
Let not light see my black and deep desires.

The witches tempt Macbeth; his wife badgers him to do the bloody deed; but the original impulse to murder Duncan arises when, before this capable and ambitious man, the king looks weak (by crying), acknowledges that he has not rewarded him commensurately with his merits and cannot do so, and at that very moment declares that he will thwart him in his most fervent wish by choosing an inexperienced successor. Duncan, and not the witches or Lady Macbeth, has opened up the fatal window of temptation through which the Thane of Cawdor will soon leap.

Most leaders discover that having a designated crown prince is a problem—either an oppositional court-in-waiting arises around the prince, or he decides to speed up the transition by some unsavory action. Henry IV suspects as much on his deathbed when Prince Hal (soon to be Henry V) reaches for the crown: "I stay too long by thee; I weary thee."[19] In this case, however, by picking his son as his successor publicly and immediately after having regained his kingdom because of Macbeth's exploits, Duncan makes a final, fatal mistake. In the play's setting at least, he has no need to make such a decision, and yet he does so.

Duncan goes to his doom as he set it up: clueless about the people around him and unwitting about what he will encounter. When he arrives for his last night on earth, he says,

> This castle hath a pleasant seat, the air
> Nimbly and sweetly recommends itself
> Unto our gentle senses.[20]

One may conceivably view this as ominous, but on rereading, it simply seems foolish, the words of an unwary king going to the slaughter at the hands of an altogether more ruthless man and making one last, fatal misjudgment.

Henry VI, as portrayed by Shakespeare, is a childlike innocent; Duncan is not as young but is similarly naive and oblivious. Richard II, our third doomed king, has elements of both, but his downfall is chiefly brought about by his arrogance. His is the overweening self-confidence of a man besotted with his own cleverness and infatuated with his own title. From the first, his sense of authority is brittle: he does not understand (as Henry V does) that to exercise power, one must persuade and inspire. At first he thinks he can calm down the feuding Bolingbroke and Mowbray, whose impending duel occupies the first scene of the play: "Lions make leopards tame."[21] Leaders who are lions, however, do not have to tell their underlings that is what they are.

Richard is all growl without the capacity to spring and rend. When the two nobles continue to spar, he barks, "We were not born to sue, but to command," and orders them to appear later for a formal duel. When that happens, he changes his mind and decides instead to banish both men. He goes on to change his mind a second time, when he reduces Bolingbroke's exile by four years. Inconstant and arbitrary, he seems to delight in indulging his whims. He too thereby sets up his downfall by mishandling his more capable subordinates, none more so than Henry Bolingbroke.

There is worse to come in his treatment of the dying John of Gaunt, Bolingbroke's father. He taunts the old man for his illness, and when Gaunt presumes to reprimand him, he replies,

> A lunatic lean-witted fool,
> Presuming on an ague's privilege!
> Darest with thy frozen admonition
> Make pale our cheek, chasing the royal blood
> With fury from his native residence?[22]

Richard, always enamored of his own wit, begins with a pun ("lean-witted" applied to a man named Gaunt), a characteristically shallow bit of verbal cleverness that betrays his underlying lack of seriousness. As he always does, he falls back on his status as king to assert his authority. His title, not his personal authority and wise command, is supposed to bring those around him to obedience. There is a triviality on display even in his indignation at having gone pale—and perhaps too a confession of weakness, if a reprimand can cause him to lose countenance.

Richard's ultimate fall to Bolingbroke stems from his obsession with his title and what he thinks it should entail. It leads him to declare, when Bolingbroke and his army have massed before his castle,

> Not all the water in the rough rude sea
> Can wash the balm off from an anointed king:
> The breath of worldly men cannot depose
> The deputy elected by the Lord:
> For every man that Bolingbroke hath press'd
> To lift shrewd steel against our golden crown,
> God for his Richard hath in heavenly pay
> A glorious angel: then, if angels fight,
> Weak men must fall, for heaven still guards the right.[23]

Richard never thinks concretely (or concretely enough) about how to deal with a rebellion, and when his belief in the power of his own majesty finally cracks, he has nothing left. Even though Bolingbroke has (insincerely, in all likelihood) offered a deal whereby he would get his lands in return for ending his uprising and acknowledging Richard's kingship, Richard collapses.

> What must the king do now? must he submit?
> The king shall do it: must he be deposed?
> The king shall be contented: must he lose
> The name of king? O'God's name, let it go.[24]

Richard, infatuated with his own kingship, falls apart when he discovers that the title and the aura of monarchical power cannot save him. At the very end of his life, it becomes clear that he does not even have an identity apart from that title; he is not an integrated personality:

> Thus play I in one person many people,
> And none contented.[25]

Richard is neither the first nor the last supreme leader whose sense of self has become so thoroughly caught up in his office that when deprived of it—particularly when he has lost it through his own arrogance and folly—his personality disintegrates.

Richard may never grow sufficiently to retain power, but even more than Henry VI, he gains through wretched experience an insight into what intoxication with the appearance of power has done to him as a human being. His famous speech—"For God's sake, let us sit upon the ground and tell sad stories of the death of kings"—culminates in these lines:

> For within the hollow crown
> That rounds the mortal temples of a king

Keeps Death his court and there the antic sits
Scoffing his state and grinning at his pomp,
Allowing him a breath, a little scene,
To monarchize, be fear'd and kill with looks,
Infusing him with self and vain conceit,
As if this flesh which walls about our life,
Were brass impregnable, and humour'd thus
Comes at the last and with a little pin
Bores through his castle wall, and farewell king![26]

Like many characters in Shakespeare—and in real life—he has acquired a measure of wisdom too late for it to be of any use. He can only now admit to himself a truth that he half-suspected before: that his public "monarchizing" and "killing with looks" were all a sham.

If Richard was particularly susceptible to the antic in his head, so too are many far more redoubtable political figures. Ashraf Ghani, the last president of the Islamic Republic of Afghanistan between two episodes of rule by the Taliban fundamentalist movement, offers a good case of the brilliant intellectual who fails utterly in practical politics. The coauthor of *Fixing Failed States*, Ghani became the head of one, Afghanistan, and proved incapable of fixing it. Despite a spectacular career in academe and nongovernmental organizations, he was not up to the task of waging war against a resurgent Taliban insurrection, focusing more on development than on the far more urgent task of ensuring that soldiers and police were properly paid and supported in the wake of the American drawdown. He did not lack self-confidence, but though brilliant as an intellectual, he lacked the political gifts needed to hold his embattled country together as the United States gradually withdrew support for it. In the summer of 2021 his reign ended in an undignified escape as the Taliban reoccupied first the country and then the capital itself.

Enoch Powell, a brilliant but ruined British scholar, soldier, and politician, once declared that all political careers end in failure. That is particularly true, one might argue, in systems in which there is no predictable end to office. The second terms of American presidencies are rarely happy, but at least they allow a measure of dignity to the incumbent, who can claim that he or she has exited office in accordance with the law rather than as a result of having been deposed.

It is different in C-suites and parliamentary politics. In the latter, in particular, sooner or later prime ministers are visited by the "men in gray suits," who, with relish or reluctance, inform them that they have been deposed by their party. The most dramatic example of that in recent times was the hurtling of Margaret Thatcher from the prime ministership in 1990 by a cabal of Conservative Party grandees, who had long bridled under her rule.[27]

Thatcher was the most consequential British prime minister after Winston Churchill, laying the groundwork for a postimperial Britain, breaking trade unions, reviving the special relationship with the United States, and shaping the European reaction to the end of the Cold War, the dissolution of the Warsaw Pact, and the collapse of the Soviet Union. Arguably she deserves much of the credit for British prosperity in the 1990s and, earlier, for the restoration of British confidence through her leadership during the 1982 Falklands War.[28]

The tale of Thatcher's fall, as recounted in the superb multivolume biography by Charles Moore, has themes that Shakespeare would have recognized. Thatcher's tenure as prime minister was long—eleven years, from 1979 to 1990. The signs were there of an approaching end: economic troubles, including rising inflation; loyal subordinates leaving office, exhausted by it (and perhaps by her); an unpopular poll tax; and most importantly, perhaps, brewing dissent among the leaders of the Conservative Party, some of whom had never been staunch supporters within it. Her favorite subordinate, John Major, was disdained as a "teacher's pet" and envied for having been made foreign secretary (at the expense of others supposedly more qualified, such as Douglas Hurd and William Waldegrave), then chancellor of the Exchequer, the second most powerful position in the British government.[29]

She had about her disgruntled subordinates, many of whom felt (rather like Macbeth) that they had been thwarted or denied the high office they deserved. Faithful friends were carried away by fate, such as Ian Gow, murdered by an Irish Republican Army bomb in July 1990. But behind it all was Mrs. Thatcher's attitude—what Nigel Lawson (who had already resigned as chancellor of the Exchequer) called her "triumphalist approach" ("she has to win, unilaterally, in the end")—which had alienated one ally after another. "The sense of an increasingly imperious leader, losing the support of her colleagues and out of touch with popular feeling, left the country uneasy."[30]

The first blow fell when Geoffrey Howe, hitherto a loyal if rather colorless politician and deputy prime minister, resigned and then denounced her in an uncharacteristically forceful speech, only a few days before the Conservative Party would meet to select its leader—which would normally have been Thatcher. Its final sentence, "The time has come for others to consider their own response to the tragic conflict of loyalties with which I have myself wrestled for perhaps too long," was correctly interpreted as an invitation to other politicians, most notably Michael Heseltine, to run against her, which he did.

The ensuing campaign was a debacle: she went to Paris rather than lobby for votes; she seemed even to her admiring biographer "unfocused on the tactics of winning the leadership battle."[31] Nominal loyalists like John Major and Douglas Hurd hinted that they would run for the leadership of the Conservative Party if she did not make it past the first round. On Thursday, November 21, a succession of political leaders trooped in to meet her, telling her that she had no chance. She later recounted, "It was the end. I was sick at heart. . . . [W]hat grieved me was the desertion of those I had always considered friends and allies and the weasel words whereby they had transmuted their betrayal into frank advice and concern for my fate." As she herself declared, it was something out of *Macbeth*.[32]

Her official biographer sums it up this way: "The effect on her was shattering. Although she was well used to scratchy relations with members of her Cabinet, she had had little idea of the resentments which swirled about her and almost no sense that some of them might be justified. As prime minister, she had been too busy, too innocent, and latterly, too haughty to give much thought to such matters."[33] The combination of the words *innocent* and *haughty* is apt, and indeed Shakespearean. Thatcher had been extraordinarily successful, winning three general elections for her party and losing none, restoring Great Britain's economic vitality and international standing, and still she found herself taken down by a cabal that included supporters upon whom she thought she could count. In the scramble that ensued, the colorless John Major won the succession, against considerably more dashing figures like Heseltine or aristocratic worthies like Hurd. He was not quite Octavius to Heseltine's Antony—he was, on the whole, more loyal to Thatcher than the rest—but in this case too, the more colorful conspirators failed. So did Major. His seven years as prime minister culminated in a crushing defeat at the hands of a rejuvenated Labor Party led by Tony Blair, a politician who had considerably more affinity with Thatcher than with her rivals.

One can be intelligent and perceptive, like Richard II and Henry VI, or experienced and accomplished, like Duncan, or possess both sets of qualities, like Margaret Thatcher, and power can still fall out of one's grip as a result of the lethal combination of innocence and arrogance. What seems solid and assured can vanish in the flash of a knife or, for that matter, a parliamentary speech. It is the nature of power to be fragile and contingent, and it is the nature of powerful men and women to forget that fact.

Arrogance and innocence often join together to dull a leader's wit and set him or her up for the final surprise. It is a mistake to think that leaders necessarily become more seasoned, more skilled, and wiser as they settle into power. They may for a time—but Shakespeare and common experience suggest that over time they become more oblivious and thus more exposed. Nikita Khrushchev, leader of the Soviet Union, was underestimated by his Politburo rivals and outmaneuvered them after the death of Joseph Stalin in 1953. He was shocked, in 1964, when he was deposed by his own protégés. He too was at the peak of his power when the blow fell. He discovered too that when the powerful fall, there is rarely any coming back. Instead they are, as Macbeth says of pity at Duncan's death, "like a naked new-born babe," lost in a world of killers. It is a matter of cold comfort that those who take them down will sooner or later, like Macbeth, or for that matter Michael Heseltine, meet similar fates.[34]

CHAPTER 9

Magic and Self-Deception

POWER HAS A DIMENSION BEYOND RATIONAL CALCULATION. WE feel it in the allure of charismatic politicians or chief executive officers and in the nonrational penumbra surrounding those whom their followers think can change the course of history. It is present in the magical thinking of leaders in desperate straits, as when Adolf Hitler and his entourage saw in Franklin D. Roosevelt's death in April 1945 a miracle, like the death of Tsar Peter III in 1762, which saved a desperate Frederick the Great of Prussia from annihilation by a triple alliance of France, Russia, and Austria. G. K. Chesterton's Father Brown remarks that rejecting rationality is bad theology. Perhaps, but disregarding belief in the suprarational is equally bad political analysis.

As Bruno Bettelheim, C. S. Lewis, and many others have pointed out, magic is woven into our understanding of the world as children. It does not leave us as adults. Henry Kissinger, supreme rationalist though he was, fell prey to it on encountering Charles de Gaulle, leader of the resistance in World War II and president of France's Fifth Republic:

> His presence at the reception tendered by [President Richard] Nixon was so overwhelming that he was the center of attention wherever he stood. Other heads of government and many Senators who usually proclaimed their antipathy to authoritarian generals crowded around him and treated him like some strange species. One had the sense that if he moved to a window the center of gravity might shift and the whole room might tilt everybody into the garden.[1]

The moment passed, but Kissinger experienced other moments of the uncanny, most notably on his pathbreaking visit to China that began the American opening to a country with which it previously had no relations. "It is not often that one can recapture as an adult the quality that in one's youth made time seem to stand still; that gave every event the mystery of novelty."[2] But so it was for Henry Kissinger in July 1971 as he made his inaugural trip to Beijing. It is not unfair to say that for Kissinger, China's magic has never quite worn off.

Power is inseparable from magic, the apparent ability to violate the laws of physics and nature, to bring to bear forces beyond the ken of mere mortals, to disarm or overthrow enemies and to enchant supporters or bystanders. It also has much to do with theater, reinforced as it is by setting, costuming, voice, and all the other tools of theatricality; when it works, even as an entertainment, it shatters one's expectations about what is possible. Whereas normal theater requires the willing suspension of disbelief, magical theater to some extent imposes it.[3] But as the use of the word *magical* in connection with everything from landscapes to boutique hotels, sunsets to luxury spas suggests, the sense of enchantment pervades our lives, even in supposedly rational societies. Our day-to-day speech is more laden with magical references than we realize. The impression of the laws of nature being violated in mysterious ways and the sentiment of astonishment and wonder are at the heart even of magical entertainment, whose purpose is to shake our sense of possibility in an admittedly innocent way.[4]

In the realm of politics, moreover, there are indeed magical moments. Winston Churchill's speeches in 1940 had, it is fair to say, a kind of magical effect, and the observer cannot but feel the tingle of the uncanny in reading or hearing them. The first landing of men on the moon, John F. Kennedy's inaugural address, a Polish pope addressing a throng of believers in a Communist country—all these moments seem to transcend the ordinary. What had seemed impossible or unheard of has become possible. There are also moments of black magic as well. The continued and widespread fascination with Nazi insignia and tropes, the unique horror evoked by a visit to Auschwitz, the invocation of Hitler as an omen of evil—these too partake of magic. Indeed, the Nazis themselves were particularly susceptible to magic and the supernatural.[5]

Shakespeare has plenty to say about magic in politics. His plays are full of magic: *The Tempest* is all about a magician, and *Macbeth* would be far less chilling a play without the three weird sisters. Yet magic is not simply a con game played by fake mediums or a mere conjuring entertainment, a matter of boxes with false bottoms, deftly palmed cards, or objects levitated by invisible threads; nor yet is it something all-powerful. Magic is, rather, liminal, lying between fantasy and reality. Shakespeare takes magic seriously, and so should we.

In one of the great comic moments in *Henry IV, Part 1*, Owen Glendower, the magician prince of Wales, has become increasingly outraged by the levity of Hotspur, Harry Percy, Prince Hal's great rival, who is orchestrating a revolt against Hal's father, Henry IV.

> Glendower: I can call spirits from the vasty deep.
> Hotspur: Why, so can I, or so can any man,
> But will they come when you do call for them?[6]

Glendower has been going on at length about how at his birth

> The front of heaven was full of fiery shapes,
> The goats ran from the mountains, and the herds
> Were strangely clamorous to the frighted fields.
> These signs have marked me extraordinary,
> And all the courses of my life do show
> I am not in the roll of common men.

He unquestionably believes in his own magical powers, but Hotspur, an impatient and choleric warrior, cannot refrain from replying,

> I think there's no man speaks better Welsh.
> I'll to dinner.

Hotspur charms us in *Henry IV, Part 1* in part because, although he is a romantic, he is also a straightforward fighter who cuts through guff and pretense. His business is war, and he disdains both the staff officer whom Henry has sent him—"A certain lord, neat, and trimly dress'd, / Fresh as a bridegroom, and his chin new reap'd"[7]—and Glendower, whom he seems to regard as a pompous fraud.

Glendower, in his brief appearance on stage, serves as something of a foil for the hotheaded but sympathetic Hotspur. But Glendower is of interest because he is an extreme example of a leader who believes not only in his own magical gifts but in their supernatural provenance. He sees in his own life signs and omens from the outset, as in the earthquake that attended his birth: "the earth did tremble." Hotspur replies,

> Why, so it would have done
> At the same season if your mother's cat had
> But kitten'd, though yourself had never been born.

They go back and forth, with Glendower barely able to contain his fury until the moment when he declares,

Why, I can teach you, cousin to command
The Devil.

To which Hotspur replies,

And I can teach thee, coz, to shame the devil
By telling truth: tell truth and shame the devil.
If thou have power to raise him, bring him hither,
And I'll be sworn I have power to shame him hence.
O, while you live, tell truth and shame the devil!

Part of Hotspur's charm lies in his contempt for pretense. He may be obsessed with honor, and he is willing to take absurd risks (for which he eventually pays the ultimate price), but he is, or thinks he is, grounded in reality. "Tell truth and shame the devil" is a compelling motto for the realist in the world of power, which is often filled with fantasy and illusion, and more narrowly, fantasists and illusionists. On the other hand, of course, it is Hotspur who accepts battle at Shrewsbury when he is fatally outnumbered because neither Glendower nor his own father, the Duke of Northumberland, is present. Perhaps his illusions are different in degree but not in kind.

Glendower is an ambiguous figure. We cannot be sure that Hotspur is right in judging him a fraud. For certain, he is no mere con man: he genuinely believes in his occult powers. We may suspect, with Hotspur, that Glendower's battlefield success has more to do with the wild warrior culture of Wales than any summoning of spirits, but Glendower probably disagrees. He is unquestionably a formidable captain but hints that his command of the weather helps account for his victories:

Three times hath Henry Bullingbrook made head
Against my power; thrice from the banks of Wye
And sandy-bottom'd Severn have I sent him
Bootless home and weather-beaten back.[8]

Hotspur cannot forebear a snicker:

> Home without boots, and in foul weather too!
> How scapes he agues, in the devil's name?

Glendower believes in his own magic. Indeed, his thralldom to the supernatural explains to members of the northern rebellion against Henry IV why he absents himself from the Battle of Shrewsbury in which Hotspur will eventually fall to the sword of Prince Hal:

> Owen Glendower's absence thence,
> Who with them was a rated sinew too,
> And comes not in, overrul'd by prophecies.[9]

This observation of the Archbishop of York, who is worried that Hotspur has too few men to win the day, is nowhere contradicted. We are left with the supposition that the mighty Glendower was, in the end, deterred from participating in a battle in which he would have made the decisive difference, by "prophecies," that is, the supernatural.

Not a few powerful people suffer from Glendower syndrome, the belief that they are "not in the roll of common men." Although they may encounter the occasional Hotspur who will have none of it, there will always be those among their followers—in some cases the majority—who nevertheless buy the tale of otherworldly powers. Where that takes them is, however, another story.

Glendower has only one scene in *Henry IV, Part 1*. Thereafter he is mentioned only in passing, and his death is announced in *Henry IV, Part 2* when the ailing king is told,

> To comfort you the more, I have received
> A certain instance that Glendower is dead.[10]

Although but a minor part of the latter play, this bit of Shakespearean manipulation of history is significant. The real Owen Glendower continued a guerrilla war against Henry IV and was never captured or, to the knowledge of the English, slain in battle. He remains to this day something of a mythic figure in Welsh history. While there may be some English chauvinism in this depiction, it has a larger significance as well, which has everything to do with Shakespeare's view of magic.

What Shakespeare gives us is a magician prince who sincerely believes in his own occult powers but provides no real evidence of them. He is deterred from a decisive strategic move by prophecies and perishes off stage without leaving much of a trace. One cannot escape the appeal of magic, Shakespeare seems to say, but to put one's faith in it presents its own perils.

In most of his plays we are never quite sure whether Shakespeare's spirits are intended to be taken literally. Is the ghost of Hamlet's father, who urges him to revenge, something real or a product of Hamlet's own intuitions? Are the ghosts that haunt Richard III the night before his last battle apparitions or the manifestation of his few shreds of a guilty conscience? We cannot tell, and neither can Hamlet or Richard. Julius Caesar is portrayed as believing in signs and portents, and indeed all manner of strange events augur his death but do not shape the actions of those who bring it about.

This in-between quality of magic in Shakespeare is uncomfortable for realists in politics. The term *fairy tale* is, after all, pejorative. But as two of the great twentieth-century authors of fantasy fiction, C. S. Lewis and J. R. R. Tolkien, both argued, fantasy, with all of its tales of magic, has a deep hold and deeper significance for adults as well as children. In Tolkien's words,

Fantasy can, of course, be carried to excess. It can be ill done. It can be put to evil uses. It may even delude the minds out of which it came. But of what human thing in this fallen world is that not true? Men have conceived not only of elves, but they have imagined gods, and worshipped them, even worshipped those most deformed by their authors' own evil. But they have made false gods out of other materials:

their notions, their banners, their monies; even their sciences and their social and economic theories have demanded human sacrifice.[11]

Science fiction writer Arthur C. Clarke once famously said that any form of sufficiently advanced technology is indistinguishable from magic and is often treated accordingly. Magical references pervade political reality as well. When Ukrainians referred to Russian invaders in 2022 as "orcs," they were conjuring the subhuman foot soldiers of Sauron in Tolkien's *The Lord of the Rings*, arguably the most powerful fantasy novel of the twentieth century.[12]

The exercise of power is facilitated by trappings designed to impose awe, from the elegance of the White House, to the magnificence of royal palaces, to the cavernous rooms and atrocious art of totalitarian meeting spaces. As did Dorothy and her friends when they approached the Wizard of Oz, through antechambers and past mysterious fires, visitors to the places of the powerful pass through waiting rooms and are admitted by impeccably turned-out secretaries and assistants. The effect can indeed be magical, although unintentionally so. One might think it would be better if a leader could hear truths frankly delivered, but his own magical aura and the majesty of his setting may deter it. Sometimes his subordinates' magic as well is a problem. For that reason Konrad Adenauer is reported to have advised President John F. Kennedy to have his generals report to him in civilian clothes rather than bemedaled uniforms.

All power is surrounded by an aura of magic. A problem—and occasionally the fatal problem—arises, however, when the person at the center forgets that it is largely, though not entirely, illusion and that the perception of immense authority is potentially perilous. At the center of power, as Shakespeare reminds us, there always and only resides a fallible human being.

This is the wisdom that Richard II comes to just as he enters the decisive confrontation with Bolingbroke. He has been talking of the angels who will defend his throne, but suddenly he is brought back to earth:

For you have but mistook me all this while.
I live with bread like you, feel want,
Taste grief, need friends. Subjected thus,
How can you say to me I am a king?[13]

Confronting his humanity, he is in no shape to overawe the vaulting Bolingbroke, although he makes one last attempt to do so.

While some of Shakespeare's figures exercise extraordinary magical power, particularly in *The Tempest*, for the most part magic turns out (in the histories and tragedies at least) to have its limits. Worse yet, it can be deeply dangerous. Belief in the magic of one's power usually turns swiftly into self-deception, and faith in it turns out to be, if not completely misplaced, then dangerously exaggerated.

The best example of this occurs in *Henry VI, Part 1*, in the figure of Joan of Arc, who leads the French in their resurgence against the invading English and is the main figure in the reversal of almost all of Henry V's gains. She appears early on, after the French have suffered (yet another) defeat. She is brought by the Bastard of Orléans to the dauphin (later king), Charles. The Bastard introduces her as a "holy maid," going on to say,

The spirit of deep prophecy she hath,
Exceeding the nine sibyls of old Rome:
What's past and what's to come she can descry.[14]

Joan picks the dauphin out from the crowd of courtiers, telling them to "be not amaz'd, there's nothing hid from me" and asking to speak with him privately. Thus Joan is introduced not as a magician or witch so much as a seer, a soothsayer who can foresee the future but not necessarily shape it.

This soon changes. Joan tells her story of being a shepherd's daughter, having a revelation from the Virgin Mary, and being blessed as a result with a beauty "which you may see"; she then offers as proof her ability to best the dauphin in a duel. Her amazing victory is preceded by a fair amount of sexual innuendo, which will surround Joan to the end. The dauphin may "impatiently burn with desire," but Joan is determined to remain a virgin. "Assigned am I to be the English scourge," she declares, and not to be his bedmate. An ancient connection between magic and sexual allure or yearning is at work here. The Vestal Virgins of Rome were required to be just that, on pain of death, while at the same time witches in many cultures are credited with suprahuman powers of seduction.[15]

Joan's self-confidence seems rooted in her belief in supernatural powers. But nothing in the play suggests that magic rather than skill accounts for her successes. She does not bewitch the dauphin: his lusts appear to be his own. She has good fortune in battle, but it is nothing unnatural. When she leads French troops, just before she wins her first battle against the English led by the doughty old warrior Talbot, she benefits from a lucky cannon shot that kills one of the ablest English commanders, Salisbury. Just as the dauphin found himself discomfited by a young shepherd's daughter in a duel, Salisbury, one of Henry V's greatest warriors, is slain by a shot fired not by the master gunner but by his son. There is nothing magical about gunpowder, an invention disdained by more than one aristocrat in Shakespeare for spoiling the elegant game of chivalric warfare.

Raging at the loss of his comrade Salisbury, Talbot himself begins the next battle this way:

> Puzel or pussel, Dolphin or dogfish,
> Your hearts I'll stamp out with my horse's heels
> And make a quagmire of your mingled brains.[16]

Joan's full name is Joan de Puzel: *pussel* can mean prostitute; Dolphin refers to the crown prince of France, and a dogfish is a small shark. Talbot may be a great warrior, but he is also something of a blowhard, who cannot respect his enemies, most particularly one who is a woman.

The newly inspired French drive the English on the battlefield, when Talbot encounters Joan:

Here, here she comes. I'll have a bout with thee—
Devil, or devil's dam, I'll conjure thee.
Blood will I draw on thee—thou art a witch—
And straightway give thy soul to him thou serv'st.[17]

Here again, sex and magic are interwoven. "I'll have a bout with thee" could mean to fight or have sex. They duel, and Talbot is appalled when he is overcome, although Joan leaves before finishing him off. Discomfited, he calls Joan a "high-minded strumpet."

My thoughts are whirled like a potter's wheel,
I know not where I am nor what I do.
A witch by fear, not force, like Hannibal
Drives back our troops and conquers as she lists.

And yet, nothing in the text makes us think that Joan has used magic as opposed to better swordsmanship to overcome the overly confident and not particularly clever Earl of Shrewsbury. Nor is she seen casting spells on the English army. She has not summoned demons, muttered incantations, or waved a magical wand. She has simply fought a man who, even as he is being beaten by her, makes crude sexual jokes and rails about witchcraft because he cannot believe what is happening. Talbot's indignation is directed partly at Joan and partly at the English soldiery for yielding to the French attack. Belief in Joan's magic is an excuse and perhaps even a small comfort for a man not used to losing.

The war seesaws back and forth. Talbot's men take Orléans by a surprise attack, and the dauphin rages at Joan, who deflects his anger by making the entirely reasonable argument that the English attacked at some weak point. She then rallies the French troops—again, without magic. Then, in Act 3, Joan leads a successful assault on Rouen, but she does it through warlike craft, dressed as a peasant with four soldiers similarly disguised: "our policy must make a breach"—not magic. She coaches her men to "talk like the vulgar sort of market men," and they come in. They open the gates as what Charles calls "this happy stratagem" succeeds. Talbot rages again at the "foul fiend of France," "Puzel, that witch, that damned sorceress," even though no magic has been used, and the French are driven out again.[18]

Yet Joan again rescues French fortunes, this time through a stroke of diplomacy, persuading the Duke of Burgundy to switch sides, leaving the English for the French.

> Then thus it must be—this doth Joan devise:
> By fair persuasions mixed with sugared words
> We will entice the Duke of Burgundy
> To leave the Talbot and to follow us.[19]

And so it happens, through a speech that is marvelously persuasive and patriotic but involves nothing of supernatural force. Burgundy has until now allied with the English, and Joan persuades him to join with France.

> Look on thy country, look on fertile France,
> And see the cities and the towns defaced
> By wasting ruin of the cruel foe . . .
> Return thee therefore with a flood of tears
> And wash away thy country's stained spots.

And it works. Burgundy switches sides, admitting,

> I am vanquished: these haughty words of hers
> Have battered me like roaring cannon-shot
> And made me almost yield upon my knees.—
> Forgive me, country, and sweet countrymen.

Thus far Joan has shown herself a skilled warrior, a clever tactician, and an able diplomat. Her enemies rail at her witchcraft, but only because they find it impossible to admit to themselves that she is skilled in the handling of arms and a capable general. It is, in fact, only when Joan is finally defeated and captured that we see her summoning up dark powers:

> Now ye familiar spirits, that are culled
> Out of the powerful regions under earth,
> Help me this once, that France may get the field.[20]

If Joan's magic were a figment of her imagination, nothing would happen. Instead, however, Shakespeare has the spirits appear, but they remain silent, hanging their heads, and eventually walking off stage. Admitting that her "ancient incantations are too weak," she is taken. And at the piteous end, when she is about to be burned, she begins inventing things—that she is the daughter of a noble, not her real father, who is a shepherd; that she "issued from the progeny of kings"; that she is a virgin who is yet with child. It is a pitiful ending, and the English nobles York and Warwick, who mock her as a witch and a whore, put her to the stake—although not before she utters one final, prophetic curse.[21] A belief in magic perhaps enabled her triumphs, which were grounded in more mundane qualities and skills, without which such beliefs were, on their own, powerless.

Joan can with reason be portrayed as a feminist hero. But for our purposes, it is more interesting to think of her as an exceptionally skillful operator, who exploited her reputation as a magician to demoralize her enemies and weld together her friends. Only in her downfall does she come to believe in her occult powers and act on those beliefs, and that is precisely the point at which she falls. Her reputation and her glory are human and therefore perishable. Indeed, she foresees her own fate early in the play:

> Glory is like a circle in the water,
> Which never ceaseth to enlarge itself,
> Till by broad spreading it disperse to nought.[22]

And yet Shakespeare still puts those silent spirits on the stage. He does not portray Joan as mad or hallucinatory until those last moments, when she repudiates her father and seems to lie about a pregnancy. Her gifts of martial skill and leadership seemed a kind of magic, perhaps, but she puts too much faith in that. Like most magicians in Shakespeare, she is reminded bitterly of the limits of her powers.

A belief in magic can be a source of comfort to the weak because it allows them to imagine that they can overcome the strong. It can lead to the kind of adulation that Robert E. Lee received as the commanding general of the Army of Northern Virginia, not only at the time but even in retrospect. The belief he inspired helped prevent a sober calculation of probabilities that might have led to a Southern surrender any time after the reelection of Abraham Lincoln—an implacable foe of secession—in late 1864. And it still can obstruct a sober assessment of his competence as a general.

For Shakespeare magic is more often the downfall of those who are actually strong and capable than consolation for the weak. Of no one is this truer than Macbeth, whose play begins with an encounter with the three weird sisters. The three witches (although Shakespeare does not use that word) do not use the powers they have, which include raising the dead (temporarily at any rate), to actually do anything—it is Macbeth and his lady who commit the murders. Rather, they entice Macbeth through a series of prophecies, obscurely worded but compelling to one who is already open to the commission of murder. His belief in their prophecies, and hence their supernatural authority, makes it far easier for Macbeth to pursue his bloody course. Indeed, given the compunctions that he shows about the actual murder, one may wonder whether he would have had the nerve to commit it without his encounters with them.

Macbeth's first encounter with the witches begins with their greetings to him as Thane of Glamis (his current title), Thane of Cawdor (the title Duncan will award him for his defeat of the rebellion), and king. His companion Banquo seems a bit more skeptical about their supernatural powers as opposed to their judgment:

If you can look into the seeds of time,
And say which grain will grow, and which will not,
Speak then to me, who neither beg nor fear
Your favours, nor your hate.[23]

Macbeth is more awestruck, but both go on their way. It is Banquo who captures what has just happened:

And often times, to win us to our harm,
The instruments of darkness tell us truths,
Win us with honest trifles, to betray's
In deepest confidence.

For Banquo, magic in the sense of foreknowledge is real—these are truths, after all—but dangerous and misleading.

Again, it is Macbeth who is tempted and terrified by the prophecy,

Whose horrid image doth unfix my hair,
And make my seated heart knock at my ribs.

He does not respond to Banquo's more skeptical and cautious view of the encounter with the witches. He finds them uncanny, even repulsive, but he believes them.

Macbeth commits the murder; he orders the deaths of others as well, including Banquo. He encounters the witches one more time, in a scene that is over the top with grisly details of their occult ceremonies as they dance around a seething cauldron whose ingredients include "liver of blaspheming Jew," as well as

Nose of Turk and Tartar's lips,
Finger of birth-strangled babe
Ditch-delivered by a drab.[24]

Macbeth speaks with the three weird sisters in the tones of someone whose nerves have already been stretched, awed, perhaps, by their gruesome doings. "Even till destruction sicken" he is desperate to hear what they have to say. Hardened warrior though he is, he wants the assurance that the supernatural can provide him.

In the end, the things he can understand are that he should be wary of Macduff, that no man of woman born can harm him, and that he cannot be vanquished until "Great Birnam Wood to high Dunsinane Hill shall come against him." For the rest—a bloody baby, a parade of kings, Banquo's ghost—he is baffled. And so he clings to what he can understand. In fact, as commentators point out, those all signify elements of the future that he cannot understand or upon which he does not choose to reflect. That too is part of the way of magic: it can short-circuit the work of thinking through one's situation.

Magical thinking betrays Macbeth. No man born of woman in the natural way can kill him—but Macduff was born by caesarean section. The soldiers of those marching against Macbeth's castle bear boughs of trees from Birnam Wood, and although he slaughters Macduff's family, he is indeed overcome by the grief-maddened Scottish lord. Macbeth's descent into murder was facilitated, not caused, by his belief in a supernaturally ordained destiny. He is betrayed, curiously, by phenomena that would seem on the surface to have no natural possibility—a man not born of woman, a forest that moves—but in fact do. The magical prognostications were right but misunderstood or insufficiently contemplated by the object of the prophecies.

Belief in magic betrayed Richard II into absurd flights of arrogance that led to his destruction; one might say the same of Macbeth. In neither case do the supernatural forces actually do anything. In the case of Prospero, the magician ruler of a desert island in *The Tempest*, the magic is real. But at least at the outset of Prospero's career, it set him up for failure in a different way.

That Prospero is a powerful magician is indubitable. He knows who is in the ships approaching his desert island; he can conjure up storms to shipwreck them and yet so arrange matters that they will not be harmed. Unlike the weird sisters, or Joan of Arc, or the ghosts of Richard III, Macbeth, and Julius Caesar, he actually can make things happen through supernatural means. But if that is so, how came he to be exiled in the first place?

Prospero, formerly Duke of Milan, was deposed by his treacherous brother while locked in magical studies. He is not, however, besotted with supernatural forces, like Richard II, who believes without warrant in angels that exist to protect him. Nor is he simply confronted by such beings, as Macbeth is. He has instead committed himself to "secret studies." Those will eventually serve him well once he and his daughter are cast away, but for the moment they prevent him from tending to the low arts of politics that are necessary to rule. Prospero's description of how his brother supplanted him is a concise list of what it takes to run a kingdom (or a corporation): selecting, promoting, or discarding subordinates, securing loyalty and motivation. They are mundane arts. But those skills too seem, in Prospero's telling, to have a particular magical virtue of their own. They enabled his brother to change or newly form the servants of the state of Milan and set all their hearts to a common tune. Political magic may exist, but it rests on some lowly skills, which Prospero had not yet acquired or had indeed despised, while he pursued loftier kinds of enchantment—also real but inadequate to hold a dukedom.

Many leaders, in all kinds of organizations but particularly in politics, inspire a belief in magic and may even have a self-confidence that reflects a magical self-conception, perhaps less flowery than Owen Glendower's pronouncements but no less sincerely felt. And it's not just the raving dictators either: the phenomenon is found among sane and otherwise sensible leaders.

A good contemporary example is Barack Obama, the forty-fourth president of the United States. His rise to the supreme office in the country is nothing short of astonishing. A dispassionate one-word assessment of his record before his election might be "promising" but nothing more. He had served as a community activist and state legislator, without any particularly notable legislative accomplishments, and had yet to complete a single term in the US Senate, where again, no notable legislative achievement lay on his record. The comparison sometimes made to Abraham Lincoln is not apt: Lincoln was perhaps the most successful lawyer in the American West, a onetime congressman who made a mark in his opposition to the Mexican-American War, a cofounder of a new political party, and a tireless and gifted exponent of the view that slavery must not be allowed to be extended into new territories being added to the Union.

Obama had a kind of magic, one that he seems to have believed in almost as much as did his supporters. "I think that I'm a better speechwriter than my speechwriters. I know more about policies on any particular issue than my policy directors. And I'll tell you right now that I'm gonna think I'm a better political director than my political director."[25] One might think of this simply as hubris, of which Obama had a fair amount, but it goes beyond self-confidence or even arrogance. When Senate Majority Leader Harry Reid congratulated the new senator on one of his speeches, he replied, "I have a gift, Harry."[26]

Obama's gifts lay in his imperturbability and his oratory. His speeches—for example, on accepting the 2009 Nobel Peace Prize or in consoling the victims of the 2015 Charleston church shooting—were moving and powerful. They contained no ringing phrases that will last, as so many of Lincoln's have, but there was eloquence and emotion, if not incandescent passion or an exalted vision.

It is easy for politicians to believe in their own magic, especially if they are surrounded by admiring subordinates who will not confront or at least contradict them. And that often gets worse over time, as the aura of political power settles around a leader who may have come into office feeling unsure and unsettled. That seems to have been the case with Obama, a highly intelligent politician, but one whose belief in his powers of persuasion and his personal example—his writings consist chiefly of three books of autobiography or memoir—was and remains enormous. Supposedly a cool rationalist, he too was touched by magic, and in more than one sense.

Some of Obama's magic resulted from an ascription to him of powers beyond the normal and merely mortal. An admiring interviewer described him at the beginning of his presidency this way: "Barack Obama moving as he wishes to move, and the world bending itself to him."[27] This characterization echoes themes of self-confidence bordering on—or lapsing into—hubris from earlier on in the campaign. As more than one commentator observed, where past presidents had embarked upon their office humbled by its gravity and a sense of their own inadequacy—any leader's inadequacy—to meet its challenges, Obama had no such reservations.

So much, one might say, was merely hubris. But the misleading magical aura of power ended up thwarting this president in a different way. It encouraged magical thinking, a belief that mere will or conviction or intelligence would translate into action. The world did not, in fact, move along with him, as a series of foreign policy failures demonstrated. He himself confessed, "A certain arrogance crept in, in the sense of thinking as long as we get the policy ready, we didn't have to sell it."[28] Obama and his entourage succumbed to magical thinking: in this case, the belief that policy could be made without persuasion, compromise, and dealing. It afflicted his foreign policy as well, with repercussions still felt a decade later.[29]

Like Prospero, Obama neglected the small arts of politics. This man—so celebrated at home and abroad—ended up with results that can only be described as mediocre. When his eight years in office came to an end, his political party suffered a devastating loss to an American Jack Cade, a populist businessman with a long history of lying and grifting. A Congress dominated by Democratic majorities in the year of his first electoral victory, 2008, was controlled in both houses by the opposition, and local and state Democratic organizations were outmatched by the competition. Abroad, audiences who had been swept off their feet by Obama—awarding him a Nobel Peace Prize in October 2009, less than a year after he had taken office—were disillusioned, as Obama's magic seemed to have no effect on civil war in Libya, Russian seizure of parts of Ukraine, and mass slaughter in Syria.

The country's enemies were no weaker, and the wars he had promised to bring to a speedy end continued. Obama's bedazzling magic did not destroy him, but it proved itself in some measure self-destructive of an administration from which so much had been hoped.

The magic of power is real but has severe limits. One is unrealistic if one ignores it altogether. It is not for nothing that some of the great politicians have magical powers assigned to them. David Lloyd George, Britain's prime minister from 1916 to 1922, was known as the Welsh Wizard—a testimony not only to the eloquence of his oratory but to the deftness of his political maneuvers in preserving his rule despite the collapse of the Liberal Party, and perhaps a tribute to the magical traditions of a country that produced not only Owen Glendower but Merlin. There are politicians like Ronald Reagan who baffle and frustrate their opponents by their apparently magical gifts—in his case a sunny, invincible optimism that resonated profoundly with the American people even as it seemed shallow and riddled with Hollywood clichés to those immune to its spells. There are others (Bill Clinton was one) who have a kind of personal magnetism that one might say bewitches those who encounter them; this can be true of democrats and of monsters as well. Hitler himself had a hypnotic effect not only on crowds but on the individuals who came into his orbit. There are leaders in the world of business who seem to have the ability to mesmerize their investors, often to their ruin—think of Adam Neumann, for example, the founder of WeWork, once the most valuable start-up in New York City. Bernard Madoff convinced otherwise sober business leaders that his investments could consistently yield 10 percent a year, no matter the vagaries of the market. This too was a kind of malign enchantment that turned on those who fell for it and on the wizard himself, who died in prison, disgraced and abandoned by family and friends.

There are soldiers who seem invested with magical powers. As Churchill put it, "There is required for the composition of a great commander not only massive common sense and reasoning power, not only imagination, but also an element of legerdemain, an original and sinister touch, which leaves the enemy puzzled as well as beaten."[30] And not just generals: during the 2022 Russo-Ukraine War, much was made in Ukrainian propaganda of "the Ghost of Kyiv," a fictitious Ukrainian fighter pilot with numerous single-combat kills to his credit. Indeed, a senior Ukrainian official informed me that psychological warfare messaging to Russian soldiers involving witchcraft and the occult was particularly effective.[31]

Often, these magical qualities—or, rather, talk of them—are immensely frustrating to the opponents of such leaders or individuals, who may think less in terms of the supernatural than sheer fraud. By so doing they miss an important part of reality. Magical qualities, such as those attributed by others and by himself to Barack Obama, helped lead him to the presidency of the United States, after all.

On the other hand, those who, like Prospero, fall so deeply in thrall to their own magic that they can no longer cope with the hard edges of intractable reality fail or are destroyed. Shakespeare teaches us that magical powers, or something that very much resembles them, can be real—but you still need to be able to count votes, fight battles, and make a prudent and clean getaway. Otherwise, you can find yourself deposed, overwhelmed in battle, or, in the worst case, burning at the stake.

CHAPTER 10

Walking Away from It

E VEN AT THE END OF A LONG AND EXCEPTIONALLY SUCCESSFUL career, relinquishing power voluntarily is painful. Powerful persons all too often believe that their successor, even their handpicked favorite, will prove inadequate to the task. In 1955 Winston Churchill was concluding his second term as prime minister. He had decided, after considerable urging and a recognition of his own failing strength, to give Anthony Eden the opportunity the younger man had long ardently desired.

There had been a time when he admired the younger man profoundly: in early 1938, when Eden had resigned as foreign secretary, Churchill was so distraught that he lost sleep—which he never did during all the strains of the crisis of France's defeat at the hands of Germany in 1940. In 1938, he thought, "There seemed one strong young figure standing up against long, dismal drawling tides of drift and surrender. . . . [H]e seemed to me at this moment to embody the life-hope of the British nation. . . .

[N]ow he was gone. I watched the daylight slowly creep in through the windows, and saw before me in mental gaze the vision of death."[1]

But seventeen years later, at age eighty, Churchill had a different premonition about the once heroic foreign secretary. On his last night at 10 Downing Street, he was lost in thought after a final dinner with Queen Elizabeth and Prince Philip. His personal secretary, John Colville, thought he was brooding about leaving public life. Instead, Churchill suddenly stared at him and "said with vehemence: 'I don't believe Anthony can do it.'" As Colville noted, the Suez Crisis barely a year later proved him right.[2]

Churchill walked away from power—reluctantly, born down by age—but he had held on longer than he probably should, chiefly because he did not trust his successor was up for the job. There is some resemblance here to Shakespeare's Henry IV, who has wrested a king-dom from his incompetent predecessor and fought off rebellion after rebellion, only to raise a son and heir whom he mistrusts and does not particularly like. Another playwright might have given him a happy, or at least a happier, ending. Shakespeare does not. The rebels have been suppressed, and the king is ill. He has been informed by his favored son, Clarence, that instead of attending upon his ailing father, Prince Hal is dining with his low-life comrades. Sick at heart, Henry declares,

> Most subject is the fattest soil to weeds,
> And he, the noble image of my youth,
> Is overspread with them; therefore my grief
> Stretches itself beyond the hour of death.
> The blood weeps from my heart when I do shape,
> In forms imaginary, th'unguided days
> And rotten times that you shall look upon,
> When I am sleeping with my ancestors.[3]

Others attempt to comfort the dying king, predicting (correctly as we later learn) that Hal will cast off his louche companions. Henry will have none of it.

'Tis seldom when the bee doth leave her comb
In the dead carrion.

Henry, like many other extremely successful leaders, has no choice about leaving but cannot believe that his heir is up to the task.

The dying king is asleep in the Jerusalem chamber in Westminster—itself an irony, because one of Henry's avowed goals had been to go on crusade to the Holy Land. Prince Hal finally arrives to sit by his father's bedside and, believing that he has breathed his last, spots his father's crown. Eyes gleaming, he takes it:

Thy due from me
Is tears and heavy sorrows of the blood,
Which nature, love and filial tenderness
Shall, O dear father, pay thee plenteously.
My due from thee is this imperial crown,
Which, as immediate from thy place and blood,
Derives itself to me.

Even in mourning, Hal is as transactional as his father—tears in return for that lovely crown. Henry awakes from something like a coma to see that Hal has snatched the crown, and when the prince protests the innocence of his motives, Henry snaps,

Thy wish was father, Harry, to that thought:
I stay too long by thee; I weary thee.[4]

The dying king reproaches his successor:

Thy life did manifest thou lov'dst me not
And thou wilt have me die assured of it.
Thou hid'st a thousand daggers in thy thoughts,
Whom thou hast whetted on thy stony heart
To stab at half an hour of my life.

It is the lament of any leader about a successor whom they think ungrateful and, let it be said, not up to the example that they believe themselves to have set.

Hal does a brilliant job of convincing his father that he is mistaken, allowing for a temporary, limited kind of reconciliation. But it is as cold and businesslike as the king, who, with little time left, reflects on his own life story:

> God knows, my son,
> By what bypaths and indirect, crook'd ways
> I met this crown; and I myself know well
> How troublesome it sat upon my head.

On his way out of power Henry is reinventing his own story. He will not admit that he sought the crown—he insists, rather, that he merely "met it." His confrontation with Richard was an encounter with kingship through "bypaths and indirect, crook'd ways," when in fact it was the result of an artfully conducted coup. It is proof that Henry has a conscience, of a kind, in the throbs of guilt that we have seen in other ways, including his avowed determination—always thwarted—to go on a crusade to the Holy Land. But Henry's self-pity about his tenure as king is real enough, as are his regrets about not achieving all that he could wish. His exit from power is for him, as for many leaders, a matter of disappointment and regret. Henry dies, a thoroughly successful and equally thoroughly unhappy man. Even after their reconciliation, the connection between father and son is never entirely free of a transactional element.

The relationship between ex-ruler and new successor can never be entirely easy, as corporate executives and politicians have found. The transition between the administrations of Ronald Reagan and his vice president, George H. W. Bush, was notoriously acrimonious. The bitterly difficult relationship between British prime minister Tony Blair and Gordon Brown, his chancellor of the Exchequer and successor, offers another good example. On a lesser scale, it is why the wise university president or dean quietly moves to the countryside or decamps to another university after stepping down from his office.

There are, however, in Shakespeare, as in life, rulers who choose to depart power of their own volition in hopes of a better end. Two in particular stand out: King Lear in the play of that name and Prospero at the end of *The Tempest*. Their motives, their methods, and the outcomes, however, could not be more different.

At the opening of *King Lear*, the aging king has decided to divide his kingdom in three. This, he says, is his "darker purpose." His motivations are striking:

> 'Tis our fast intent
> To shake all cares and business from our age,
> Conferring them on younger strengths, while we
> Unburdened crawl toward death.[5]

Lear has a problem: he has three daughters but no sons, and he presumably wishes to avoid division among them. But his reasons for setting aside his power are essentially selfish. He wishes to divest himself of "cares and business," and the last line foreshadows the madness that will overcome him. The desire to "unburdened crawl toward death" suggests a man stricken with a kind of despair beneath his surface brusqueness and command. He does say that he wishes to prevent "future strife," but notably, there is nothing here about his responsibility for the welfare of his subjects.

Lear's purpose is ignoble but understandable: he wants to retire to the good life. What makes his decision utterly irresponsible is the method he has selected for allocating the parts of the kingdom. The lion's share will flow to whichever of his daughters "shall we say doth love us most." His wicked daughters, Goneril and Regan, play the game, whereas the faithful Cordelia refuses, and matters go downhill from there.

In one interpretation, Lear is already in the early stages of senility, and the story of Lear is a meditation on what Charles de Gaulle once referred to as the shipwreck of old age. But it is truer to say that it is a study not of anyone's old age but of the old age of a king, someone used to enormous power and prestige who either no longer wishes or no longer can carry the burdens of office.

Lear's behavior is not atypical of leaders. It is not enough that he be respected or even feared as a king: he is desperate to be told that he is loved. This wish is not uncommon among those who have exerted power, often in unlovable ways. They want to have it all. When Niccolò Machiavelli said that it is best to be feared and loved, but that if one must choose, one should choose fear, he did not reckon fully with the desire for love (or what passes for it) in royal hearts. The exercise of power itself, it turns out, has not satisfied some deeper craving in Lear. He, like Henry IV, is desperate to be loved by his children, who are also his successors. He soon learns, however, that power often disrupts the most fundamental relationship between parent and child.

Lear has been corrupted by years of flattery. His loyal servant Kent has already warned him of this at the beginning of the play:

> What wouldst thou do, old man?
> Think'st thou that duty shall have dread to speak,
> When power to flattery bows? To plainness honour's bound
> When majesty falls to folly.[6]

To no avail: Lear erupts in rage at the faithful Kent and banishes him. Kent probably never had much of a chance of convincing the furious king that he had made a terrible mistake, but the fatal words were "old man." No ruler likes to be reminded that they too are frail and human, prone to error and misjudgment, and most of all, coming to the end of their allotted period of rule, even if they have confessed that.

In this foolish demand for declarations of his daughters' love, Lear shows that if he once knew what genuine love is, he no longer does. And when Cordelia is honest—"I love your majesty / According to my bond, no more or less"—Lear is outraged and disinherits her. His power has corrupted him, and he no longer deals with Cordelia with a good father's sensitivity and compassion. When his loyal servant Kent protests, he warns, "Come not between the dragon and his wrath!" One of the most powerful of all bonds, that between parent and child, has been deformed beyond recognition when a father can refer to himself as a "dragon." But that is what power has made him. He is incapable of self-understanding and reflection and will have a terrible journey before he reaches that point.

Lear's retirement from power is finally compromised by his vision of what leaving power will be: a roistering party with his fifty knights and a continuation of the honors and deference due a king. Goneril and Regan will soon strip these companions away from him, however, in shocking and painful fashion. The loss of power leaves, for many men and women, a hole never to be filled.

There are few sadder meetings in Washington than those with the former high official who has an idea he demands to press on the secretary of state, even though he no longer understands the intricacies of personalities and policies, the underlying subtleties and conditions that shape policymaking. When I was counselor of the Department of State, I took a number of these meetings (thereby shielding the secretary, who had far better uses for her time, from them). I did so with initial annoyance and then with pity. Even worse are the functions and conferences where the once powerful and famous can be seen sitting alone, their peers retired or dead, their protégés having moved on, erstwhile supplicants and sycophants no longer needing them, and a new generation simply ignorant of who they once were.

Like many retirees, Lear soon discovers that the image of an unceasing party is far from the reality. The sisters share their irritation with his retinue and his illusions about who he now is. Goneril is the harshest:

Idle old man,

That still would manage those authorities

That he hath given away![7]

Her sister Regan is little better:

O sir, you are old,

Nature in you stands on the very verge

Of his confine. You should be rul'd and led

By some discretion that discerns your state

Better than you yourself.[8]

Lear is not just the tragedy of a choleric old man in his dotage; it is also the story of the troubles that come hurtling down on a kingdom when its leader has taken leave of his senses. Gloucester, who will endure his own terrible sufferings, captures the moment: "Love cools, friendship falls off, brothers divide: in cities, mutinies; in countries, discord; in palaces, treason; and the bond cracked 'twist son and father. . . . We have seen the best of our time. Machinations, hollowness, treachery and all ruinous disorders follow us disquietly to our graves."[9]

Lear's daughters, Goneril and Regan, strip Lear of his train of knights and squires: Goneril describes them as "disordered," "debauched," and "bold," whereas Lear sees only "men of choicest and rarest parts that all particulars of duty know."[10] It is up to the director how to stage that scene: the knights can be restrained, a bit noisy, or indeed riotous. It may be that Goneril has a point and that what Lear thinks of as a dignified retinue is, in fact, a drunken band of hangers-on. If so, it is evidence again that over time he has come to misjudge his own court, not seeing in his attendees what others do.

Lear does not come to a happy end, but at least he does return to a kind of humanity. At the beginning of the play, even that seems to have drained out of him. He loses the trappings of a king, as his knights are evicted—and interestingly, none of them cling to the old man. Shooed off by Lear's daughters, none are inclined to resist. Lear himself is stripped of all the externals of kingship and, above all, of a court. He finally sees himself as he is:

> You see me here, you gods, a poor old man,
> As full of grief as age, wretched in both.[11]

Even then, recalling his vanished powers as king, he still engages in fantasies of revenge, assuming he has a power that he does not:

> No, you unnatural hags,
> I will have such revenges on you both
> That all the world shall—I will do such things—
> What they are yet I know not, but they shall be
> The terrors of the earth!

This is mere venting. Regan and Goneril come to bad ends, to be sure, but not as a result of anything that Lear does or can do—their own human flaws bring on their doom. Lear's true return to humanity comes as he struggles through the storm on the heath.

> Poor naked wretches, whereso'e'er you are,
> That bide the pelting of this pitiless storm,
> How shall your houseless heads and unfed sides,
> Your looped and windowed raggedness, defend you
> From seasons such as these? O, I have ta'en
> Too little care of this. Take physic, pomp,
> Expose thyself to feel what wretches feel.[12]

It is too late for Lear to undo the damage he has done as a foolish, feckless king, who has proven himself unable to read the people around him and whose egotism has landed him, and those who truly love him, in the deepest peril. He realizes too that he has failed in other kingly responsibilities, having taken too little care of what befalls his poorest subjects. But he becomes human at the end. "I am a very foolish, fond old man," he tells Cordelia, and they are reconciled.[13] But that can only happen when he has left all of the trappings of power—not only his escort of knights but his pride, his vanity, and most of all the illusions of mastery that power brings.

The exercise of power distorts all normal human relationships. Consider, for example, Henry IV's guidance on his deathbed to Prince Hal following their reconciliation:

> Thou art not firm enough, since griefs are green,
> And all my friends, which thou must make thy friends,
> Have but their stings and teeth newly ta'en out,
> By whose fell working I was first advanced
> And by whose power I well might lodge a fear
> To be again displaced; which to avoid,
> I cut them off, and had a purpose now
> To lead out many to the Holy Land.[14]

One sees here that Henry has no idea of what real friendship is. His life to this point has guaranteed that he cannot. His closest collaborator in the overthrow of Richard II, for example, the Duke of Northumberland, ends up leading a conspiracy against him. As a result, for Henry, friends are those whose "stings and teeth" must be extracted in order to be sure of their friendship. His is a world of enemies, followers, and supporters for the moment. He is a man with no real human connection even to his own family, save perhaps his younger son John of Lancaster, who has no chance of inheriting the crown. He needs other people, and he uses them—it was after all by their "fell working" that he came to the throne—but he fundamentally trusts no one and has no emotional bonds with anyone.

There is, however, one character in Shakespeare who chooses to abandon power and seems to do it well. Prospero, the magician ruler of a desert island, has by the end of *The Tempest* accomplished all that a prince might hope for. Overthrown from his erstwhile post as Duke of Milan, he has made himself the ruler of this island, where he commands servants who include an androgynous spirit, Ariel, who craves freedom but does his bidding, as well as the far more dangerous and mutinous Caliban. Neither can challenge him.

Knowing, thanks to his magic arts, that his erstwhile enemies, including his treacherous brother and the faithless King Alonso, are in a nearby ship, he calls up a storm that shipwrecks them. After various adventures he brings all to a happy conclusion. He has presided over a love match between Alonso's son Ferdinand and his daughter Miranda. He has exposed his brother's betrayal and won Alonso's apology and the restoration of his dukedom. He has rewarded the faithful Gonzalo, who had been his friend when he was duke. He has thwarted all plots against him, and in one final feat of magic, he has summoned elves, dimmed the noonday sun, called forth raging winds, ordered thunder and lightning, and called forth the dead from their graves. All this has been done by his "so potent art."

He is at the peak of his powers. And then he makes a sudden and surprising decision:

> But this rough magic
> I here abjure; and when I have required
> Some heavenly music (which even now I do)
> To work mine end upon their senses that
> This airy charm is for, I'll break my staff,
> Bury it certain fathoms in the earth,
> And deeper than did ever plummet sound
> I'll drown my book.[15]

The question that cries out for an answer is why? Why should a magician with such extraordinary powers relinquish them? Prospero can, if he wishes, stay on this enchanted island or (as will be the case) be restored to his dukedom by a chastened and grateful king of Naples.

No one is compelling him to leave behind his occult powers, which we know he found utterly enthralling in Milan, and which have been so useful to him. Why does he have to retire?

Prospero, like Lear, has been dehumanized by power. But there is a large difference between the two, in that Prospero intuits what has happened to him. At the outset of the play, he has caused the terrific storm that will shipwreck Alonso and the other nobles; his daughter Miranda has pity for the sailors caught in the storm, and Prospero tells her that "there's no harm done." At this point the magician decides to inform his daughter of his own history and how they came to the island.

He begins by admitting that he has kept her in partial ignorance and that she knows of him only that he is "master of a full poor cell, and thy no greater father."[16] He has thus far, in other words, presented himself to her not as the powerful enchanter of the island but in a far more humble light and as her "no greater father." He proceeds:

> 'Tis time
> I should inform thee further. Lend thy hand
> And pluck my magic garment from me. So,
> Lie there my art.

Prospero cannot fully relate to Miranda as father to daughter while wearing his magical robe; he has to remove it (or ask her to remove it) before he can do so. It is the hint at the very beginning of the play that foreshadows its end. Prospero knows that power and the most important relationships of our lives are incompatible.

Prospero has been deeply wronged and is in the end forbearing where he cannot be forgiving. He will show generosity too, in freeing Ariel, his messenger who yearns to escape even Prospero's gentle dominion. But in the interim he is also moody, imperious, and threatening. Thus, when Ariel early in the play reminds Prospero of his promise to free him and of his dedicated service thus far, Prospero can only respond,

Dost thou forget
From what a torment I did free thee?[17]

Ariel assures him that he does not, to which Prospero responds, "Thou liest, malignant thing," and berates his faithful servant, who fairly grovels in apology.

If thou more murmur'st, I will rend an oak
And peg thee in his knotty entrails till
Thou hast howled away twelve winters.

He secures two more days of good work out of Ariel and promises him his release then. But his first response to the spirit's desire for freedom is a reproach and then a cruel threat.

Toward Caliban, son of Sycorax, the witch who previously dominated the island, he is more brutal. "Hag-seed, hence: Fetch us fuel and be quick." Before Caliban, whom he has taught to speak, can reply, Prospero snarls,

Shrug'st thou malice?
If thou neglect'st, or dost unwillingly
What I command, I'll rack thee with old cramps,
Fill all thy bones with aches, make thee roar,
That beasts shall tremble at the din.

Ariel can be abused and bullied into gratitude, Prospero believes; Caliban, on the other hand, submits to his rule purely out of fear, and he has no compunctions about that. Caliban is incapable of gratitude to Prospero, although not necessarily to others—he will fall in with the drunken courtiers who get separated from Alonso in the storm, flattering and groveling to them. In modern renditions of *The Tempest*, Caliban even becomes a sympathetic figure, a representative of the peoples of the New World being despoiled by European invaders. This strains the text, much as an attempt to render Shylock the hero of *The*

Merchant of Venice does. But, as is so often the case in Shakespeare, the villain or near villain gets his due, or at least has a complicated story to tell. Caliban points out,

> This island's mine by Sycorax my mother,
> Which thou tak'st from me. When thou cam'st first,
> Thou strok'st me and made much of me, wouldst give me
> Water with berries in't, and teach me how
> To name the bigger light, and how the less,
> That burn by day and night; and then I lo'd thee
> And show'd thee all the qualities o'th'isle,
> The fresh springs, brine pits, barren place and fertile.[18]

It is not the whole story: Caliban also attempted to rape Miranda. But even so, there is a kind of injustice here. Moreover, Prospero may not be entirely right when he describes Caliban as a being one "whom stripes may move, not kindness!" The word Prospero uses to describe him is *filth*. By contrast, the courtiers with whom Caliban later associates are ruffians, but they do indeed move Caliban with a sort of kindness. What is unquestionable is that Prospero's rule of the island depends upon the exercise of coercive power. At the beginning of the play, he shows no regret about that and only slight awareness of what it has done to him.

Even toward his future son-in-law, Ferdinand, Prospero behaves harshly, albeit presumably with the higher purpose of ascertaining whether he is a worthy match for Miranda. The magician dissimulates, accusing him of being a spy, threatening him with manacles and seawater for drink, then setting for him the exhausting task of moving logs about. Ferdinand confides to Miranda,

> And he's composed of harshness. I must remove
> Some thousands of these logs and pile them up,
> Upon a sore injunction.[19]

But Prospero is harder yet on Caliban and the motley gang clustered around him. He summons spirits:

> Go, charge my goblins that they grind their joints
> With dry convulsions, shorten up their sinews
> With aged cramps, and more pinch-spotted make them
> Than pard or cat o'mountain.[20]

And, as the spirits chase Caliban, Stephano, and Trinculo off stage, he quietly says to Ariel, "Let them be hunted soundly." With not a little satisfaction, Prospero observes, "At this hour lies at my mercy all mine enemies." If the play ended here, it could portray Prospero as a ruler driven somewhat mad by injustice, but it does not.

Prospero admits that he is torn between vengeance and a reasonable forgiveness: "Yet with my nobler reason 'gainst my fury do I take part."[21] He reconciles with King Alonso, although his brother, Antonio, is strangely mute in that final scene. He frees Ariel, whom he will miss, and even his behavior toward Caliban changes: "This thing of darkness I acknowledge mine," he says to Alonso. The tone is very different from that he takes at the beginning of the play. He has blessed the engagement of Miranda to Ferdinand and will return with the king to Naples, there to see the wedding.

> And thence retire me to my Milan, where
> Every third thought shall be my grave.

The discharge of all of his responsibilities is a premonition of death, and like Lear, Prospero admits it.

In the epilogue, he addresses the audience.

> Now my charms are all o'erthrown,
> And what strength I have mine's own,
> Which is most faint . . .

Now I want
Spirits to enforce, art to enchant;
And my ending is despair,
Unless I be relieved by prayer,
Which pierces so that it assaults
Mercy itself, and frees all faults.
As you from crimes would pardoned be,
Let your indulgence set me free.[22]

This passage is often interpreted as Shakespeare's own farewell to the theater. As it has become clear that *The Tempest* was not, in fact, his last play, that becomes a more difficult interpretation to sustain.

A more straightforward reading is the more plausible: Prospero's renunciation of magical power is tied to his awareness that it has involved a certain degree of brutality. If the audience has its crimes from which it would like to be pardoned, so too does Prospero, and he knows it—the gentleness of his speeches at the end to his brother, the king, Miranda, and, above all, the two creatures he has ruled, Ariel and even Caliban, reveals it. He cannot be truly human while clinging to the magical powers that have enabled him to rule the island. That is why he had to remove his magical cloak before speaking with his daughter and why he has to break his staff and drown his book.

Power is "rough magic," in Prospero's words. It makes those who wield it solipsistic. But Prospero, faintly at the beginning and more strongly at the end, realizes that it had its beginnings and ends, its uses, but also that his wielding of it inflicted a kind of damage on himself. He knows that retirement is a step toward death—but unlike Lear, who can only see himself hurtling downward, he is simply realistic. When one is old and has stepped back from worldly affairs and grave responsibilities, death is, as one retired chief executive officer once put it to me, "the next big job." Lear attempts to ward off this reality with riotous living but succumbs instead to morbid brooding and madness; Prospero faces this last phase of life without illusions. He does not expect, and does not get, a completely happy ending. His relationship with his treacherous brother is unresolved, although one assumes that Antonio has been rendered harmless. But if there is some sadness and regret in Prospero, there is predominantly peace. That is a gift (or rather, an achievement) that escapes Henry IV on his deathbed and that Lear discovers in only small measure when he and Cordelia are reconciled.

Exiting power is difficult. Many leaders persist until debilitation or death: Franklin Delano Roosevelt, for example, was in increasingly poor health toward the end of his life, including at the critical Yalta Conference in 1945. During his second premiership (1951–1955), and particularly toward its end, Winston Churchill began showing signs of age. The diary of his loyal secretary, John Colville, began to use words like "advancing senility" and "visibly ageing." By the end he had lost the ability to focus on much more than the newspapers and one of his favorite card games, bezique.[23] Business leaders and university presidents have been known to linger too long. Charles de Gaulle had famously lost touch with a France in the throes of student revolt in 1968, exited power a year later, and died suddenly a year after that. Aging or sick leaders can be a menace, their conditions too often concealed not only from the public but from themselves.[24] In an age that foolishly insists that physical age has nothing to do with mental vigor, artificial constraints on tenure in the highest office have become more difficult to sustain, but they are wise. Bechtel Corporation, for example, a remarkably successful construction firm that has remained in the same family for over 125 years, requires its employees—including the CEO—to retire at age sixty-five and to sell their shares in the company.[25] Still, none of these arrangements can ensure that whenever one leaves power, one does it at the right time and with some kind of equanimity.

Without those artificial constraints on tenure in office, one is forced back on simple good judgment and strength of character to shape retirement, and there are examples of that. The best is George Washington, both as commanding general of the forces of the new United States and its first president. Two of his biggest decisions were to formally return his commission to Congress and to step down from the presidency. Both were accomplished with a degree of theatricality that marked a man who loved plays and not only was the father of his country but studiously played that part.

From the outset of his career, Washington had an actor's sensibility, which was not surprising for a man who had what Ron Chernow describes as "an instinctive command of the theatrical gesture . . . a magisterial way of directing the major scenes of his life."[26] Consider costuming, for example. In May 1775 the Second Continental Congress convened following the battles at Lexington and Concord. The question was whether the Congress would take charge of the army now milling around Boston and besieging the British garrison there—to that the answer was self-evidently yes. But who should command? Washington seized the moment, showing up in the dress uniform of a colonel of the Virginia militia.[27] A towering figure, he looked good in uniform and knew it; he did not have to solicit command but signaled that he was quite prepared to have it offered him—which, of course, it was.

Throughout his public career Washington calculated his appearance on the public stage with extraordinary finesse. For example, when commanding the Continental Army surrounding Boston in 1775, he found himself, in some respects, the first American. Yet there he was, a Virginia gentleman leading an army composed chiefly of New Englanders who could have been citizens of an altogether different country—egalitarians who elected their own officers and had little use for aristocrats. Washington decided that in the new army New Englanders would man and lead his personal bodyguard, thereby demonstrating a kind of intracolonial identity that had been tenuous to this point. After the Revolution, when the Constitutional Convention met in 1788, he led the members who had gathered a week before the event to services—at a Catholic church, thereby signaling the centrality of religious toleration in the new country. For his inauguration as president, he dressed not in luxurious robes but in dignified American homespun, as befitted the leader of the world's newest and largest republic. And he made great theatrical gestures. In March 1783 at Newburgh, New York, in one of his greatest strokes of theatrical genius, he quelled a potential mutiny of army officers furious at the failure of Congress to follow through on its promises of payment to them. Never a great orator, he began to read his remarks from a prepared text, and then, fumbling for his glasses, said, "Gentlemen, you must pardon me, for I have not only grown gray but almost blind in service to my country." The officers present were reduced to tears, and the threatened insurrection dissolved.[28] Historians have wondered whether the gesture was spontaneous or calculated.

Yet, in some ways, the two greatest pieces of stagecraft in his career had to do with the way in which he walked away from power. In September 1783, the Treaty of Paris officially ended the War of American Independence, and several months later the last British troops evacuated New York City. In December of that year, Washington arrived in Annapolis, Maryland, with the intent of resigning his commission. A committee of Congress agreed with him that this should take place at a public ceremony on December 23, at which the members of Congress would remain seated with their hats on, while he stood before them. There could have been no clearer demonstration of the superiority of the civilian to the military power. But Washington added one dramatic touch, uncalled for, and probably unexpected, by Congress. He took his original commission from Congress out of his pocket and handed it to the presiding officer, Thomas Mifflin, together with a copy of the speech.

This symbolic gesture, so laden with humility and subordination, was profoundly at odds with the extraordinary adulation that he otherwise received on his progression from New York to Annapolis and in the town itself. It made, and was intended to make, an enduring point about the place of an individual leader in a free republic. It was repeated again when he decided to retire from the presidency at the end of two consecutive terms, having been twice unanimously elected to that office. His precedent of serving only two terms was broken only once thereafter, by Franklin D. Roosevelt, and that in turn led to an amendment of the Constitution to prevent it happening ever again. As he finally bid adieu to public office, he staged one last gesture, a farewell address intended as a legacy and testament, to be read and pondered rather than heard.

Washington's exits from power and their manner won the unqualified admiration of the most unlikely critic of all: King George III. During the war he had asked the Loyalist Benjamin West what Washington would do should the Americans prove victorious. When West predicted that he would retire from public life, the king replied, "If he does that he would be the greatest man of the age." And when Washington retired from the presidency in 1797, he confirmed that he had become "the greatest character of the age."[29]

Washington's withdrawal from power was, like Prospero's, not entirely happy. He was old and often ill; his house was overrun with uninvited guests; his plantation had suffered in his absence; he had growing qualms about his own prosperity, which rested on the labor of slaves. His last years in office were unhappy as well, as his brilliant subordinates Alexander Hamilton and Thomas Jefferson clawed at each other, while his vice president brooded in resentment, believing he had made this man. He took few pleasures in the trappings of power but rather felt its burdens acutely. Extraordinarily ambitious as a young and then a middle-aged man, he had accomplished the tasks that had been set before him and was able to conclude his career, drawn and haggard as he was, with satisfaction.

Washington was not the most brilliant of America's founding generation—Alexander Hamilton, Thomas Jefferson, James Madison, and John Adams, among others, could plausibly claim to be a lot smarter. Yet interestingly enough, they all (even Adams) accepted his superiority. He had his strengths as a general but also his weaknesses and more than once brought the American cause close to catastrophe. He kept the Union together as the first signs of tension between North and South began to emerge and presided over a partial reconciliation with Great Britain that angered many. His policy of neutrality toward European politics even meant a personally painful betrayal of his imprisoned protégé the Marquis de Lafayette, on whose behalf he refused to appeal in order to avoid further complications with a dangerous revolutionary French regime. He, in turn, was bullied and betrayed by his subordinates, Hamilton and Jefferson, both trying to use him for their own ends.

And yet, in the end, he concluded his career on his own terms, not escaping the ills attendant on old age and an exhausting career of public service but knowing how to walk off the stage. Washington was, perhaps not coincidentally, a great admirer of Shakespeare (he possessed a bust of the playwright) and quoted him frequently, particularly *The Tempest*, echoes of which his biographer finds in his famous farewell address.[30]

If Shakespeare teaches anything about politics, it is the preeminent importance of character in all of its complexity. One has to think Washington would have been an excellent subject for him—the slave owner who created a country built on principles that would eventually destroy the institution upon which he depended for his livelihood; the insular Virginia gentleman who would become the first American; the man of explosive temper who learned, at considerable internal cost, to control it. In short, he would have found another character who, like Prospero, having exercised his own rough magic, wisely knew that he had to relinquish it and did so with dignity, grace, and humility.

AFTERWORD

Shakespeare's Political Vision

WE DO NOT KNOW SHAKESPEARE'S POLITICAL VIEWS OR, INDEED, whether he had any. We cannot know them because he never wrote them down, and attempts to infer them usually run upon the rocks of his characters' brilliant ambiguity. Yet we can discern the questions that his plays explore and the recurrent themes that illuminate the acquisition, use, and limits of all kinds of power, especially political power.

Repeatedly Shakespeare explores the tension between power that is legitimate and power that is effective. In *Richard II*, most notably, but in other plays as well, a legitimate king proves to be appallingly incompetent. Brilliant but utterly unserious, Richard makes one mistake after another: his incompetence breeds rebellion at the cost of both his crown and his life. His successor is far more effective but is haunted for the rest of his life, across *Henry IV, Part 1* and *Part 2*, by his illegitimate acquisition of the throne. His son, Prince Hal, who becomes Henry V, goes off to war pledging to atone for the way his father achieved the crown.

In the same vein, Julius Caesar may have seized power on his own, but he has a certain legitimacy, at least insofar as the population of Rome is concerned. Yet, in the opening scene of the play, the senators rebuke the crowds for forgetting Pompey, the man whom Caesar slew in pursuit of the dictatorship. And the conspirators' fears about him seem justified, for Caesar clearly craves the crown, an abhorrent thing in republican Rome. Shakespeare gives more than enough hints in Caesar's utterances and behavior to serve as confirmation that Brutus's theory of "the serpent's egg"—that, left unchecked, Caesar will become a tyrant—is correct. And so the plot proceeds. The conspirators remedy, or perhaps anticipate, one problem but create another in the form of a civil war that will ravage Rome and lead to their own deaths.

In neither case does Shakespeare seem to offer a judgment about who was right. He is silent on the question of whether one should accept incompetent but legitimate rule or overthrow it, with the result of unleashing a chain of second- and third-order consequences that may be unforeseeable but are likely to be perilous. At least he points out for us the tension between those unsatisfactory courses of action, which are well worth contemplating in any C-suite prone to conspiracy. The cases that he treats warn us that even when there is a good reason to cast aside rules, precedent, and custom, the price may, in the end, not be worth it—or, at the very least, a price will have to be paid.

Shakespeare deals with the politics of courts, and courts are universal in all human organizations. He does not, however, neglect the masses, average people and their interests and desires. This is why Falstaff is not only an immensely entertaining figure but an important one. There is in him not merely a comic but an unillusioned, sensual Everyman. It is Prince Hal's genius that he appreciates the need to understand Falstaff and, so to speak, study with him, learning what average people are like. Yet, even so, a gap remains, as his soliloquy after walking around the campfires suggests:

O hard condition,
Twin-born with greatness, subject to the breath
Of every fool whose sense no more can feel
But his own wringing!

This is a soliloquy, so presumably Henry is not lying to his audience, but he may be deceiving himself when he declares,

What infinite heart's ease
Must kings neglect, that private men enjoy!
And what kings, that privates have not too,
Save ceremony, save general ceremony?[1]

He knows enough of common men to be able to manipulate them, but even as skilled a leader as he cannot fully empathize with them. Hal, now Henry V, resents the fact that his yeomen archers do not see the world as he does. He recovers and offers them a kind of diluted glory, accommodating their coarser appetites, but it remains manipulation.

The tension between elites and masses is as old as politics: patricians and plebs; before that, the demos of Athens and leaders like Pericles and Alcibiades. Repeatedly in Shakespeare, the elites, no matter how brilliant or skilled, fail to appreciate why normal people do not think the way they do or share their values. That fatal misapprehension is the downfall of Coriolanus, the magnificent general who is an appallingly poor consul. The only patrician in his play who understands the plebeians and can communicate with them effectively is Menenius, but he is a drunken, garrulous intermediary. One cannot imagine him carrying any weight in the Senate.

This book goes to press at a time when the tension between elites and masses is large and growing. The success of Brexit—the referendum that eventually took Great Britain out of the European Union in 2020—and the surprising election and subsequent popularity of Donald Trump in 2016 and beyond reflected a populist surge. One fascinating aspect of both events is how shocked elites were by the outcome—and their spluttering disgust was not entirely different in kind from Caska's when he reports on Caesar's reluctant refusal of the crown: "He put it the third time by, and still he refused it; the rabblement hooted and clapped their chapped hands, and threw up their sweaty nightcaps, and uttered such a deal of stinking breath because Caesar refused the crown, that it had almost choked Caesar; for he swooned and feel down at it; and for mine own part, I durst not laugh for fear of opening my lips and receiving the bad air."[2] In many plays this contempt for the mob recurs. Yet Shakespeare mitigates, or even rebukes, it in subtle ways.

The elite, after all, have their own grave faults. In the end, it is Coriolanus who commits treason, not the Roman people. It is Brutus and his comrades who commit political murder and Mark Antony who cold-bloodedly unleashes civil war. And it is the average man who often displays more common sense than those at the top, as when the gardeners in *Richard II* reflect on what has happened to the kingdom under Richard's rule. Bolingbroke, the older man says,

> Hath seiz'd the wasteful King. O, what pity is it
> That he had not so trimm'd and dress'd his land
> As we this garden! We at time of year
> Do wound the bark, the skin of our fruit-trees,
> Lest being over-proud in sap and blood,
> With too much riches it confound itself;
> Had he done so to great and growing men,
> they might have liv'd to bear and he to taste
> Their fruits of duty.[3]

These average men have a conservative wisdom that the feckless Richard did not. They understand that with better management he might have kept Bolingbroke's loyalty, and they regret that he failed to do so.

Leaders and led, elites and mass are ubiquitous. Shakespeare gives us elites who have their own forms of blindness, corruption, and even wickedness; the masses are often fickle, shortsighted, and even brutal, as in the mayhem that follows Mark Antony's speech by Caesar's corpse or in their blind adherence to Jack Cade's murder and riot. Shakespeare himself is no elite author. He is accessible, rather, to all—he has proved no less resonant with dangerous criminals serving life sentences in solitary confinement for murder than with professors of literature.[4]

Although Shakespeare does not spare us the dark side of leaders, and although he is a scholar of human weakness and folly, he does not deny the possibility of real political greatness. Far from it: he captures its moods and its moments. There is nothing insincere in Antony's description of Brutus as "the noblest Roman of them all," and we see enough to realize that the leader of the conspiracy has the stuff of greatness in him.

Here, too, Shakespeare administers a useful inoculation against the tendency—more pronounced now than in centuries past—to cut leaders down to size. There are biographers eager to say that Abraham Lincoln stumbled into his largest decisions during the Civil War and that Winston Churchill was an incompetent alcoholic; there are local politicians willing to dispatch the statue of Thomas Jefferson to a warehouse because he was a slave owner without considering his role in writing the document that would ultimately destroy American slavery. There is, particularly in this postheroic age, a tendency to dismiss the very idea of greatness.

Shakespeare gives us a way back. Some of his great figures are deeply flawed: Henry V is the best example, but there are others. Because he is indeed a mirror of the world, Shakespeare captures, as few can, the weaknesses of those at the top of the heap. At the same time, even his villains display a kind of virtuosity that elicits a grudging admiration, since in their own way, villains can be great too. The fascination of performances of *Richard III* is in how often the audience finds itself chuckling along with Richard as he marvels at the success of his own duplicity and crime.

And Shakespeare reveals to us the better side of those we would as often dismiss. Richard II, a hollow king bewailing the loss of his hollow crown, is given remarkable insight and, at the end, courage, dispatching one of his assassins with a snarl: "Go thou and fill another room in Hell." This cry of defiance may be the most winning line in a career filled with far more brilliant speeches. In a deeper way, the desperate goodness of Edgar, legitimate son of Gloucester in *King Lear*, or the willingness of a Cassius to die rather than submit to Caesar and his minions elicits our admiration.

All this is another way of saying that Shakespeare teaches us to see leaders in the round, not concealing their faults and vices but admiring and even wondering at their virtues. Shakespeare teaches the student of those at the pinnacle of power to be realistic, which should mean neither offering over-the-top praise nor engaging in mere cynical diminishment. For those who have to navigate their way through the world of power, that is a powerful lesson. His closely observing subordinates—a Kent in *Lear*, an Enobarbus in *Antony and Cleopatra*—are frustrated and alarmed by the failures of those they must follow, but they nonetheless understand and appreciate their merits.

Political leaders of a certain character themselves share this view. In his famous "Man in the Arena" speech in 1910, Theodore Roosevelt declared,

It is not the critic who counts; not the man who points out how the strong man stumbles, or where the doer of deeds could have done them better. The credit belongs to the man who is actually in the arena, whose face is marred by dust and sweat and blood; who strives valiantly; who errs, and comes short again and again, because there is no effort without error and shortcoming; but who does actually strive to do the deeds.[5]

And if that man fails, says Roosevelt, he "at least fails while daring greatly." It is a Shakespearean way of viewing the world of action, one quite detached from that of journalists, pundits, and academic students of power, because it attaches value to action. As a formidable historian in his own right, Roosevelt understood that the detached observer misses something of great importance.

Shakespeare has very few illusions about those who seek power and those who wield it. But he offers a view that is not cynical. Many of his powerful men and women fail—they go mad or are murdered, fall from power and die despairing, or nearly so. But not all: Cardinal Wolsey, with whom this book began, comes quickly to a kind of peace. When Thomas Cromwell, his loyal assistant, asks, "How does your Grace?" he replies,

> Why, well;
> Never so truly happy, my good Cromwell;
> I know myself now, and I feel within me
> A peace above all earthly dignities.[6]

The loss of power, it would appear, frees Wolsey to know himself at last, and therein to find tranquility.

If those who fall from power often find some kind of peace, in Shakespeare those who succeed often do so only to have their achievements crumble away, as happens to Henry V after his untimely death. But Shakespeare's vision never ends there. Cardinal Wolsey, who swam too long upon a sea of glory, never fully understood just how fragile his hold on power was. Yet even his tale is not entirely one of failure. He has at least acquired self-knowledge and perspective, even at the expense of regret. Between becoming wise too late and failing to become wise at all, one should prefer the former. And in Wolsey's decline and fall, there is still a measure of hope for the future.

Wolsey was stripped of his titles and many of his possessions. He died surrounded by only a few servants and exiled from the court. We do not need to take his word for the peace that he finds in losing power. The verdict on his life is given by Griffith, the gentleman usher to Queen Katherine, Henry VIII's wife, who will herself come to a sad end, set aside by the king for Anne Boleyn. Wolsey had been no friend to Katherine, but Griffith nonetheless speaks up to her after his fall. "Noble madam / Men's evil manners live in brass, their virtues we write in water." Griffith speaks of Wolsey's rise from humble beginnings, his scholarship, his generosity, and his philanthropy in endowing what became Christ Church college in Oxford. But in his fall he too returned to humanity:

> His overthrow heaped happiness upon him,
> For then, and not till then, he felt himself,
> And found the blessedness of being little.
> And, to add greater honours to his age
> Than man could give him, he died fearing God.[7]

Prospero renounced the rough magic of power; Wolsey had it ripped away from him. In the end, however, great as their achievements were with that art, Shakespeare shows us that they could only regain their souls when they walked away from it. Like others who have exited power, both found in their final surrender a "blessedness of being little."

Shakespeare is neither monarchist nor republican, liberal nor conservative. He is immersed in politics because politics is part of life, and it was part of his life. He was not a political philosopher or a pundit, and few people study or enjoy him because of the politics. Rather, we share that view of him as a mirror of life, one who observes all with an understanding eye and a kind of sympathy even with characters who are unattractive.

In the end Shakespeare is so powerfully compelling about power because he knows it is not the most important thing about our lives and characters. He can describe power with insight and empathy precisely because he understands that it is not what makes us human. He teaches us that power is necessary and unavoidable, but it always comes with a price. He teaches us most importantly that the wisest wielder of it will, with or without regrets, set aside the bargain of power at the expense of his or her soul, and happy or not, walk away free.

Acknowledgments

The completion of this book coincided with the conclusion of my teaching career at Johns Hopkins University's School of Advanced International Studies. This led me to reflect on what I owe my own teachers throughout the years. For well over half a century, they encouraged my curiosity, instilled in me the courage to embark on intellectual adventures, and imparted skill in writing. Almost all are departed now, but I dedicate this book to them in grateful memory.

Two wise friends, literary scholars both, who taught me much about Shakespeare, insisted that I should write this book, which is, as we say in Washington, a bit out of my lane. Dale Salwak not only did that but read the original manuscript with exceptional care. Alas, Mel Plotinsky, learned and gentle, passed away before the book was finished. Both gave me the encouragement a military historian and recovering dean needed to undertake this project.

The manuscript received a careful reading from other friends who brought a variety of practical and literary perspectives to bear on Shakespeare and power. Kenneth Adelman, William Bodie, Charles Edel, Eric Edelman, Brian Gunderson, John McLaughlin, and Elizabeth Samet shared their insights much to the improvement of the manuscript.

Five terrific students helped this book along: Jeb Benkowski in the initial phase, then Will Quinn, Sarah Crawford, and Stephen Honig. A special thanks goes to Jacqueline Roeder, who did the bulk of the research work, while Will and Sarah were outstanding teaching assistants in the course "Rough Magic: Shakespeare on Getting, Using and Losing Power," which shaped much of my thinking about Shakespeare. In the last few years I have had the good fortune to teach that course to scores of students, from first-year undergraduates to mid-career professionals, and I owe all of them a debt of gratitude for their typical Johns Hopkins curiosity, intelligence, and spirited interest in how a giant of English literature could illuminate the world in which they live. Their enthusiasm and insights shaped many of my own ideas.

At the *Atlantic*, Yoni Appelbaum, Adrienne LaFrance, Juliet Lapidos, and Jeffrey Goldberg have encouraged my literary interests, including my writing of a number of Shakespeare-themed articles that helped develop my thinking on the matters covered by this book. Directly and indirectly, they have helped me branch out beyond my usual subjects and reach an ever-wider audience.

Ron Daniels, president of Johns Hopkins University, kindly subsidized a stay at the Mishkenot Sha'ananim guesthouse in Jerusalem, an ideal venue in which to write—and so I did, finishing the manuscript there. Moti Schwartz, Rita Kramer, and the entire staff were hospitality personified.

My editor in chief, Lara Heimert, is a kindly if implacable task master, imposing, as she did, rigor on what was initially a set of musings. Brandon Proia was a superb editor, much improving my prose, and Andrew Wylie, my agent, was, as he always is, a source of encouragement and support. The professionalism of the entire team at Basic Books has, as ever, made it a pleasure to work with them.

Finally, to our children, their spouses, and our grandchildren, I owe so much joy of a kind that, alas, usually escapes Shakespeare's heroes, not to mention his villains. But the Bard knew more than a little of love, and so for my wife, Judy, let me just quote a sonnet that speaks to me more than ever:

Acknowledgments

Haply I think on thee, and then my state,
Like to the lark at break of day arising
From sullen earth, sings hymns at heaven's gate;
For thy sweet love remembered such wealth brings
That then I scorn to change my state with kings.

Notes

The Arc of Power

1. See the exhaustive discussion in Gordon McMullan, ed., *King Henry VIII*, Arden Shakespeare, 3rd series (London: Bloomsbury, 2000), 113ff.

2. *Henry VIII*, Act 3, Scene 2.

3. From "The Prince's Dog," in Edward Mendelson, ed., *W. H. Auden: The Dyer's Hand and Other Essays* (New York: Vintage, 1989), 182.

4. *Richard III*, Act 4, Scene 2.

5. Nathan Hodge, "Putin's Use of Crude Language Reveals a Lot About His Worldview," CNN, February 8, 2022, www.cnn.com/2022/02/08/europe/putin-coarse-remarks -ukraine-intl/index.html.

6. William Hazlitt, *Characters of Shakespeare's Plays* (London: Oxford University Press, 1916), 262–263.

7. See John Lukacs, *The Duel: The Eighty-Day Struggle Between Churchill and Hitler* (New York: Ticknor & Fields, 1990), esp. 35–52.

8. James Shapiro discusses this episode in *Shakespeare in a Divided America: What His Plays Tell Us About Our Past and Future* (New York: Penguin, 2020), esp. 201–222.

9. Hazlitt, Preface, xxxvii.

10. Hazlitt, Preface, xxxiv.

Chapter 1. Why Shakespeare?

1. Abraham Lincoln to James H. Hackett, August 17, 1863, in Roy P. Basler, ed., *The Collected Works of Abraham Lincoln* (New Brunswick, NJ: Rutgers University Press, 1953), 4:392.

2. Michael Anderegg, *Lincoln and Shakespeare* (Lawrence: University Press of Kansas, 2015), 94–95.

3. See Anderegg, *Lincoln and Shakespeare*, 48–49.

4. This story and others are recounted in Robert Berkelman, "Lincoln's Interest in Shakespeare," *Shakespeare Quarterly* 2, no. 4 (October 1951): 303–312.

5. See the discussion in Fred Kaplan, *Lincoln: Biography of a Writer* (New York: Harper-Collins, 2008), 346–349.

6. This story, told repeatedly by Burton, may be found at "Richard Burton on a Curious Meeting with Churchill," BBC, July 30, 1965, www.bbc.co.uk/programmes/p02yd5zr.

7. Winston S. Churchill to Clementine Churchill, March 31, 1918, in Martin Gilbert, ed., *Winston S. Churchill: Companion Volume IV, Part 1, January 1917–June 1919* (Boston: Houghton Mifflin, 1978), 291.

Notes

8. Isaiah Berlin, *Mr. Churchill in 1940* (London: John Murray, 1949), 13.

9. See Albert Furtwangler, *Assassin on Stage: Brutus, Hamlet and the Death of Lincoln* (Champaign: University of Illinois Press, 1991).

10. See Rodney Symington, *The Nazi Appropriation of Shakespeare: Cultural Politics in the Third Reich* (Lewiston, NY: Edwin Mellen Press, 2005); Anselm Heinrich, "'It Is Germany Where He Truly Lives': Nazi Claims on Shakespearean Drama," *New Theatre Quarterly* 28, no. 3 (August 2012): 230–242.

11. See the transcript of their discussion at "Derek Jacobi and Mark Rylance: Reasonable Doubt About the Identity of William Shakespeare," *Critical Stages/Scènes critiques*, www .critical-stages.org/18/reasonable-doubt-about-the-identity-of-william-shakespeare. For an extremely well-executed presentation of the facts as known to scholars, see James Shapiro, *Contested Will: Who Wrote Shakespeare?* (New York: Simon & Schuster, 2010).

12. See the discussion in Jonathan Bate, "Essex Man? A Political Tragedy in Five Acts," in *Soul of the Age: The Life, Mind and World of William Shakespeare* (London: Penguin, 2008), 249–286.

13. See Jonathan Bate, *How the Classics Made Shakespeare* (Princeton, NJ: Princeton University Press, 2019).

14. Shapiro, *Contested Will*, 277.

15. *Henry IV, Part 1*, Act 1, Scene 2.

16. See, for example, Paul A. Cantor, *Shakespeare's Rome: Republic and Empire* (Chicago: University of Chicago Press, 1976).

17. Leo Tolstoy, *War and Peace*, trans. Anthony Briggs (New York: Penguin, 2005), vol. 3, pt. 1, chap. 19, p. 700.

18. Katsuji Nakazawa, "Analysis: Xi Becomes 'Mao' in Tienanmen Visual Effect," *Nikkei Asia*, July 8, 2021, https://asia.nikkei.com/Editor-s-Picks/China-up-close/Analysis-Xi -becomes-Mao-in-Tiananmen-visual-effect.

19. *Henry VI, Part 3*, Act 3, Scene 2.

20. I attempted a bit of this in analyzing the final days of President Donald J. Trump: "The Feckless King," *The Atlantic*, October 5, 2020, www.theatlantic.com/ideas/archive /2020/10/trump-shakespeare/616612.

21. The full text can be found at "Transcript of Nixon's Farewell Speech to Cabinet and Staff Members in the Capital," *New York Times*, August 10, 1974, www.nytimes.com/1974 /08/10/archives/transcript-of-nixons-farewell-speech-to-cabinet-and-staff-members.html.

22. *Richard II*, Act 5, Scene 5.

Chapter 2. Inheriting It

1. For a discussion of this, see Adrian Woolridge, *The Aristocracy of Talent: How Meritocracy Made the Modern World* (New York: Skyhorse, 2021).

2. The story is told in a number of places, but see in particular Walter Isaacson, *Steve Jobs* (New York: Simon & Schuster, 2011). See also Tim Bajarin, "How Steve Jobs Helped Guarantee Tim Cook's Success at Apple," *Forbes*, September 2, 2021, www.forbes.com /sites/timbajarin/2021/09/02/how-steve-jobs-helped-guarantee-tim-cooks-success-at-apple.

3. "'You've Got to Find What You Love,' Jobs Says," *Stanford News*, June 12, 2005, https://news.stanford.edu/2005/06/12/youve-got-find-love-jobs-says.

4. The basic account can be found in Thomas Gryta and Ted Mann, *Lights Out: Pride, Delusion, and the Fall of General Electric* (New York: Mariner Books, 2020). The story continues to reverberate. See the Exchange section of the *Wall Street Journal*, Saturday/ Sunday, November 13–14, 2021, including Jason Zweig, "The Fall of the Colossus," and Thomas Gryta, Ted Mann, and Cara Lombardo, "He Rewired GE. Then He Unwound It," pp. B1, B6–B7. A quick summary of the criticisms of Immelt can be found in David

Gelles, "Jeff Immelt Oversaw the Downfall of G.E. Now He'd Like You to Read His Book," *New York Times*, February 5, 2021, www.nytimes.com/2021/02/05/business/jeff -immelt-general-electric-corner-office.html.

5. The best recent account of this is Vladislav Zubok, *Collapse: The Fall of the Soviet Union* (New Haven, CT: Yale University Press, 2021).

6. *Cymbeline*, Act 3, Scene 5.

7. *Cymbeline*, Act 2, Scene 1.

8. *Cymbeline*, Act 4, Scene 2.

9. *Cymbeline*, Act 3, Scene 3.

10. *Henry IV, Part 1*, Act 1, Scene 1.

11. *Henry IV, Part 1*, Act 1, Scene 2.

12. *Henry IV, Part 1*, Act 1, Scene 3.

13. *Henry IV, Part 1*, Act 1, Scene 3.

14. *Henry V*, Act 4, Scene 3.

15. Harold Bloom, *Shakespeare: The Invention of the Human* (New York: Riverhead Books, 1998), 286. The play within the play is *Henry IV, Part 1*, Act 2, Scene 4.

16. *Henry IV, Part 2*, Act 5, Scene 5.

17. Scutcheon here is a decorative coat of arms deployed in a memorial. *Henry IV, Part 1*, Act 5, Scene 1.

18. *Henry IV, Part 2*, Act 4, Scene 3.

19. *Henry IV, Part 2*, Act 4, Scene 3.

Chapter 3. Acquiring It

1. *Richard II*, Act 1, Scene 1.

2. See the discussion in Charles R. Forker's Arden Shakespeare (3rd Series) version of *Richard II* (London: Bloomsbury, 2009), 183.

3. *Richard II*, Act 1, Scene 3.

4. *Richard II*, Act 3, Scene 3.

5. *Richard II*, Act 4, Scene 1.

6. *Richard II*, Act 5, Scene 6.

7. *Richard II*, Act 5, Scene 4.

8. See Lynne Olson, "A Question of Loyalty," in *Troublesome Young Men: The Rebels Who Brought Churchill to Power and Helped Save England* (New York: Farrar, Straus and Giroux, 2008), 322ff.

9. *Henry IV, Part 2*, Act 4, Scene 3.

10. *Henry IV, Part 1*, Act 3, Scene 2.

11. First Debate, August 21, 1858, in Don E. Fehrenbacher, ed., *Abraham Lincoln: Speeches and Writings, 1832–1858* (New York: Library of America, 1989), 512.

12. William H. Herndon, *Herndon's Life of Lincoln* (1888; repr., New York: Da Capo Press, 1983), 269–270.

13. To William Kellogg, December 11, 1860, in Don E. Fehrenbacher, ed., *Abraham Lincoln: Speeches and Writings, 1859–1865* (New York: Library of America, 1989), 190.

14. The best account is Harold Holzer, *Lincoln at Cooper Union: The Speech That Made Abraham Lincoln President* (New York: Simon & Schuster, 2024).

15. William H. Herndon and Jesse K. Welk, *Herndon's Lincoln: A True Story of a Great Life* (1889; repr. Cosimo, 2009), 375.

16. This story is found in Don E. Fehrenbacher and Virginia Fehrenbacher, eds., *Recollected Words of Abraham Lincoln* (Stanford, CA: Stanford University Press, 1996), 365, citing the recollections of James B. Fry.

17. *Coriolanus*, Act 1, Scene 1.

18. *Coriolanus*, Act 1, Scene 1.

19. *Coriolanus*, Act 1, Scene 1.

20. *Coriolanus*, Act 2, Scene 3.

21. *Coriolanus*, Act 3, Scene 3.

22. Ariel Sharon with David Chanoff, *Warrior: The Autobiography of Ariel Sharon* (New York: Simon & Schuster, 2001), 286.

23. Charles de Gaulle's *The Edge of the Sword*, trans. Gerard Hopkins (London: Faber & Faber, 1960), is a particularly interesting meditation on these issues. See, in particular, 96–101.

24. *Coriolanus*, Act 5, Scene 6.

25. James Kirby Martin, *Benedict Arnold: Revolutionary Hero* (New York: New York University Press, 1997), 415.

Chapter 4. Seizing It

1. *Macbeth*, Act 1, Scene 7.

2. *Julius Caesar*, Act 5, Scene 5.

3. *Julius Caesar*, Act 1, Scene 2.

4. *Julius Caesar*, Act 1, Scene 3.

5. *Julius Caesar*, Act 1, Scene 3.

6. *Julius Caesar*, Act 1, Scene 2.

7. *Julius Caesar*, Act 2, Scene 1.

8. *Julius Caesar*, Act 2, Scene 1.

9. *Julius Caesar*, Act 4, Scene 3.

10. Henry Adams, *History of the United States of America During the Administrations of Thomas Jefferson* (1889; New York: Library of America, 1986), 1:132.

11. Gore Vidal, *Burr* (New York: Random House, 1973).

12. Bob Woodward, *The Secret Man: The Story of Watergate's Deep Throat* (New York: Simon & Schuster, 2005), 106.

13. *Julius Caesar*, Act 2, Scene 1.

14. *Julius Caesar*, Act 2, Scene 2.

15. *Julius Caesar*, Act 3, Scene 1.

16. *Julius Caesar*, Act 2, Scene 1.

17. *Julius Caesar*, Act 3, Scene 1.

18. *Julius Caesar*, Act 4, Scene 1.

19. *Julius Caesar*, Act 3, Scene 2.

20. *Julius Caesar*, Act 5, Scene 5.

21. *Macbeth*, Act 1, Scene 2.

22. *Macbeth*, Act 1, Scene 3.

23. *Macbeth*, Act 1, Scene 5.

24. *Macbeth*, Act 2, Scene 3.

25. *Macbeth*, Act 2, Scene 2.

26. The phrase is from the speech cited below, "If it were done, when 'tis done," etc.

27. *Macbeth*, Act 1, Scene 7.

28. *Macbeth*, Act 5, Scene 5.

29. Jeffrey Gettleman, "The Global Elite's Favorite Strongman," *New York Times*, September 4, 2013, www.nytimes.com/2013/09/08/magazine/paul-kagame-rwanda.html.

30. See Michela Wrong, *Do Not Disturb: The Story of a Political Murder and an African Regime Gone Bad* (New York: Public Affairs, 2021).

31. Nicholas Shakespeare, "The Making of a Monster: Paul Kagame's Bloodstained Past," *The Spectator*, March 27, 2021. The article author's name is a coincidence.

Chapter 5. Inspiration

1. *Julius Caesar*, Act 1, Scene 2.
2. *Richard II*, Act 4, Scene 1.
3. *Richard II*, Act 5, Scene 1.
4. Michael Shaara, *Killer Angels* (1974; repr. New York: Ballantine Books, 2011), 231.
5. John Lukacs, *The Duel: The Eighty-Day Struggle Between Churchill and Hitler* (New Haven, CT: Yale University Press, 1990).
6. Lukacs, *The Duel*, 136.
7. "Inaugural Address, January 20, 1961," John F. Kennedy Presidential Library and Museum, www.jfklibrary.org/archives/other-resources/john-f-kennedy-speeches /inaugural-address-19610120.
8. Ted Sorenson, *Counselor: A Life at the Edge of History* (New York: Harper Collins, 2008), 220.
9. "President John F. Kennedy's Inaugural Address (1961)," National Archives, www .archives.gov/milestone-documents/president-john-f-kennedys-inaugural-address.
10. *Henry V*, Act 4, Scene 3.
11. Winston S. Churchill, *Into Battle* (1941; repr. New York: Rosetta Books, 2013), 404.
12. *Henry V*, Act 4, Scene 3.
13. *Henry V*, Act 3, Scene 1.
14. *Henry V*, Act 3, Scene 1.
15. *Henry V*, Act 3, Scene 2.
16. Militiaman Thomas Young, quoted in Lawrence E. Babits, *A Devil of a Whipping: The Battle of Cowpens* (Chapel Hill: University of North Carolina Press, 1998), 55.
17. William Slim, *Defeat into Victory* (1956; repr. New York: Cooper Square Press, 2000), 211.
18. Among the classical texts would have been the works on rhetoric by Aristotle, Cicero, and Quintilian.
19. Charles Eade, ed., "The Fall of France: Notes of a Speech to the House of Commons June 20, 1940," in *Secret Session Speeches* (Toronto: McClelland & Stewart, 1946), 14.
20. Churchill, *Into Battle*, 349.
21. Isaiah Berlin, "Winston Churchill in 1940," in *Personal Impressions* (Princeton, NJ: Princeton University Press, 1980), 7. This essay was written as a review of the first volume of Churchill's war memoirs in 1949.
22. For a good contemporary account, see Nigel Nicolson, ed., *Harold Nicolson: Diaries and Letters*, Vol. 2: *The War Years, 1939–1945* (New York: Atheneum, 1967).
23. Berlin, "Winston Churchill in 1940," 4.
24. I have discussed this and other aspects of Churchill's wartime leadership in Chapter 4 of *Supreme Command: Soldiers, Statesmen, and Leadership in Wartime* (New York: Free Press, 2002).
25. Joseph Wood Krutch, *Modern Temper: A Study and a Confession* (1929; repr. New York: Harcourt, Brace, 1956), 91.
26. There have been many profiles of Zelensky; the best at the time of writing is Simon Shuster, "Inside Zelensky's World," *Time*, April 28, 2022, https://time.com/6171277 /volodymyr-zelensky-interview-ukraine-war.
27. Shuster, "Inside Zelensky's World."
28. Available at "Ukrainian President Volodymyr Zelensky: 'We Are Still Here,'" video posted to YouTube by WFAA, February 26, 2022, www.youtube.com/watch?v =wgCNKhtZYks.

29. Robin Givhan, "President as Everyman: Zelensky's Mastery of the Direct Appeal," *Washington Post*, March 3, 2022, www.washingtonpost.com/world/2022/03/03/president-everyman-zelenskys-mastery-direct-appeal.

30. "'Thirteen Days of Struggle': Zelenskiy's Speech to UK Parliament—Transcript," *The Guardian*, March 8, 2022, www.theguardian.com/world/2022/mar/08/thirteen-days-of-struggle-volodymyr-zelenskiys-speech-to-uk-parliament-transcript.

31. Catie Edmondson, "Annotated Transcript: Zelensky's Speech to Congress," *New York Times*, March 16, 2022, www.nytimes.com/2022/03/16/us/politics/transcript-zelensky-speech.html.

32. Quoted in Aaron Blake, "Zelensky's Scathing Speech to Germany," *Washington Post*, March 17, 2022, www.washingtonpost.com/politics/2022/03/17/zelenskys-scathing-speech-germany.

33. *Henry V*, Act 4, Scene 6.

Chapter 6. Manipulation

1. James Gould Cozzens, *Guard of Honor* (New York: Harcourt, Brace & Co., 1948), 394.

2. *Henry V*, Act 1, Scene 2.

3. *Henry V*, Act 1, Scene 1.

4. *Henry V*, Act 1, Scene 1.

5. *Henry V*, Act 2, Scene 2.

6. *Henry V*, Act 3, Scene 5.

7. *Henry V*, Act 3, Scene 3.

8. *Henry V*, Act 1, Scene 1.

9. *Henry V*, Act 5, Scene 2.

10. *Henry V*, Act 5, Scene 2.

11. *Henry V*, Act 5, Scene 2.

12. *Henry V*, Act 4, Scene 1.

13. *Henry IV, Part 2*, Act 4, Scene 3.

14. I have described this in "They Won't Miss You When You're Gone," *The American Interest*, January 5, 2016, www.the-american-interest.com/2016/01/05/they-wont-miss-you-when-youre-gone.

15. *Henry IV, Part 1*, Act 2, Scene 4.

16. *Henry IV, Part 2*, Act 5, Scene 2.

17. *Henry V*, Act 2, Scene 1.

18. *Henry IV, Part 2*, Act 3, Scene 1.

19. *Henry V*, Act 3, Scene 6.

20. *Henry V*, Act 4, Scene 2.

21. *Henry V*, Act 4, Scene 1.

22. *Henry V*, Epilogue.

23. Caro's biography, *The Years of Lyndon Johnson*, currently runs to four volumes: *The Path to Power* (1982), *The Means of Ascent* (1990), *Master of the Senate* (2002), and *The Passage of Power* (2012), all published by Alfred Knopf. A fifth and final volume is being written.

24. Caro, *Master of the Senate*, 120.

25. Caro, *Master of the Senate*, 491.

26. Caro, *Master of the Senate*, 232.

27. Caro, *Master of the Senate*, 161.

28. Caro, *Master of the Senate*, 158.

Notes

Chapter 7. Murder

1. Jan Kott, *Shakespeare, Our Contemporary*, trans. Boleslaw Taborski (New York: Doubleday, 1964), 3.

2. See Stéphane Courtois et al., *The Black Book of Communism: Crimes, Terror, Repression*, trans. Jonathan Murphy and Mark Kramer (Cambridge, MA: Harvard University Press, 2000).

3. *Richard III*, Act 5, Scene 6.

4. Niccolò Machiavelli, *The Prince*, trans. Harvey Mansfield, 2nd ed. (Chicago: University of Chicago Press, 1998), 37.

5. Machiavelli, *The Prince*, 37.

6. *Henry VI, Part 3*, Act 3, Scene 3.

7. *Richard III*, Act 1, Scene 3.

8. Machiavelli, *The Prince*, 5.

9. Machiavelli, *The Prince*, 28.

10. *Richard III*, Act 5, Scene 3.

11. *Richard III*, Act 1, Scene 3.

12. *Richard III*, Act 4, Scene 3.

13. *Macbeth*, Act 2, Scene 3.

14. Quoted in Sandra Clark and Pamela Mason, eds., *Macbeth*, Arden Shakespeare, 3rd Series (London: Bloomsbury, 2015), 192.

15. *Macbeth*, Act 3, Scene 1.

16. *Macbeth*, Act 3, Scene 1.

17. *Macbeth*, Act 3, Scene 4.

18. *Macbeth*, Act 4, Scene 1.

19. *Macbeth*, Act 5, Scene 3.

20. *Macbeth*, Act 5, Scene 5.

21. *Macbeth*, Act 5, Scene 8.

22. *Macbeth*, Act 5, Scene 2.

23. Volker Ulrich, *Hitler: Ascent, 1889–1939*, trans. Jefferson Chase (New York: Alfred A. Knopf, 2016), 384.

24. Ulrich, *Hitler*, 6.

25. Ulrich argues, correctly, that Hitler was far from the intellectual and political mediocrity depicted in many of the biographies written in the half century after his death. In this he follows John Lukacs, who in a series of books about World War II, culminating in *The Hitler of History* (New York: Vintage, 2011), makes the case for recognizing Hitler's genius—limited and evil, to be sure, but genius nonetheless.

26. There are many accounts of these events. The best recent account is to be found in Richard Evans, *The Third Reich in Power* (New York: Penguin, 2005).

27. Richard Evans, *The Third Reich at War* (New York: Penguin, 2010), 27. Evans documents all this and more, as does the German official history published after the war, *Germany in the Second World War*.

28. See Omer Bartov, *Hitler's Army: Soldiers, Nazis and War in the Third Reich* (Oxford: Oxford University Press, 1992).

29. See Volker Ulrich, *Hitler: Downfall, 1939–1945*, trans. Jefferson Chase (New York: Random House, 2020), 756n126, on the question of Hitler's viewing of the films.

30. Ulrich, *Hitler: Downfall, 1939–1945*, 535.

31. See Richard MacGregor, *Xi Jinping: The Backlash* (Sydney: Penguin Random House Australia, 2019).

32. Anatoly Rybakov, *Children of the Arbat*, trans. Harold Shukman (London: Hutchinson, 1988), 559.

Notes

Chapter 8. Innocence and Arrogance

1. Charlie Warzel, "Elon Musk's Texts Shatter the Myth of the Tech Genius," *The Atlantic*, October 3, 2022, www.theatlantic.com/technology/archive/2022/09/elon-musk-texts-twitter-trial-jack-dorsey/671619.

2. *Henry VIII*, Act 3, Scene 2.

3. *Henry VI, Part 1*, Act 1, Scene 1.

4. *Henry VI, Part 1*, Act 1, Scene 1.

5. *Henry VI, Part 1*, Act 1, Scene 1.

6. *Henry VI, Part 1*, Act 3, Scene 1.

7. *Henry VI, Part 1*, Act 5, Scene 4.

8. *Henry VI, Part 2*, Act 2, Scene 3.

9. *Henry VI, Part 2*, Act 4, Scene 9.

10. *Henry VI, Part 3*, Act 2, Scene 5.

11. *Henry VI, Part 3*, Act 5, Scene 6.

12. *Henry VI, Part 3*, Act 4, Scene 8.

13. *Henry VI, Part 2*, Act 5, Scene 1.

14. Isaiah Berlin, "Political Judgment," in Henry Hardy, ed., *The Sense of Reality: Studies in Ideas and Their History* (New York: Farrar, Straus and Giroux, 1977), 46.

15. *Henry VI, Part 2*, Act 4, Scene 2.

16. *Macbeth*, Act 1, Scene 7.

17. *Macbeth*, Act 1, Scene 4.

18. *Macbeth*, Act 1, Scene 4.

19. *Henry IV, Part 2*, Act 4, Scene 3.

20. *Macbeth*, Act 1, Scene 6.

21. *Richard II*, Act 1, Scene 1.

22. *Richard II*, Act 2, Scene 1.

23. *Richard II*, Act 3, Scene 2.

24. *Richard II*, Act 3, Scene 3.

25. *Richard II*, Act 5, Scene 5.

26. *Richard II*, Act 3, Scene 2.

27. See the masterful account in Charles Moore, *Margaret Thatcher: Herself Alone* (New York: Knopf, 2019).

28. What follows is drawn chiefly from Moore, *Margaret Thatcher*.

29. Moore, *Margaret Thatcher*, 562.

30. Moore, *Margaret Thatcher*, 647–649.

31. Moore, *Margaret Thatcher*, 669.

32. Quoted in Moore, *Margaret Thatcher*, 702.

33. Moore, *Margaret Thatcher*, 729.

34. *Macbeth*, Act 1, Scene 7.

Chapter 9. Magic and Self-Deception

1. Henry Kissinger, *White House Years* (Boston: Little Brown, 1979), 104. On fairy tales and our imaginary lives, see Bruno Bettelheim, *The Uses of Enchantment: The Meaning and Importance of Fairy Tales* (New York: Random House, 1975); C. S. Lewis, *The Reading Life: The Joy of Seeing New Worlds Through Others' Eyes*, ed. David C. Downing and Michael G. Maudlin (New York: HarperOne, 2019), including, in particular, "Why Fairy Tales Are Often Less Deceptive Than 'Realistic Stories'" and his admiring review of J. R. R. Tolkien's *The Lord of the Rings*.

2. Kissinger, *White House Years*, 742.

3. There is a rich literature by professional entertaining magicians on this subject. For a good introduction to how magicians think about these matters, see Darwin Ortiz, *Strong Magic: Creative Showmanship for the Close-Up Magician* (Washington, DC: Kaufman and Company, 1994).

4. Some of the most serious contemporary magician entertainers, such as Eugene Burger, have thought deeply on this point. See, among other works, his book with Robert Neale, *Magic and Meaning* (Seattle, WA: Hermetic Press, 1999).

5. See Eric Kurlander, *Hitler's Monsters: A Supernatural History of the Third Reich* (New Haven, CT: Yale University Press, 2017).

6. *Henry IV, Part 1*, Act 3, Scene 1.

7. *Henry IV, Part 1*, Act 1, Scene 3.

8. *Henry IV, Part 1*, Act 3, Scene 1.

9. *Henry IV, Part 1*, Act 4, Scene 4.

10. *Henry IV, Part 2*, Act 4, Scene 2.

11. J. R. R. Tolkien, "On Fairy Stories," 26. There are many editions of this essay in print and on the Internet. I have used that on the Internet Archive at https://archive.org/details /on-fairy-stories_202110/page/n25/mode/2up.

12. On fairy tales for children, see Bettelheim, *The Uses of Enchantment*.

13. *Richard II*, Act 3, Scene 2.

14. *Henry VI, Part 1*, Act 1, Scene 3.

15. *Henry VI, Part 1*, Act 1, Scene 3.

16. *Henry VI, Part 1*, Act 1, Scene 4.

17. *Henry VI, Part 1*, Act 1, Scene 5.

18. *Henry VI, Part 1*, Act 3, Scene 2.

19. *Henry VI, Part 1*, Act 3, Scene 3.

20. *Henry VI, Part 1*, Act 5, Scene 2.

21. *Henry VI, Part 1*, Act 5, Scene 3.

22. *Henry VI, Part 1*, Act 1, Scene 2.

23. *Macbeth*, Act 1, Scene 3.

24. *Macbeth*, Act 4, Scene 1.

25. Ryan Lizza, "Battle Plans," *New Yorker*, November 8, 2008, www.newyorker.com /magazine/2008/11/17/battle-plans.

26. Quoted in Gene Healy, "Obama's Arrogance of Power," *Washington Examiner*, November 10, 2009.

27. Jon Meacham, "Meacham: A Conversation with Obama," *Newsweek*, May 15, 2009, www.newsweek.com/meacham-conversation-obama-79757.

28. Quoted in Chris Cillizza, "President Obama Admits His Biggest Mistake: Arrogance," *Washington Post*, November 17, 2015.

29. I discuss these in my review of the first volume of his presidential memoirs in "H-Diplo Roundtable XXIII-33 on Obama. A Promised Land," H-Diplo, April 11, 2022, https://networks.h-net.org/node/28443/discussions/10079498/h-diplo-roundtable -xxiii-33-obama%C2%A0-promised-land.

30. Winston S. Churchill, *The World Crisis*, Vol. 2: *1915* (1923–1931; repr. New York: RosettaBooks, 2013), 8.

31. Personal communication.

Chapter 10. Walking Away from It

1. Winston S. Churchill, *The Second World War*, Vol. 1: *The Gathering Storm* (Boston: Houghton Mifflin, 1948), 257–258.

Notes

2. John Colville, *The Fringes of Power: 10 Downing Street Diaries, 1939–1955* (New York: W. W. Norton, 1985), 708.

3. *Henry IV, Part 2,* Act 4, Scene 4.

4. *Henry IV, Part 2,* Act 4, Scene 3.

5. *King Lear,* Act 1, Scene 1.

6. *King Lear,* Act 1, Scene 1.

7. *King Lear,* Act 1, Scene 3.

8. *King Lear,* Act 2, Scene 4.

9. *King Lear,* Act 1, Scene 2.

10. *King Lear,* Act 1, Scene 4.

11. *King Lear,* Act 2, Scene 2.

12. *King Lear,* Act 3, Scene 4.

13. *King Lear,* Act 4, Scene 7.

14. *Henry IV, Part 2,* Act 4, Scene 3.

15. *The Tempest,* Act 5, Scene 1.

16. *The Tempest,* Act 1, Scene 2.

17. *The Tempest,* Act 1, Scene 2.

18. *The Tempest,* Act 2, Scene 1.

19. *The Tempest,* Act 3, Scene 1.

20. *The Tempest,* Act 4, Scene 1.

21. *The Tempest,* Act 5, Scene 1.

22. *The Tempest,* Epilogue.

23. Colville, *The Fringes of Power,* 649, 655, 707.

24. This is the topic of David Owen, *In Sickness and in Power: Illnesses in Heads of Government During the Last Hundred Years* (New York: Praeger, 2008). Trained as a doctor and having served as foreign secretary of the United Kingdom, Owen has a unique vantage point on these matters.

25. Shawn Tully, "Meet the Company That Has Changed the Face of the World," *Fortune,* May 17, 2016, https://fortune.com/longform/bechtel-construction.

26. Ron Chernow, *Washington: A Life* (New York: Penguin, 2010), 452.

27. This episode is described well in Chernow, *Washington,* 183ff.

28. This is well described at "Newburgh Conspiracy," George Washington's Mount Vernon, www.mountvernon.org/library/digitalhistory/digital-encyclopedia/article/newburgh-conspiracy.

29. Andrew Roberts, *The Last King of America: The Misunderstood Reign of George III* (New York: Viking, 2021), 454.

30. See Chernow, *Washington,* 756 and *passim.*

Afterword: Shakespeare's Political Vision

1. *Henry V,* Act 4, Scene 1.

2. *Julius Caesar,* Act 1, Scene 2.

3. *Richard II,* Act 3, Scene 4.

4. See Laura Bates, *Shakespeare Saved My Life: Ten Years in Solitary with the Bard* (New York: Sourcebooks, 2013).

5. Theodore Roosevelt, "Citizenship in a Republic," Address at the Sorbonne, Paris, April 23, 1910, in Louis Auchincloss, ed., *Theodore Roosevelt: Letters and Speeches* (New York: Library of America, 2004), 781–782.

6. *Henry VIII,* Act 3, Scene 2.

7. *Henry VIII,* Act 4, Scene 2.

Index

Index

Index

Frederick the Great of Prussia, 203
Free France, 65
French Revolution, 102

General Electric (GE), 42
generals, as politicians, 73–74, 78
George III, King, 77, 244
Germany, 174–176. *See also* Hitler, Adolf
gerrymandering, 134
Gettysburg, Battle of, 13, 68, 112
Ghani, Ashraf, 197
Ghost of Kyiv, 223
Glendower, Owen, 205–209, 219, 222
glory, 54, 55
Glossman, James, 128
Gloucester, Duke of, 184, 185–186, 187, 190, 252
Gloucester, Earl of, 232
Godfather, The, 140
Goethe, Johann, 17
Goneril, 229, 231–232, 233
Gonzalo, 235
Goodwin, Richard, 155
Gorbachev, Mikhail, 43, 101–102
Gore, Al, 40
Gow, Ian, 199
Grant, Ulysses S., 14, 68, 73–74
Great Dictator, The, 174
Grey, 138–141
Griffith, 253–254
Guard of Honor (Cozzens), 133

Hackett, James H., 13–14, 15
Halifax, Edward, 63
Hall of Mirrors, 25
Hamilton, 46
Hamilton, Alexander, 86–87, 244, 245
Hamlet (character), 209
Hamlet (Shakespeare), 8, 15, 17, 209
Harfleur, siege of, 120, 121, 141–143, 149
Haroun al-Rashid, 24
Harry Percy (Hotspur), 20–21, 47, 49, 50, 55, 205–208
Hay, John, 14
Hazlitt, William, 9, 10
Heine, Heinrich, 17
heirs, 39–56
Henriad, 20
Henry IV (character)
  Caesar compared to, 88
  complexity of, 57–58
  death of, 193, 241

deception and, 49–50
guidance from, 234
harshness of, 24
lack of inspiration from, 111–112
Lincoln compared to, 67–69
murders and, 161–162, 166, 167
rise of, 63–64, 81
son and, 47–48, 54–55, 64–65, 147, 148, 149
succession and, 226–228
See also Bolingbroke, Henry
Henry IV, Part 1 (Shakespeare), 13, 20–21, 46–49, 51–52, 64, 66, 205–208, 211–216, 247
Henry IV, Part 2 (Shakespeare), 5, 20, 46–47, 52–55, 64, 66, 148, 208, 247
Henry IV, Part 3 (Shakespeare), 162–163, 165
Henry V (character)
  death of, 183–184
  Falstaff and, 52–54
  as flawed, 251
  inspiration and, 9, 114–123, 124, 127–128
  manipulation and, 134–154, 157
  multiple roles of, 26
  succession and, 47, 66
  See also Prince Hal
Henry V (Shakespeare), 20, 51, 119, 122, 132, 134–154
Henry VI (character), 46, 163, 183, 185–190, 194
Henry VI, Part 1 (Shakespeare), 20, 182, 183–184
Henry VI, Part 2 (Shakespeare), 20, 22, 182, 190–191
Henry VI, Part 3 (Shakespeare), 15, 20, 27–32, 182–183
Henry VIII (Shakespeare), 2–4, 15, 20, 34, 182
Herndon, William, 67
Heseltine, Michael, 199, 200, 201
Hitler, Adolf
  Caesar and, 89
  Churchill and, 9, 18
  communism versus, 161
  empathy and, 174–175
  fear versus inspiration and, 112
  hypnotic effect of, 222
  invocation of, 205
  lack of awareness and, 101
  magical thinking and, 203
  Richard III and, 176
  use of power and, 30
Ho Chi Minh, 161

272

Index

Index

Index

Index

Index

Eliot A. Cohen is the Arleigh A. Burke Chair in Strategy at the Center for Strategic and International Studies and the Robert E. Osgood Professor of Strategic Studies at Johns Hopkins University's School of Advanced International Studies, where he also served as the school's ninth dean. Formerly a director on the Defense Department's policy planning staff and Counselor of the Department of State, he is the prize-winning author of several books, including *The Big Stick*, *Supreme Command*, and *Conquered into Liberty*. He lives in the Washington, DC, area.